# Federalism and the Westminster Tradition

# Federalism and the Westminster Tradition

*Reformed Orthodoxy at the Crossroads*

MARK W. KARLBERG

*Wipf & Stock*
PUBLISHERS
*Eugene, Oregon*

FEDERALISM AND THE WESTMINSTER TRADITION
Reformed Orthodoxy at the Crossroads

Copyright © 2006 Mark W. Karlberg. All rights reserved. Except for brief quotations in critical publications or reviews, no part of this book may be reproduced in any manner without prior written permission from the publisher. Write: Permissions, Wipf & Stock Publishers, 199 W. 8th Ave., Suite 3, Eugene, OR 97401.

ISBN 10: 1-59752-904-4
ISBN 13: 978-1-59752-904-4

*Cataloging-in-Publication Data:*

Karlberg, Mark W.
    Federalism and the Westminster tradition: reformed orthodoxy at the crossroads / Mark W. Karlberg.

xiv + 158 p.; 23 cm.

Includes bibliography

ISBN 10: 1-59752-904-4
ISBN 13: 978-1-59752-904-4

1. Covenant theology. 2. Orthodox Presbyterian Church. 3. Vos, Geerhardus, 1862–1949. 4. Kline, Meredith G. 5. Elliott, Paul M. 6. Westminster Seminary. I. Title.

BT155 K36 2006

Manufactured in the U.S.A.

In memory of the faculty
That served at (Old) Westminster
Whose voice is still heard

*Soli Deo gloria*

# Table of Contents

*Preface / ix*

*Acknowledgments / xiii*

1. The Significance and Basis of the Covenant of Works / 1
   *Exegetical and Theological Factors*

2. New Vistas in Old Testament Narrative / 25
   *Geerhardus Vos and Meredith G. Kline as
   Exemplary Reformed Interpreters*

3. Westminster Seminary / 36
   *A Fractured Foundation—A Divided House*
   **With Addendum**—*A response to the 2006 OPC study report on justification* / 48

4. Paul Elliott's *Christianity and Neo-Liberalism* / 61
   *Drama in the Orthodox Presbyterian Church*

5. Westminster and Washington / 82
   *Church and State in American Calvinism*

*Appendix A*  Book review of Sandlin / 101
*Appendix B*  Book review of Horton (with Addendum) / 107
*Appendix C*  Book review of Moore / 124
*Appendix D*  Book review of VanDrunen / 131
*Appendix E*  Book review of Mathison / 136
*Appendix F*  Book review of Engelsma / 142

*Table of Contents*

*Supplemental Bibliography / 151*

*Name Index / 155*

# Preface

THE TERM "federalism" is the synonym for Reformed covenant theology, one that highlights the representative principle of headship associated with the First and Second Adams. Biblical history opens with the account of the creation of the world—with particular attention to the origin of humankind, fashioned in the likeness of God. It closes with the arrival of the Eschaton, the eternal kingdom of heaven. Hence, biblical history is eschatological, looking forward to the consummation of God's purposes in creation and recreation. As the account of God's relationship with humankind, biblical history is also covenantal. These two features, covenant and eschatology, are of signal importance in the interpretation of God's revelation.

The unfolding of the history of the world is distinguished by various events—and is, accordingly, subject to several divisions or schematizations. There is "the world that once was" (from creation to the great flood in the days of Noah) and "the world that now is" (from the flood to the close of the age). Never again would God destroy the earth as he did in the days of Noah. Rather, God would preserve the world until the final Day of Judgment. The rainbow is the covenant sign of God's pledge (in the Covenant of Common Grace). There is also the threefold division between Creation, Fall, and Redemption. The fall of our first parents resulted in the abrogation of the first covenant, the Covenant of Works. God's gracious provision in the offering up of the Savior of the world as substitute for the sins of humanity required the making of a new covenant, the Covenant of Grace, extending over the entire course of postlapsarian history. Equally important is the division between old and new ages, the latter inaugurated in eschatological glory (though not yet consummate fullness) with the first advent of Jesus Christ. (Hence, the new covenant age is, properly speaking, "semi-eschatological.") On any of these schematizations, the divine covenants occupy a central role in the unfolding of biblical history, the account of God's engagement with humanity. The pivotal figure in this history is the incarnate Christ, the Second and Last Adam—the Alpha and Omega.

*Preface*

More than any other theological tradition, Reformed federalism has recognized the importance of the biblical teaching on the covenants in its system of doctrine. This tradition came to mature confessional status in the writing of the Westminster Confession of Faith (and Catechisms). The place of the Westminster tradition in the stream of Christian history and theology is remarkable indeed. Westminster not only gained recognition as the epitome of Calvinist teaching at the close of the Protestant Reformation (the middle of the seventeenth century), it also earned the reputation for precision and comprehensiveness in doctrinal formulation. It became the measure by which biblical interpreters defended their systems of doctrine—either in agreement or disagreement with the theology of the Westminster divines.

With little exception (the Puritan doctrine of the sabbath being the notable one), the Westminster documents bear testimony to Reformed catholicity. And they continue to speak for historic Reformed orthodoxy (*i.e.*, international Calvinism) down to the present day. This is not to suggest that Westminster Calvinism is not open to revision and correction—in places. And, to be sure, the Westminster theology has found its ardent critics. Today, no where are the Westminster standards faulted more than in the doctrine of the covenants (including the juridical interpretation of justification and the law of God). The chief focus of this collection of essays is the doctrine of the law of God—law as covenant. More specifically, our theological concern is the relationship between the Law and the Gospel. Of equal interest is the subject of the divine institutions of church and state, which introduces us to the important and perennial question concerning the relationship between church and state in the postlapsarian world. (Prior to the Fall, there was only theocracy—God's immediate rule over his people. The institutions of church and state arise after the Fall.)

While the first chapter lays out the biblical warrant for the Reformed doctrine of the Covenant of Works, the second features the work of the leading modern-day exponents of federalism, Geerhardus Vos and Meredith G. Kline. Division within the Westminster Seminaries over the doctrine of covenant, justification, and election—including its impact upon the Orthodox Presbyterian Church—is the subject of the third and fourth chapters. The closing chapter takes up the subject of the relationship between church and state, pointing out differences in theological viewpoint based upon divergent and conflicting understandings of the doctrine of the covenant. Central to all this discussion is the teaching concerning the spiritual nature of the church as the gathered saints, the covenant people of God called out from the world as the instrument of God's reconciliation and redemption. The appendixes contain reviews of books addressing the subject of the theology of the covenants (including justification, predestination, and the sacraments). Here additional light is shed on differences and contradictions in contemporary Reformed formulation. Of crucial importance in these articles and reviews is the teaching of the (New) Westminster School, which presently holds multiple perspectives on basic Reformed doctrine—views reflecting the diverse meandering of (neo-)Calvinism and (neo-)evangelicalism more broadly over the last three decades.

These writings are the climax of three decades of research and study; they appear as the third in the series of collections published by Wipf and Stock, beginning with *Covenant Theology in Reformed Perspective,* followed by *Gospel Grace: The Modern-day Controversy.* The critical teaching in dispute in each of these studies is the classic Protestant antithesis between the Law and the Gospel, what serves as the basis for the Reformed doctrine of the twofold covenants, the Covenant of Works and the Covenant of Grace. Protestant-Reformed Orthodoxy now stands at the crossroads; the plight of Westminster Seminary (East and West) is merely illustrative of the depth and the intensity of the contemporary theological dispute, one impacting the future of Protestant evangelicalism as a whole. The battle is between historic Reformed-Protestantism and modern-day revisionism of a radical sort. The rise of postmodernism (or nonfoundationalism) is indicative of the rapidly changing mood and posture in ("evangelical") biblical scholarship at the opening of this third millennium of Christian interpretation. Without question, the modern church continues to lose her biblical moorings. Forsaking the basic theological convictions of the Protestant Reformation it has attempted to subject the Word of God to vigorous academic (*i.e.*, "scientific") investigation (the return of rationalism). In doing so, it has abandoned the Scripture principle, which recognizes the uniquely authoritative and inerrant character of the Word of God. Lost in the shuffle is the uncompromising proclamation of the one, true Gospel—the Gospel of justification by grace through faith alone. Lost also is the doctrine of the perspicuity of Scripture. Nothing less than a new Reformation in our day will halt travel down the road leading to destruction.

[A summary exposition of the issues in dispute can be found in my two-part essay: "Today's Church: Standing or Falling?" [Part 1] in *The Outlook* 54.4 (April 2004) 5–8; and "Judgment According to Works: The Crux of Today's Dispute" [Part 2] in *The Outlook* 54.5 (May 2004) 6–8.]

# Acknowledgments

*The following are published here with permission:*

Review of Michael Horton, *God of Promise: Introducing Covenant Theology* (Grand Rapids: Baker, 2006), in *Journal of the Evangelical Theological Society* (forthcoming).

Review of Russell D. Moore, *The Kingdom of Christ: The New Evangelical Perspective* (Wheaton: Crossway, 2004), in *Journal of the Evangelical Theological Society* 48 (2005) 410–15.

Review of *The Pattern of Sound Doctrine: Systematic Theology at the Westminster Seminaries*, ed. David VanDrunen (Phillipsburg: Presbyterian and Reformed, 2004), in *Southern Baptist Journal of Theology* (forthcoming).

Review of Keith A. Mathison, *Given for You: Reclaiming Calvin's Doctrine of the Lord's Supper* (Phillipsburg: Presbyterian and Reformed, 2002), in *Journal of the Evangelical Theological Society* 48 (2005) 174–78.

Review of David J. Engelsma, *The Covenant of God and the Children of Believers: Sovereign Grace in the Covenant* (Grandville, Mich.: Reformed Free Publishing Association, 2005), in *Journal of the Evangelical Theological Society* (forthcoming).

ONE

# The Significance and Basis of the Covenant of Works

*Exegetical and Theological Factors*

THE REFORMED doctrine of the Covenant of Works was introduced in the late sixteenth century, with intimations of a pre-Fall covenant appearing in earlier writers, notably, in Augustine, Heinrich Bullinger, and John Calvin. Study of the history of biblical interpretation from the time of the Reformation onwards shows that the doctrine of the Covenant of Works developed in close conjunction with exposition of the old, Mosaic economy of redemption. In their controversy with the Anabaptists, who held a low view of the Old Testament (partly reminiscent of the teaching of Marcion, an expositor from the early period of church history), Reformed theologians vigorously challenged their erroneous reading of the Bible and championed a positive assessment of the Old Testament, companion to the New. Despite obvious differences between the old and new covenants —chiefly, the legal cast of the former—there stands the underlying unity between the two Testaments, summed up in the theological terminology of the Covenant of Grace.

Once it surfaced, the doctrine of the Covenant of Works—the covenant of law established with Adam at creation and (partially) reinstituted with Israel under Moses—very quickly became a theological commonplace in international Calvinism, a vital and essential element in the system of biblical teaching. Debates did arise how best to formulate the old, Mosaic covenant as part on the single, ongoing revelation of the Covenant of Grace, while retaining within its administration a legal (or works) principle, antithetical to the principle of grace ("grace"= saving faith in Christ as Redeemer and Reconciler).[1]

## The Significance of the Doctrine of the Covenant of Works

Precursor to this distinctively Reformed teaching was the Protestant understanding of the foundational doctrine of justification by faith alone (*sola fide*), what is called the material principle of the Reformation. The doctrine of the Covenant of Works within Reformed theology, in other words, was the inevitable systematico-theological outworking of the Protestant law/gospel contrast, which theological contrast was critical to all debates with Rome and other detractors regarding the nature and content of the Gospel of sovereign grace. And so it remains down to modern times. Evangelical Protestants maintain with one, unified voice the position affirming that the grounds of the sinner's justification before our holy and righteous God is supplied by another Person, namely, Jesus Christ. Salvation rests on an alien righteousness imputed to all who are identified (through spiritual union) with the sacrificial, substitutionary Lamb of God. Good works, though necessary in the life of the believer, are not the grounds of life and salvation, but are evidential of true, justifying faith. (Under the first covenant, the Covenant of Works, Adam as federal head of the entire human race would have earned or merited eternal life, the reward of successful probation in the Garden of Eden. More on this below.)

### *Theological summary*

The Reformed system of doctrine teaches these essential points: The Mosaic covenant is *in some sense* a covenant of works, even though it is part of the unfolding Covenant of Grace in the history of redemption. The consistent portrayal in Old and New Testaments of the old covenant is as a legal arrangement, antithetical to the new covenant administration of life and blessing (the old is a ministration of death and condemnation). The legal requirement associated with the old economy of redemption, specifically, regulation of *temporal life* in the land of Canaan *on grounds of Israel's compliance with the law of Moses*,[2] is wholly abrogated with the inauguration of the new covenant in Christ's blood. The law came through Moses, grace and truth through Jesus Christ. The principle of works-inheritance, antithetical to faith-inheritance, is expressive of the law of nature, man's duty to render full, perfect obedience to his Creator. This requirement is contained in the moral law of God. Protestant theology distinguishes three kinds of law: the moral, the civil, and the ceremonial. And alongside this threefold classification of the law of God is its *threefold usage*—the civil, the pedagogical, and the normative.[3]

*The Significance and Basis of the Covenant of Works*

The inability of sinners, individually and corporately as the people of God, to satisfy the divine demand for righteousness—such righteousness being the grounds of meritorious reward proffered in the covenant—points to the need for Another to perform the work that Adam, and later corporate Israel, was unable to fulfill as God's image-bearer. What the law could not do for sinners, Christ has done, once-for-all. God's covenant made with the two Adams (in the Covenant of Creation and in the Covenant of Redemption) entails the federal or representative principle, the one acting on behalf of the many. Under the former economy of redemption Moses as mediator of the old covenant did not act as federal head on behalf of the Israelite nation, although on certain occasions in Israelite history the obedience of Moses, as well as that of others (including corporate Israel), were pointers to the future, messianic work of Christ.[4] In each instance the representative obedience typified the obedience of the (coming) "Servant of the Lord." (Typology is an integral element in Reformed covenant theology.) The purpose of the Sinaitic covenant was to frustrate Israel in seeking righteousness on grounds of works-obedience. As her history proved, Israel was unable to secure the temporal blessing of God on this legal basis. Babylonian exile dramatized the futility of works-righteousness as the way to secure blessing from God. (Here it must be stressed that the Sinaitic law never stipulated works-obedience as the grounds of *eternal* blessing, only as the grounds of *temporal* blessing in the land of Canaan—and this for purely pedagogical purposes.)

The latter prophets were the agents of God's covenant lawsuit against disobedient, wayward Israel. Calling the Israelites to repentance and covenant-faithfulness, the prophets were not heeded, their message ignored. Even the messenger of God's final ultimatum with Israel, John the Baptist, was rejected.[5] What the old covenant could not achieve on Israel's behalf was realized through the work of the great Prophet and High Priest, Jesus Christ—by the establishment of the new and better covenant. The sacrificial system of the levitical institution pointed to the final sacrifice for sin, the Lamb of God. Christ's work of atonement involves the vicarious satisfaction of the penal and legal obligations of the covenant first broken by Adam in the Garden. (That primal history was played out again in the theocratic life of Israel in the typological Garden of God, Canaan, the land flowing with milk and honey.[6] This earthly Garden typified the eternal dwelling of God with his people in the new heavens and new earth which is to come. The typological picture in the Bible is rich, diverse and complex.)

Christ in his life and death fulfilled the requirements of God's law on behalf of the elect, and them alone. Salvation is *actualized*; it is *accomplished*. All this to say, the work of Christ on the cross did not make salvation possible (dependent upon those who might respond on their own volition favorably to the free offer of the Gospel), but certain for the elect. The Holy Spirit—the Spirit of Christ—applies the benefits of the crucified, risen Lord to all those chosen in him. If God were to save a fallen people, it was necessary that he satisfy divine justice, paying the penalty for sin and removing the guilt of transgression. This is the meaning of the Reformed doctrine of the *consequent, absolute necessity of the atonement*. The divine purpose and good pleasure of God was "contracted" in the plan of redemption, the so-called Counsel of Peace or Covenant of Redemption established in eternity between the Father and the Son—in the Spirit. The plan of God entails a threefold imputation: (1) the imputation of Adam's sin to all humanity; (2) the imputation of the sins of the elect to the Second Adam when he made satisfaction for the sins of the world on Golgatha's hill; and (3) the imputation of the meritorious obedience of Christ to the elect, his obedience being the exclusive grounds of life and salvation. The obedience of the messianic Son of God includes both his life of active obedience (keeping of the law) and passive obedience (suffering and satisfaction for sin).

The justification of sinners is by faith alone. Faith is the sole instrument of soteric justification; the (scholastic) term "instrument" identifies the precise manner in which sinners receive the righteousness of Christ as a free gift of grace. Salvation is by grace through faith alone. Good works, though not instrumental in the justification of sinners, are evidential of true, saving faith. They are necessary. The justification of the godly is realized in time, as the outworking of God's eternal purpose. From this vantage point, the proper purpose of redemptive covenant is election. In terms of the institution and administration of covenant in the history of salvation, however, *redemptive covenant is broader than election.*

Baptism as the sign and seal of the Covenant of Grace identifies and secures, according to its *proper purpose,* the salvation of those chosen in Christ (in the mystery of God's electing purpose). Hence, not all recipients of the baptismal ordinance receive the saving benefits of Christ's atonement. Baptism, like circumcision previously, enunciates the dual sanctions of the covenant, blessing for obedience and curse of disobedience. In all cases Christian baptism is the sacrament of initiation into the covenant family of God, the church visible. It does not guarantee salvation for all who receive the sign.[7] The fruits of justification (and regeneration which precedes justification) are manifested in converted lives—lives evidencing true repentance, faith and obedience. Here we must distinguish properly the benefits of the Covenant of Redemption to the elect and the wider (common grace) benefits of the Covenant of Grace to the unregenerate who find themselves included within the covenant family in its historical formation.[8]

## *Biblical panorama: covenant and eschatology*

Idyllic paradise in the original Garden of Eden was the beginning—not the end—of God's purpose in creation. The climax of the creation-days was the fashioning of Adam, progenitor of the human race, in the image of God. After successful probation, namely, faithful guardianship of the holy place of God's meeting/dwelling in the midst of his image-bearers, humankind would have been confirmed in righteousness and equipped to pursue the cultural mandate free from sin and its destructive consequences. Humankind would have enjoyed perfect dominion over all creation as God's vicegerents, without the ravaging effects of sin, disease, corruption, and natural catastrophe. Procreation would likewise have proceeded without sorrow or pain in child-bearing. Unlike the angelic host, humankind was created a race of peoples; its destiny would be determined by the outcome of Adam's representative obedience (his "one act of righteousness") or disobedience.

Creation is eschatological from the start. There would have been movement from glory to greater glory by means of Adam's own glorification of God in the days of probation. The principle of the Covenant of Works was legal, not gracious (what is descriptive of the postlapsarian situation *exclusively*). God was pleased after Adam's transgression to establish an altogether different covenant, what Reformed theologians have categorized as the Covenant of Grace, extending from the Fall to the Consummation. Upholding divine justice and righteousness, the Son of God (Second Adam) would satisfy the legal requirement associated with the first covenant made with Adam. He would fulfill all righteousness on behalf of God's elect. The way of divine blessing is the way of works-righteousness; salvation would require an alien righteousness, the meritorious obedience of Christ imputed to sinners by grace through faith.

Preparatory to the accomplishment of redemption in the fullness of time, God mediated his covenant of law to theocratic Israel through Moses. (The attending angels on Mount Sinai—those who successfully passed their prior time of probation—were part of the theophanic glory-Council, ministering as God's servants in creation and recreation.) The old economy was Israel's time of probation, anticipatory of the probationary circumstance that would qualify Jesus' earthly mission as the true Servant of the Lord.

Where there is probation, there is a covenant-of-works arrangement. Such was the case with Adam at creation, Israel at Sinai, and Jesus, "born of a woman, born under the law" (Gal 4:4).

The original Temple of God, God's dwelling with his people, was manifested in the Garden of Eden, later prophetically and eschatologically portrayed in the refashioning of the people of Israel in the wilderness (a situation echoing the first creation, when order was brought out of chaos). Israel's safe passage to and settlement in the land of Canaan was prelude to Christ's greater exodus from Egypt (the house of bondage) and entrance into the eternal, heavenly Kingdom of God (the saints already enjoy the heavenly session at Christ's right hand). The Solomonic temple was merely provisional and typological. Establishment of the new covenant brought about the reshaping and reordering of the covenant life of God's people in the present (semi-)eschatological age of the Spirit. The paradigm of this glorious work of God in creation and recreation is the Glory-Spirit, God as overshadowing Protection and Giver of life. The everlasting Temple of God dawns with the coming of the Spirit in consummate power and perfection. Those united to Christ presently enter into that reality, though now only as a foretaste of things to come on the Great Day of his appearing.

# The Basis of the Doctrine of the Covenant of Works

We indicated above that the origin of the Reformed doctrine of the Covenant of Works is found in expositions of the Mosaic covenant of law, a covenant that stands in contrast to the new covenant, even as it is wholly consistent with the unfolding revelation of the single Covenant of Grace in the history of redemption. In simple terms, this means that there is only one way of salvation in the old and new economies, the way of justification by grace through faith. The legal cast of the Mosaic covenant, however, is apparent throughout the literature of the Old and New Testaments, nowhere more clearly than in the Book of Deuteronomy. Only blindness or obstinacy would lead one to dissolve or obscure the biblical antithesis between the principle of works-inheritance associated with the Mosaic law (restricted to temporal life in the land of Canaan) and the principle of faith-inheritance associated with the Abrahamic promise (the good news of the Gospel—salvation and eternal life in Christ as the free, unmerited gift of God's saving grace to undeserving sinners).

Modern-day repudiation of the Reformed doctrine of the twofold covenants, the Covenant of Works and the Covenant of Grace, immediately registers itself among other loci within the system of doctrine. Detractors of traditional covenant theology contend that the doctrine of the Covenant of Works is speculative, rationalistic, scholastic—in a word, unbiblical. In the final analysis, the present-day dispute must be answered from Scripture, not the history of doctrine. At the same time, it is a matter of moral and scholarly integrity that we represent fairly and accurately the teachings of historic Calvinism, from the time of the Protestant Reformation onwards.[9] The discipline of historical theology is not our immediate concern in this essay. Rather, the question is: What evidence is there from Scripture—summarily stated—to support the teaching of historic Reformed orthodoxy? To that question we now turn.

The context for the unfolding drama of human history is the eternal, decretive purpose of God, his sovereign and absolute control of whatsoever comes to pass. The decree(s) of God, which is one and many, provides for the historical differentiation between the elect and the reprobate over the passage of time. Redemption was not an afterthought; it was not a quick fix to a sad and surprising development at the opening of human history. The Fall was inevitable; it was decreed by God to take place. The responsibility for the sin of Adam and Eve belongs entirely to them, not to God. How do we reconcile the sovereign decree of God and human responsibility? We are obliged to receive both truths as divinely revealed in Scripture. Special and general revelation (specifically, the law of nature) provide indisputable testimony to every fallen son and daughter of Adam that he/she is guilty and accountable to God for transgression, personal and federal.

The apostle Paul in Romans 5 explicitly teaches the representative headship of Adam; his sin is the sin of Everyman. Given the reality of this universal predicament, God enters into covenant with Israel at Sinai for the purpose of Israel—identified as the "Old Man" in Romans 6—to relive the experience of the First Adam. In the seventh chapter of Romans the apostle portrays Israel *metaphorically* as Adam, the man of sin, who broke covenant with God by willful disobedience, thus mirroring his father the devil. Once Israel was alive (in the time of promise, from Abraham to Moses); then Israel died (in the time of law, climaxing in the days of Babylonian captivity). The resurrection of dry bones was a miraculous work of God, bringing life from the dead, what was prelude to the death and resurrection of Jesus, Second Adam, who would come to make atonement for sin and achieve victory over Satan and his evil hordes—all in fulfillment of the promise to our first parents in the Garden after the Fall (Gen 3:15).

Israel as a child of the times (pre-Messianic) was introduced to a picture world of types and symbols. The time of law was shadowy in contrast to the time of grace, which is reality (John 4:21-24 and Heb 10:1). The law of Moses, inadequate and temporary though it was, would govern the Israelite theocracy until the Seed should come. The establishment of the new covenant in Christ's blood necessarily resulted in the abrogation of the old (Heb 8). Why was the law incapable of bearing fruit for salvation? Why was the new covenant described as a ministration of life and righteousness, in contrast to the old as a ministration of death and condemnation (2 Cor 3)? It was not because the Spirit of grace was not working effectually in the lives of true believers in the former economy of redemption. He was. There could be no salvation apart from the Spirit's regenerating work (under the old and new economies). The reason for the weakness of the law as a covenant of works was the operation of the principle of inheritance obligating obedience, that is, works-righteousness (*not* works-salvation), as grounds for blessing. The purpose of the giving of the law under Moses was to demonstrate that the works of sinners cannot secure the temporal inheritance, let alone the eternal. (There are instances, however, when Israelites individually or corporately were rewarded for their obedience; but these were instances of typological anticipation of the saving work of the coming Messiah—part of the pedagogy of the law in the former economy of redemption). In addition, the levitical institutions regulating temple-worship, ritual and sacrifice were of temporary duration (Heb 10:1-25). The benefit(s) of the new covenant, however, is of eternal duration; and the principle of inheritance associated with the gospel of Christ as revealed in the Covenant of Grace is that of saving faith (the gospel is more fully and clearly revealed under the new).

The pivotal text in the Old Testament enunciating the legal principle of the Sinaitic covenant is Leviticus 18:5 (note the numerous citations of this text in the Old and New Testament literature). We consider here only one reference, that found in Paul's letter to the Galatians, chapters 3 and 4. The apostle states emphatically and unequivocally that the works-inheritance principle, "do this and life," is antithetical to the gospel-principle, "believe in the Lord Jesus Christ and you shall be saved" (Rom 10:1-10).[10] This aspect of the Mosaic covenant of law, however, does not exhaust its meaning and content. As we noted earlier, Moses is both a preacher of Law and a preacher of Gospel. The purpose of the law is, in part, pedagogical; the law is Israel's schoolmaster until Christ comes. The pentateuchal writings also contain the good news of gospel-grace, salvation and life everlasting in the strong arms of the Lord's Anointed. The prophets, likewise, foretell the coming of this Servant of the Lord, Israel's Redeemer and Advocate. The principle of works-inheritance characteristic of the Mosaic law is a reinstitution of the legal principle operative in the first covenant with Adam before the Fall. Adam would live, commune with God, and receive the gift of life everlasting on the grounds or merit of his own obedience, not that of another. Doing the will of God as federal head, Adam would earn life eternal for himself and his posterity. The reward of eternal life was to be earned (that is, merited) by Adam; it was not a gift of unearned grace. (The theological term "grace" refers to redemptive provision. Moreover, the notion of non-soteric, prelapsarian grace is a contradiction in terms; it is an oxymoron.)

The giving of the law did not annul the Abrahamic promise; somehow the dual principles of inheritance, legal and gracious, were administratively compatible in the Mosaic economy. It is the task of systematico-biblical exegesis and interpretation to elucidate further the meaning and significance of the law at Sinai. (The canonical writings do not provide all that needs to be said by way of theological exposition and amplification. Church doctrine and canonical teaching work in tandem, though only the teaching contained in Scripture is inspired and inerrant [free from error]. That said, the theological work of the Christian church throughout her history is a valid and necessary extension of biblical teaching, teaching that manifests the deepening *understanding* of the mind of the church[11]). It is the great apostle Paul who supplies the most systematic and comprehensive reading of the history of redemption, most notably in his letter to the Romans, the pinnacle of Paul's theological reflection and work as apostle to the Gentiles.

The books of Exodus and Deuteronomy, containing respectively the first and second giving of the law mediated through Moses, place before Israel the *temporal* blessings of life in the land of Canaan, obtained on the meritorious grounds of Israel's covenant obedience; disobedience elicits the *temporal* curses, chastisement and ultimately exile from the land (see especially Deut 28). Securing the spiritual, eternal inheritance is wholly a matter of faith-righteousness, a gift of God's grace, that not of works. (Recall, Moses is a preacher of Law and Gospel.) If the principle of inheritance respecting temporal life in Canaan was that of grace (not its opposite, works), then the temporal blessing would have been secure and indefectible. Such clearly was not the case.[12] In this concrete, temporal, physical way God taught his children—the covenant people of God under age—that the way of salvation from sin and (ultimate) destruction is the way of faith and obedience, the latter being the *fruit* of true, justifying faith. When God's covenant people come of age with the arrival of Christ in the fullness of times, they are no longer children, but sons. One of the distinguishing features of the new, eschatological age is new covenant sonship, attained by believers by means of union with the resurrected Christ (Gal 3:23-4:7 and Rom 8:15-25).[13] And maturity is a mark of sonship. That is our standing as the new covenant people of God, or so it should be (Eph 3:14-19 and 4:11-16).

The history of theocratic Israel demonstrates the folly of human wisdom and the inability of human works to secure the blessing of God (1 Cor 1:18-31; Rom 4:1-25 and 8:1-14). But with the coming of Christ and the establishment of the new covenant comes growth in maturity and increase in covenantal responsibility and accountability. (The popular notion of gradation or rewards in heaven is a remnant of Romish theology. Our reward is Christ; there is no additional reward to be gained than the Savior himself. In the Covenant of Grace personal reward and loss pertain to the present, historical circumstance, governed and superintended by God in his providence, special and general. What bears fruit and endures throughout eternity is that which is derived from the true Vine—fruit produced by the Spirit of Christ [see John 15:1-11 and 1 Cor 3:10-15]. The good works of believers have themselves been prepared by God beforehand [Eph 2:10].) With the establishment of the new covenant no longer are the people of God in need of that which is merely shadowy and typical. Theocracy, ceremonial law, sacrificial offerings, legal obedience as grounds for temporal blessing, all come to an end. The new supplants the old, even as the moral law of God is reestablished in Christ and the civil code of Moses continues to serve as a *guide,* not as the rule or standard, in shaping public, social policy within the political institutions of this world (including America!).[14]

Returning to the legal principle of the Mosaic covenant, "do this and live," we see that Israel could not keep the law and thus secure the promise of life, temporal or eternal. However, the Gentiles did obtain the righteousness which is by faith, the gift of sovereign, saving grace (Rom 9:25-33). The picture for theocratic Israel is grim indeed, so declare the latter-day prophets. Isaiah announces utter doom and destruction: Israel has transgressed God's laws, violated the commandments of the Lord, broken the everlasting covenant (what is a reference to the original Covenant of Works and the eternal law of nature, summed up in the principle, "do this and life, or die"). God's wrath and curse are meted out. The earth is devoured; those who live in it—each and everyone—are held accountable. Every man is guilty (Isa 24:5-6; Rom 3). This is not good news for Israel, or for any of the fallen sons of God. This is Law, not Gospel. The image of sonship has been marred, communion with God severed. In a disputed passage, Hosea the prophet declares that Israel, like Adam, has transgressed the covenant.

## The Significance and Basis of the Covenant of Works

Which covenant? The covenant of Sinai, the covenant of works mediated to Israel through Moses, the covenant reinstituted (in some measure) from the earliest days of creation when God placed Adam on probation in the Edenic Garden. All humanity stands before God as covenant-breakers. Hence the need for a different covenant, the Covenant of Grace.

Fortunately for the fallen sons and daughters of Adam, including the children of Israel, God's word of judgment was not his final word. God's grace to Israel announces the enlargement of the gates of Shem (Gen 9:27), despite the curse of exile and death (compare, for example, Ezek 11:14-25; 34:11-31; and Isa 49:1-13). The prophet Jeremiah announces the coming day when the new covenant institution will be inaugurated (Jer 31:27-40). The Glory of the Lord will be revealed from everlasting to everlasting, this being the crown jewel of God's creative/recreative design and purpose, cosmic in scope. The Glory is the Lord himself dwelling with his people, world without end (John 1:14-19 and Col 1:13-29). How is this work achieved? Through the Lord's Anointed, Jesus the Christ, the exact image/representation of God, God's true Son (Heb 1:1-4). The original purpose of God in creation is not frustrated. Adam and his seed—made a little lower than the angels (which is to say, first placed in a state of probation analogous to the angels now participant in the Glory-Council of God when Adam was fashioned in that same image)—have now *in Christ* been elevated above the angels, in anticipation of the final judgment (see Gen 1: 26 and Ps 8:5; on the *ministerial* role of the angels in the giving of the law, see Gal 3:19,20). The angels had previously been confirmed in righteousness, subsequent to their successful probation. Now the saints reign with Christ, ruling and judging over all creation (Eph 1:3-14; Col 3:1-4; and Rev 20:1-6).

What is lost in the First Adam, and in Israel (as typological Adam) under the temporal covenant of works, is regained and secured forever by the Second Adam. The elect of God are the New Adam (what is a corporate metaphor). The covenant between the Father and the Son—in the Spirit—was contracted and ratified in eternity, in the Covenant of Redemption. The Son has freely and voluntarily offered up his own life as atonement for the sins of the elect, and them alone. The Spirit efficaciously applies those saving benefits of the Cross to all those chosen in Christ. What is of special note is the principle of works-inheritance informing the oath assumed by the Lord of the covenant. Divine justice requires that payment be made for sin and perfect fulfillment of the law be rendered by the God-man, Christ in our stead. Here is the exact parallel between First and Second Adams (Rom 5:12-21). The reward of the covenant is a matter of *meritorious accomplishment* on the part of the federal head, either in the case of Adam (who failed in his probationary test) or Christ (who succeeded). Christ's obedience is *meritorious;* Adam's would likewise have been, had he obeyed.

Several additional features are to be noted in the Romans 5 passage. Firstly, the law which came through Moses served as a *parenthesis* in the history of redemption. The time from Abraham to Moses is the time of grace and promise, the period wherein sins are forgiven and remembered no more. The time from Moses to Christ is the time of law and condemnation, wherein sins are reckoned *in the temporal sphere of life in Canaan* (verse 13). The people of God from Abraham to Moses were under the Covenant of Grace and recipients of God's forgiveness; under the Covenant of Law they experienced temporal death and condemnation. Secondly, *physical death* (as an expression of the common curse) reigned over the entire period, even over those who did not sin like Adam under law—on probation, under a covenant of works (verse 14). Thirdly, the First and Second Adams are alike, in that they were both under a covenant of works in their time of probation. Fourthly, the imputation of Christ's righteousness cancels out sin and guilt accruing to sinners by virtue of the imputation of Adam's sin and personal, moral depravity. Fifthly, the sons of Adam were *constituted* sinners, not made sinners (verse19). The focus is on the "one act" of Adam imputed to all humankind. We are guilty of the sin of Adam, our federal head. (Elsewhere we learn that the Fall introduced moral corruption as well, so that sinners are born in sin, born under the wrath and curse of God, incapable of pleasing him in their own natural strength.) Similarly, those who are in Christ are *constituted* righteous, not made righteous, through the imputation of Christ's "one (superlative) act," wherein the grace of God abounds far more gloriously to the many who are its recipients.[15] This grace extends to Gentiles and to Jews (compare Rom 11).

Soteric justification is by grace through faith, not by obedience as required in the Covenant of Works (Rom 5:16, 18; compare Rom 4:25). It is *grace* that qualifies the covenant God established with our first parents after their fall into sin. "Grace" as a term descriptive of God's beneficence is not applicable to the pre-Fall situation. To be sure, God's work in creating all things and fashioning his covenant-son, Adam, in his own image, is exceedingly good and beneficent (Gen 1:31), but it is not "gracious." *Grace is what is bestowed upon undeserving sinners*. Hence, the vital and necessary distinction between the Covenant of Works and the Covenant of Grace. Apart from the classic Protestant law/grace (*gospel-grace*) contrast, we cannot rightly formulate the biblical doctrine of justification by grace through faith. That is one of the chief lessons to be learned—and learned anew—from of our theological heritage.

Before turning to our final section, we note two others arguments supporting the biblical, historic Reformed doctrine of the Covenant of Works. In the first place there is the literary-treaty form of the Mosaic documents themselves. This is especially clear in the book of Deuteronomy, an outline of which follows precisely the form of the ancient suzerain treaties common in the Near East at that time: preamble, historical prologue, stipulations, sanctions, and dynastic succession.[16] This treaty pattern is replicated creatively in so many different ways and in so many different contexts throughout Scripture, Old and New Testaments.[17] The recurring theme in the ancient treaties is blessing for obedience to the great king, and punishment for violation. Prosperity is a matter of earned reward for allegiance and fidelity to the sovereign. In the second place, there is the analogy of human marriage.[18] God's covenant relationship, whether pre- or post-Fall, is analogous to the marriage-bond between a man and a woman. The prophet Ezekiel is especially fond of employing this biblical imagery to depict God's covenantal love and pledge to Israel, his bride. It is likewise employed by the apostle Paul in his edifying words of instruction regarding the Christian family—the relationship of husband to wife, parents to children, masters to slaves (Eph 5:22—6:9). Like covenants, marriage is a bond, a pledge, a commitment, a relationship. It carries privilege and responsibility. The marriage feast of the Lamb to be celebrated with his Bride at his return serves as the fitting and superlative metaphor for the inauguration of the consummate life of God with his people through all eternity. The covenant is filial, as it is legal (having some "contractual" features). There are conditions to be met in the covenant relationship. How those conditions are met (or satisfied) in God's covenant depends upon the particular arrangement in view, be it the Covenant of Works or the Covenant of Grace.

## The Great Debate Today: Challenge and Confrontation

Christian theology is at one and the same time proclamatory and apologetic. Confessional theology, including the writing of churchly dogmatics, is a statement of faith written from the standpoint of a particular theological tradition, be it Reformed, Lutheran, Arminian, or some other persuasion. The ongoing task of the church is to state clearly and boldly the teachings of the Bible on matters of faith and life—and only what the Bible teaches, nothing more, nothing less.[19] Christians write and teach theology for the benefit of the church; they are responsible and accountable in the church body (under the appropriate courts of jurisdiction) for their public teaching in the classroom, in conversation, and in publication. And, of course, the church is subject to the authority and teaching of Scripture. History has proven time and again that ecclesiastical bodies all too often succumb to new ideas and teachings that undermine the faith once-for-all delivered to the saints. In such cases they refuse to submit to Scripture and the historic orthodox creeds, preferring false doctrine which appeals to the times. Frequently, attempts are made to reinterpret Scripture and creed to one degree or another—some more radically than others. That is very much the situation we currently find among Reformed bodies professing allegiance to the confessions.

Who determines true doctrine? Scripture, to be sure, requires interpretation. Who then ultimately decides which interpretation is correct, especially when new controversies arise challenging old notions? Three considerations need to be borne in mind: (1) historic, international Calvinism bears witness to biblical truth through her confessional statements, to which appeal can and must be made in the ongoing elucidation of scriptural teaching; (2) the Holy Spirit is the final and ultimate interpreter of the inscripturated Word of God, convincing and assuring the saints of God's revelation; and (3) too often the courts of the church (from the local judicatory upwards) fail to assume their duty to guard and defend the faith, for any number of reasons, or they embrace the wrong position. The latter circumstance in large measure accounts for the present, widespread discord among Reformed churches today. This can best be illustrated in the rise of the New Westminster theology associated with the theology of Norman Shepherd and Richard B. Gaffin, Jr., teaching that has infiltrated the churches and seminaries. Related contemporary theological movements include the Federal Vision and the New Perspective on Paul. Having dealt extensively with the first of these three, we close this essay by commenting upon the New Perspective and its growing impact.[20]

The apostle Paul in Romans 10 clearly contrasts the two principles of inheritance, that set forth in the law of Moses and regulative of temporal life in the land of Canaan, and that set forth in the gospel, declaring salvation by grace through faith (apart from works, even the good works of the saints). The Jews in the time of Christ, as a whole, rejected the message of salvation through faith in Israel's Messiah, God-come-in-the-flesh. They misinterpreted the law of Moses by applying the works-principle of inheritance operative in the temporal sphere to the spiritual, eternal sphere (where it did not pertain), and thus sought salvation through works of the law (Rom 9:27-33; *cf.* 2 Cor 3:12-18). Even so, there remained a remnant of election, those Jews who were of true, spiritual Israel (Rom 2:25-29,

*The Significance and Basis of the Covenant of Works*

and chapter 11). Accordingly, there is an unbridgeable chasm between Old Testament religion—the faith of Abraham, Moses, and David—and the religion of Judaism.[21] That was true in the time of Christ and in all subsequent times.

The New Perspective reinterprets (or rather distorts) the New Testament witness in accordance with the distinctive teachings of Second Temple Judaism, which teachings Jesus himself boldly refuted. Testimony against Judaism—and the Judaizing doctrine of salvation by works—is prominent in John's Gospel, written to challenge and confront the false teachers. Complementing John's account is that of Matthew. His gospel highlights the fulfillment of the Old Testament in the New, offering a historical and theological account of the life and teachings of Christ replete with Old Testament citation. In the apocalyptic genre, the Book of Revelation portrays the consummation of God's covenant promise, "I will be their God, and they will be my people," in symbolic terms, drawing widely and diversely from the Old Testament, all pointing to the building of the true and living Temple of God in the Spirit.[22]

"Woe to the scribes and the Pharisees," declares the Lord (Matt 23). In deference to the Pharisees, those claiming to be "pure" in doctrine and in practice, Jesus invites the weak and needy to come to him to find rest and have their yoke lifted. It was the Pharisees who placed the burden upon the people to keep the law of Moses for the maintenance of their covenant-standing. Membership into God's covenant was viewed by Second Temple Judaism as a gift of divine grace and election, but maintenance was a matter of compliance with the law (hence the cooperative effort of divine grace *and* human works). In this school of religion the way of justification became the way of the faith and works, divine gift and human achievement. Similarly, the New Perspective (mis)construes the Pauline phrase "the obedience of faith" to include both faith and works in justification.

The Book of Acts, likewise, testifies to the intense antagonism (and jealousy) that arose between Judaism and early Christianity. Despite the efforts of those opposing the Gospel, God's grace prevailed and continues to prevail over the forces the evil and falsehood. Occupying a special place in Luke's inspired, historical record is the story of the conversion of Saul, called by God to be the apostle to the Gentiles. Paul recounts his Jewish upbringing and his divine calling in his letter to the Galatians (chapters 1–2) and his letter to the Philippians (chapter 3). Death to the law (as a covenant of works) and union with Christ through faith is the heart of Paul's gospel to the Gentiles and to the Jews, his brethren in the flesh (see Rom 10–11).

Second Temple Judaism and biblical Christianity are two different religions (the Protestant reformers understood that correctly).

The New Perspective misreads the exile of Israel, both in the days of Babylonian captivity and the dispersion, leading up to the time of Christ. The error in their interpretation centers upon their misreading of the covenant at Sinai. Contrary to the teachings of the Protestant-Reformed tradition, the New Perspective insists that the covenant of God with ancient Israel gave expression to electing grace, pure and simple. No works-principle here, or anywhere in the Bible. As a consequence, this school of interpretation rejects the biblical doctrine of probation, applicable to Adam at the opening of human history, to Israel reconstituted as corporate Adam (the Old Man) in the wilderness of Sinai, and to Christ in his earthly mission.[23] The Bible plainly teaches, however, that the exile of Israel was meted out in accordance with divine justice, in accordance with the curse-sanction of the Sinaitic covenant (compare Isa 40:1ff. and Dan 9). The destruction of the temple in AD 70 brought to an end the old covenant and its symbolic institutions. The new covenant is built on "better promises"—that of grace, not law. Christ under the law obeyed the will of his Father, passed probation, made satisfaction for the sins of the elect, and led the captives free. He ushered in a new, eschatological age.

Common to each of the three, deviant movements presently bearing down upon the work and witness of the church today—the New Perspective, the Federal Vision, and the Shepherd-Gaffin theology—is a mutually-shared understanding of the *gratuity* of God's (covenantal) work in creation and redemption. According to this new reading on Paul and the Mosaic law, the covenant between God and Israel (like the covenant with Adam) is a dispensation of *pure grace*, with no element of works-inheritance. On first appearances, this interpretation may sound like nothing different than what was widely taught in latter-day Puritanism, culminating in the twentieth-century theological formulations of John Murray, Westminster Seminary's most revered systematician.[24] The two views, however, are radically different. What is distinctive in the new theology is the insistence that "grace" (not "works") informs all God's dealings with humankind, before and after the Fall.[25] Neither Adam nor Israel was ever in a position to merit reward, so we are told.

To be sure, here is where argumentation in the current dispute becomes ambiguous and slippery. While Shepherd denies merit altogether (even with respect to Christ's substitutionary obedience in the procurement of redemption), Gaffin regards the obedience of the Second Adam as "meritorious" (loosely speaking), the obedience of the First Adam being similar, yet different. There is only an *analogy*, not an exact parallel, respecting the principle of inheritance as it relates to the two federal heads. Strictly speaking, maintains Gaffin, Adam as a creature of the dust could not merit blessing and reward from God (whereas the obedience of the Son is inherently meritorious).[26] And unlike Murray, who taught that the merit principle did operate in the order of nature, if not in the (subsequent) covenantal administration, Gaffin insists that God's covenant with Adam and his race is wholly a matter of divine condescension—that is, divine *gratuity* (not "works"). Contrary to Gaffin's conceptualization, the principle of inheritance is either works or grace—one or the other. There is no third way.[27]

If this point of dispute remains unclear or elusive in the mind of readers, we have only to consider the role the law/gospel antithesis plays—or does not play—in the Shepherd-Gaffin theology. Any fair reading will lead the reader to conclude that it does not function at all, certainly not as is does in historic Protestant thinking. Adopting the Barthian or neoorthodox conception of *law in grace* (or *grace in law*), the new theology jettisons the classic Protestant law/grace contrast altogether. The only reason one would set the "Law" against the "Gospel," argues the modern-day revisionist, is to be found in the sinful, human inclination to pervert the law of God, to misinterpret God's law in the attempt to establish human works (that is, obedience) as the grounds of justification before God.

Crucial to the resolution of this long-standing dispute among Reformed interpreters is acknowledgment of the probationary task originally assigned to Adam in the covenant at creation, one requiring perfect, personal obedience from the federal head (perfect righteousness is what Christ imputes to believers as the Second Adam; it is an *alien* righteousness). There is a radical discontinuity between the Covenant of Works and the Covenant of Grace in terms of the principles of inheritance, works versus faith. From the standpoint of the history of redemptive revelation, the Mosaic covenant occupies a singular place and function preparatory to the advent of Christ and the institution of the new covenant.[28]

# Conclusion

How significant is the doctrine of the Covenant of Works? Very. Without this biblical teaching the system of Reformed doctrine is fatally flawed, the Gospel of sovereign grace nullified. The new theology rejects traditional Protestant doctrine concerning the antithesis between the "Law" and the "Gospel," justification by faith (*sola fide*), and the legal cast imposed upon the old, Mosaic covenant. (The biblical doctrine of justification by faith alone acknowledges the unique instrumentality of faith in soteric justification, and the purely evidential value of obedience.) With respect to the fundamentals of the Reformed faith and the basic contour of biblical theology, there is nothing difficult here to grasp, nothing too complicated for the average reader of the Bible to understand concerning the way of salvation, contrary to what many are led to believe hearing today's detractors.

The most influential source of the new doctrine in Reformed circles is Westminster Seminary in Philadelphia. Shepherd tells us straightforwardly that confessional Reformed orthodoxy is wrong; Gaffin tells us it merely needs improvement and reformulation. Improvement where, and at what price? Whether from the New Perspective on Paul, the Federal Vision, or semi-Barthianism, teaching on the single covenant of grace, however disguised in theological formulation by exponents of the New Theology, is destructive of Gospel-grace.[29] Here there can be no fudging, no compromise on basic principles. Grace is God's gift to undeserving sinners. The ground of the believer's righteousness is Christ alone, faith receiving the perfect righteousness of Christ who is our justification. May this Gospel of grace—the one, true Gospel—be fully recovered in our churches and seminaries in our day.

## NOTES

[This paper was first written for publication in a collection of essays elsewhere. See chapter 4, endnote 27.]

[1] Our focus in this paper is not the history of the interpretation of the covenant of works established at creation and at Sinai (which I have furnished elsewhere), but rather the setting forth of the basic contour and significance of the doctrine within the Reformed tradition, past and present. Covenant theology is the unique contribution of international Calvinism. For thorough exegetical and theological discussion of the issues and concerns raised in this essay, see my *Covenant Theology in Reformed Perspective: Collected Essays and Book Reviews in Historical, Biblical, and Systematic Theology* (Eugene, Ore.: Wipf and Stock, 2000) available online at www.twoagepress.org; and its sequel, *Gospel Grace: The Modern-day Controversy* (Eugene, Ore.: Wipf and Stock, 2003).

[2] Obedience to the law of Moses brought blessing and prosperity for the Israelites living in the land of promise. Disobedience provoked God's wrath and displeasure, bringing chastisement and judgment (ultimately, exile from the land). The Israelite theocracy recalled the original state of humankind in Eden, where God ruled directly over his vassal people. There are no other theocracies in history other than these two. Here our Puritan forefathers were wide of the mark. See my "Moses and Christ: The Place of Law in Seventeenth-Century Puritanism," *TrinJ* 10 NS (1989) 11–32, republished in *Covenant Theology in Reformed Perspective* 73–93.

[3] The Mosaic law, summed up in the Ten Commandments, provides the moral standard for the theocratic people of God (intertwined with ceremonial and civil aspects). It also serves as a guide to all nations and peoples (this being its "civil use"). The governance of human

societies is ultimately the outworking of God's direct, providential superintendence. After the Fall, the requirement of *perfect obedience* in order to enjoy communion with a holy God results in the elenctic or pedagogical usage of the law, whereby the law convicts sinners, declaring them guilty of disobedience against God. In Reformed theology the order of usage is the following: civil (the first), pedagogical (the second), and moral (the third). With respect to the salvation of sinners the moral law can be truly fulfilled only in Christ, in whom there is justification and sanctification.

[4] Consult the work of Sidney Greidanus, *Preaching Christ from the Old Testament: A Contemporary Hermeneutical Method* (Grand Rapids: Eerdmans, 1999); and Leonhard Goppelt, *Typos: The Typological Interpretation of the Old Testament in the New* (trans. D. H. Madvig; Grand Rapids: Eerdmans, 1982). The latter work I have reviewed in *JETS* 26 (1982) 490–93, republished in *Covenant Theology in Reformed Perspective* 259–63.

[5] Meredith G. Kline, *By Oath Consigned: A Reinterpretation of the Covenant Signs of Circumcision and Baptism* (Grand Rapids: Eerdmans, 1968). This stands as the finest study on the subject of Christian baptism.

[6] See Mark W. Karlberg, "Israel's History Personified: Romans 7:7-13 in Relation to Paul's Teaching on the 'Old Man,'" *TrinJ* 7 NS (1986) 65–74; republished in *Covenant Theology in Reformed Perspective* 181–91; and Chris Alex Vlachos, "Law, Sin, and Death: An Edenic Triad? An Examination with Reference to 1 Corinthians 15:56," *JETS* 47 (2004) 277–98. Consult further, Meredith G. Kline, *Kingdom Prologue: Genesis Foundations for a Covenantal Worldview* (Overland Park, Ks.: Two Age, 2000); Kline, *Images of the Spirit* (Baker biblical monograph; Grand Rapids: Baker, 1980); and Gregory K. Beale, *The Temple and the Church's Mission: A Biblical Theology of the Dwelling Place of God* (New Studies in Biblical Theology; ed. D. A. Carson; Downers Grove: InterVarsity, 2004). Beale's biblical-theological study draws heavily on the work of Kline.

Throughout its history, Reformed exposition has proven to be exceedingly diverse in its unpacking of the theology of the covenants—on numerous aspects and details. Not withstanding this diversity (within confessional bounds), there is broad consensus, as evidenced in the Westminster standards, the epitome of confessional writing in seventeenth-century Calvinism. The interpretation of twentieth-century Old Testament theologian Meredith G. Kline represents one voice, one of the most insightful, speaking from within this theological tradition (see Chapter 2). Kline's latest (and perhaps final work) is *God, Heaven and Har Magedon: A Covenantal Tale of Cosmos and Telos* (Eugene, Ore.: Wipf and Stock, 2006); see my brief comments in the *Addendum* of Appendix B.

[7] See further, Kline, *By Oath Consigned*. Peter writes: "baptism now saves you," which is to say, "Christ saves." What is attributed to baptism rightfully and exclusively belongs to Christ alone (1 Pet 3:21; *cf.* 1 Cor 10:1-4; Titus 3:4-7). In sacramental language, what is true of Christ is posited to baptism, the sign and seal of the covenant, in terms denoting its *proper purpose*, namely, election unto salvation. The Federal Visionists fail to distinguish between the sign and the reality, ending up confusing the two. Their doctrine is similar to Roman sacramentalism. On a Reformed understanding of the sacrament of the Lord's Supper, see my review of Keith A. Mathison's *Given For You: Reclaiming Calvin's Doctrine of the Lord's Supper* (Phillipsburg: Presbyterian and Reformed, 2002) in Appendix E.

[8] There are three leading covenants in the Bible—the Covenant of Redemption, the Covenant of Works, and the Covenant of Grace. The question is often raised: Is the new covenant made with Christ and the elect, Christ being the mediator of the historical covenant? How are we to view the new covenant in Christ's blood, the fulfillment in history of the eternal Covenant of Redemption? First it must be said that the administration of the historical

*Notes*

Covenant of Grace is not restricted to the elect. (Here is a place where the Federal Visionists, once again, confound matters—alongside many other theological misconceptions and deviations they erroneously draw from Scripture. To be sure, our tradition is partly to blame for current misinterpretations and misformulations.)

The Covenant of Redemption is the "compact" made between the Father and the Son, involving the full participation of the Spirit in the accomplishment and application of Christ's redeeming work on behalf of the elect, and them alone. The Covenant of Grace in its historical outworking—as part of what Cornelius Van Til has described as the process of differentiation between the elect and reprobate in history—is broader than election. That is to say, its administration over the course of history includes some nonelect within the *visible* church (whether old or new economies). From this conception of the Covenant of Grace we then can move on to consider the warning passages, the threat of apostasy from the household of faith, and other related issues. Parenthetically, Ralph Smith's study, *The Eternal Covenant: How the Trinity Reshapes Covenant Theology* (Moscow, Ida.: Canon, 2003) and his earlier work, *Paradox and Truth: Rethinking Van Til on the Trinity* (Moscow, Ida.: Canon, 2002) are based on a misreading of the Bible and Reformed theology. Smith's interpretation is a prime example of eisegesis, a reading into Scripture and into Van Til views contrary to the author's meaning and intent. Smith's thinking does reflect the mindset and hermeneutical methodology of the revisionists with exceptional clarity and conviction.

Considering the Westminster Larger Catechism (31), it would appear that Meredith G. Kline's line of interpretation, shared by some of the Puritan divines, did not win the day at the Westminster Assembly—or so it would appear. But here is where matters become much more subtle and complex. As one studies the literature of the period (and in the time leading up to the Assembly), various theological nuances must be acknowledged. The answer to question 31 of the Larger Catechism provides insight into what is the *proper purpose* of redemptive covenant, namely, election to salvation. However, redemptive covenant, as historically administered over the course of time, is broader than election. Q & A 31 must be read in the light of what is taught in Q & A 61–66. Tension? Yes. Need for reformulation and clarification? Yes. Although the Covenant of Redemption is not explicitly identified in the Confession, the substance is taught in chapter 8. In the final analysis, the answer to the Federal Visionists is not exegesis of the Westminster Standards *per se*, but engagement with Scripture and the confessions, the former being the final arbiter. Theological formulation does not end with these confessional writings, important as they are in the life and witness of the church and in the history of doctrine. (Many of the comments in this note were first communicated in a recent exchange with my provocateurs Fowler White and Cal Beisner.)

[9] Evident in the work of Norman Shepherd, former professor of systematic theology at Westminster Seminary (dismissed for deviant teaching), is the distortion of the reading of the history of doctrine, notably with regard to the doctrine of covenant, election, and justification. Another instance of blatant historical revisionism is found in Peter A. Lillback's reformulation of Calvin's teaching on the covenants. (Lillback is now president of Westminster Seminary.) For critical reviews of Lillback's *The Binding of God: Calvin's Role in the Development of Covenant Theology* (Texts & Studies in Reformation & Post-Reformation Thought, gen. ed. R. A. Muller; Grand Rapids: Baker, 2001) see Cornelis Venema in the *Mid-America Journal of Theology* 13 (2002) 201–9; and David J. Engelsma in the *Protestant Reformed Theological Journal* (November 2001) 47–58, republished in *Trinity Review* (January/February 2002) and posted on www.trinityfoundation.org.

On the Westminster controversy, see especially, *Covenant and Justification: A Westminster Seminary California Faculty Symposium,* ed. R. Scott Clark (Phillipsburg: Presbyterian and Reformed, forthcoming), a collection of papers read at a conference on the campus of

*Notes*

Westminster in California critical of the teachings of Norman Shepherd; David J. Englesma, "The Account of a Fallen Seminary and a 'Falling' Church," *Standard Bearer* (April 15, 2004) 320–21; O. Palmer Robertson, *The Current Justification Controversy* (Unicoi, Tenn.: Trinity Foundation, 2003), an account of the early phase of the seminary dispute, written by a former professor of Westminster in Philadelphia; A. Donald MacLeod, *W. Stanford Reid: An Evangelical Calvinist in the Academy* (Montreal: McGill-Gween's University Press, 2004 (chapter 15 [pages 257–79] highlights Reid's role in the Westminster dispute); David VanDrunen, ed., *The Pattern of Sound Doctrine: Systematic Theology at the Westminster Seminaries* (Phillipsburg: P&R, 2004), a collection of essays by professors at Westminster (East and West) providing further insight into the divisions between the two seminaries, chiefly over the Shepherd-Gaffin theology; Mark W. Karlberg, "Westminster Seminary: A Fractured Foundation—a Divided House," paper read at the 2005 national meeting of the Evangelical Theological Society (Valley Forge, Pa., November 2005), published here as chapter 3; and Guy Prentiss Waters, *Federal Vision and Covenant Theology: A Comparative Analysis* (Phillipsburg: Presbyterian and Reformed, 2006). Additionally, see my two books listed in note one above.

In a newly published book co-authored by Mark Noll and Carolyn Nystrom, *Is the Reformation Over? An Evangelical Assessment of Contemporary Roman Catholicism* (Grand Rapids: Baker, 2005) the argument is advanced that times have changed significantly. Concerning perceived agreement among two former theological rivals, they highlight the consensus now reached on the basics of Christian doctrine and salvation. In particular, they note: "It is the same for justification by faith, about which many Catholics and evangelicals now believe approximately the same thing. . . . Thus, on the substance of what is actually taught about God's saving work in the world, if not always on the exact terminology used to describe that saving work, many evangelicals and Catholics believe something close to the same thing. If it is true, as once was repeated frequently by Protestants conscious of their anchorage in Martin Luther or John Calvin that *iustificatio articulus stantis vel cadentis ecclesias* (justification is the article on which the church stands or falls), then the Reformation is over" (p. 232). In large measure, the modern-day rapprochement among Catholics and Protestants has resulted in the blurring, if not the obliteration, of the biblical distinction between justification and sanctification.

[10] For a prime example of exegetical mishandling of this crucial biblical text—what is a strained reading—see Moisés Silva, *Explorations in Exegetical Method: Galatians as a Test Case* (Grand Rapids: Baker, 1996), chapter 11; compare his prior comments in *Philippians* (The Wycliffe Exegetical Commentary, gen. ed. K. Barker; Chicago: Moody, 1988) 127–28.

For representative thinking by faculty members of the Old Testament department at Westminster in support of the New Perspective (with some modification), see Peter Enns, in "Expansions of Scripture," *Justification and Variegated Nomism* ("The Complexities of Second Temple Judaism," vol. 1, ed. D. A. Carson et al.; Grand Rapids: Baker, 2001) 73–98, and Doug Green, "N. T. Wright—A Westminster Seminary Perspective," www.ntwright.com/Green_Westminster_Seminary_Perspective.pdf. Compare my earlier study, "The Search for an Evangelical Consensus on Paul and the Law" *JETS* 40 (1997) 563–79, republished in *Covenant Theology in Reformed Perspective* 209–26.

For an argument against the biblico-theological concept of "merit," compare James B. Jordan, "Maturity, Not Merit," Center for Cultural Leadership: www.christianculture.com/cgi-local/npublisher/viewnews.cgi?category=3&id=1038912-130; and Tim Gallant, "Monocovenantalism? Multiple Covenants, No Adamic Merit," www.timgallant.org: Biblical Studies Center: file:///A:\Gallant%20on%20monocovenantalismhtm.

*Notes*

[11] Mark W. Karlberg, "Doctrinal Development in Scripture and Tradition: A Reformed Assessment of the Church's Theological Task," *CTJ* 30 (1995) 401–18, republished in *Covenant Theology in Reformed Perspective* 357–77.

[12] Shepherd, Gaffin, and the Federal Visionists contend that the Mosaic law (with its divine sanctions of blessing and curse) teaches that election, like temporal enjoyment in the land of promise, is losable. They fail to distinguish between national election (which is losable) and decretive election, that is, election to salvation (which is unlosable).

For recent discussion of the Reformed doctrine of the Mosaic covenant (as in some measure a covenant of works) see the exchange between Patrick Ramsey, "In Defense of Moses: A Confessional Critique of Kline and Karlberg" (*WTJ* 66 [2004] 373–400), and Brenton C. Ferry, "Cross-Examining Moses' Defense: An Answer to Ramsey's Critique of Kline and Karlberg" (*WTJ* 67 [2005] 163–68).

[13] Sonship is not an entirely new covenant blessing. It is already enjoyed in the old economy, in anticipation of greater things to come (compare Heb 11:39-40). At the beginning, Adam was created a son of God (Luke 3:38). Those renewed in the image of Christ are the true sons of God. As Kline rightly maintains, covenant and sonship are twin concepts (see his *Images of the Spirit*).

[14] See my "Reformation Politics: The Relevance of Old Testament Ethics in Calvinist Political Theory," *JETS* 29 (1986) 179–91; "Covenant and Common Grace: A Review Article," *WTJ* 50 (1988) 323–37; and "Moses and Christ: The Place of Law in Seventeenth Century Puritanism." All are republished in *Covenant Theology in Reformed Perspective*. See also Chapter 5.

[15] Imputation is a crucial element in the formulation of the covenant between God and humanity. For the importance of this doctrine, see my "Covenant and Imputation: The Federal System of Doctrine," paper read at the Eastern regional meeting of the Evangelical Theological Society in Lancaster, Pa. (April 4, 2003), published in *Gospel Grace* 235–77. This essay includes a critique of John Piper's widely-read *Counted Righteous in Christ: Should We Abandon the Imputation of Christ's Righteousness?* (Wheaton: Crossway, 2002). The beneficiaries of the imputation of Christ's righteousness are the elect of God. By way of comparison, the election of angels is not "in Christ." Whether in the case of angels or humankind, election is foreordained by God in eternity past, and is not contingent upon human decision. Election is according to God's sovereign, good purpose and for the manifestation of his own glory (compare WCF, chapter 3).

Once again—after a reversal from the November 2001 public meeting of the Evangelical Theological Society—Don Garlington renounces the doctrine of imputation in "Imputation or Union with Christ," *The Tanglewood Journal: A Quarterly Publication of Tanglewood Baptist Church* 1.1 (2003) republished in *Reformation and Revival Journal* 12 (2003) 45–113; and in his *Exegetical Essays* (third edition; Eugene, Ore.: Wipf and Stock, 2003) 375–431. John Piper's response to Garlington, "Imputation or Union with Christ: A Response to John Piper," appears in the same issue of *Reformation and Revival Journal* 12 (2003) 121–27. Garlington issues "A Rejoinder to Piper," in *The Tanglewood Journal* 2.1 (2004). (Piper's theology, it must be said, fails to make a solid, substantial case for the biblical doctrine of imputation.)

[16] See especially, Meredith G. Kline, *Treaty of the Great King: The Covenant Structure of Deuteronomy* (Grand Rapids: Eerdmans, 1963).

[17] Consult further, Meredith G. Kline, *The Structure of Biblical Authority* (Grand Rapids: Eerdmans, 1972).

*Notes*

[18] All divine revelation is an accommodation to the capacity of human understanding. Further, God's self-revelation is replete with human analogies, analogies all-too-often misconstrued as conveying an equivalence or equity between God and man. This false notion destroys the basic distinction between the Creator and the creature taught throughout Scripture and witnessed by human conscience. The distinction informs ontology and epistemology, whereby we think God's thoughts after him.

[19] Theological formulation by an individual writer is unique and personal. No two theologians think exactly alike. The confessions of the church, however, help preserve essential unity and soundness on the basics of doctrine, none better than the Westminster standards.

[20] For a critique of the Federal (Re)Visionists, see my review of *Backbone of the Bible: Covenant in Contemporary Perspective*, a collection of papers edited by P. Andrew Sandlin (Nacogdoches, Tx.: Covenant, 2004) in Appendix A. John Frame, for one, anticipates a new consensus that will overturn the traditional Protestant (or as he sees it, Lutheran) contrast between Law and Gospel, a theological construct he regards as false and unscriptural.

Some today insist that we debate theological issues without naming individuals who teach controverted doctrine within our ecclesiastical circles. Or if we do, we do so without leveling the charge of heresy against anyone (except in cases where heretical teaching of individuals has already been named, identified, and determined by the courts of the church). What happens when the courts of the church themselves become thoroughly corrupted? There are times—far too numerous to recount in the history of the Christian church—when those few in number must take their stand against the majority. Scripture and conscience remain supreme in the interpretative life of the church, regardless of ecclesiastical maneuverings. For the latest developments within the Westminster school, see Chapters 3 and 4.

[21] See my review article, "Paul, the Old Testament and Judaism: A Review Article," in *Foundations: A Journal of Evangelical Theology* 43 (1999) 36–44; republished in *Covenant Theology in Reformed Perspective* 247–58.

[22] See further: Kline, *Images of the Spirit*; Beale, *The Temple and the Church's Mission*; and Beale, *The Book of Revelation: A Commentary on the Greek Text* (The New International Greek Testament Commentary; Grand Rapids: Eerdmans, 1999).

[23] Illustrative is the work of N. T. Wright. See his *The Climax of the Covenant: Christ and the Law in Pauline Theology* (Minneapolis: Fortress, 1993); *The New Testament and the People of God* (Minneapolis: Fortress, 1992); and *Jesus and the Victory of God* (Minneapolis: Fortress, 1996). An alternative, though similar, reading is offered by Frank Thielman in *Paul and the Law: A Contextual Approach* (Downers Grove: InterVarsity, 1994). Compare my "Israel Under Probation: An Evaluation of Frank Thielman's *Paul and the Law*," paper read at the Eastern regional meeting of the Evangelical Theological Society in Valley Forge, Pa. (April 4, 1995), available at www.tren.com.

[24] As I have argued in various places, Murray's interpretation of the Mosaic covenant marks a dead-end, the end of the line in English-Puritan interpretation. His position is exegetically and theologically untenable. Among my writings, see "Paul's Letter to the Romans in the *New International Commentary on the New Testament* and in Contemporary Reformed Thought," *EvQ* 71 (1999) 3–24; republished in *Covenant Theology in Reformed Perspective* 227–45.

[25] In Barth's version of monocovenantalism there is no transition from wrath to grace in history. In the Shepherd-Gaffin theology the transition is partially muted; there is no significant difference in the pre- and post-Fall covenants with respect to divine promise and

command, and the role of faith and works in soteric justification. Murray's adherence to the merit principle in the order of creation, works being the meritorious grounds of reward (what for Murray is the reward of ongoing life and communion with God), provides the basis for the doctrine of the active obedience of Christ, which obedience is requisite for the atonement for sin—vicarious obedience being imputed to those who believe. Diverse and incompatible views in the contemporary debate are offered in *Justification: What's at Stake in the Current Debates*, eds. M. Husbands and D. J. Treier (Downers Grove: InterVarsity, 2004) and in *The Glory of the Atonement: Biblical, Historical and Practical Perspectives, Essays in Honor of Roger Nicole*, eds. C. E. Hill and F. A. James III (Downers Grove: InterVarsity, 2004). On the subject of imputation, compare also, Michael F. Bird, "Incorporated Righteousness: A Response to Recent Evangelical Discussion concerning the Imputation of Christ's Righteousness in Justification," *JETS* 47 (2004) 253–75. Mark A. Seifrid, in *Christ Our Righteousness: Paul's Theology of Justification*, New Studies in Biblical Theology 9; series editor, D. A. Carson (Downers Grove: InterVarsity, 2000), upholds the classic law/gospel distinction, but questions the doctrine of imputation as misleading and inadequate. Seifrid's treatment of the subject is unsystematic, lacking any coherent theology of the covenants. In this regard, Seifrid's position is much like that of the (quasi-)Lutheran exegete and theologian Douglas Moo.

[26] This formulation hearkens back to the dualistic conception of nature and covenant held by the scholastic Reformed federalists. See my "The Original State of Adam: Tensions in Reformed Theology," *EvanQ* 59 (1987) 291–309; republished in *Covenant Theology in Reformed Perspective* 95–110.

[27] Even though the Westminster Confession of Faith (7.1) uses the language of "condescension" to describe the covenant with Adam, the divines categorized the first covenant as a Covenant of Works, one requiring perfect, personal obedience as the way to blessing and reward. And even though they viewed the covenant relationship as superimposed upon a prior state of nature, they nevertheless (and more importantly) maintained the vital law/gospel contrast in their doctrine of the covenants and justification by faith alone. See note 25 above.

[28] Lutheran theology has no doctrine of the covenants or probation; hence it holds a static conception of creation (with no adequate doctrine of biblical eschatology). The works-principle functions in the Lutheran system only as a bare, legal principle, not a covenantal principle. Lutheran teaching fails to do full justice to the biblical data. The Lutheran and Reformed, however, do agree on the essential, foundational law/gospel contrast.

[29] Common to all covenants (pre- and post-Fall), according to the monocovenantalists, are the elements of promise and stipulation; hence, they contend, all covenants are conditional. Divine blessing is contingent upon the exercise of faith and good works (the "obedience of faith"). In his highly-acclaimed and magisterial study, *Theology in America: Christian Thought from the Age of the Puritans to the Civil War* (New Haven: Yale University, 2003), historian E. Brooks Holifield reads the Puritans aright on the critical doctrines of justification and the dual covenants, teaching that conveys the classic Protestant understanding of the antithesis between Law and Gospel. But as Holifield notes, there were numerous debates over the role of works in justification, some ministers and teachers espousing views similar to that of Shepherd and Gaffin. All this to say, heterodox doctrine on justification has been around for centuries in the history of Christian doctrine, and will continue to threaten and undermine sound preaching and teaching of the Gospel.

# TWO

# New Vistas in Old Testament Narrative

*Geerhardus Vos and Meredith G. Kline
as Exemplary Reformed Interpreters*

NARRATIVE IS basic to the unfolding of redemptive revelation. Holy Scripture, Old and New Testaments, is inconceivable without storytelling. After all, the Bible is His Story, the remarkable account of God's saving intervention in the fallen world. All creation testifies to God's power and majesty, his grace and wrath. From the standpoint of the history of Christian teaching, "narrative theology" is the new kid on the block. This fact leads us to suspect that narrative in this school of interpretation is more than just retelling stories, recalling urgent pleas for divine forgiveness in seasons of great distress, or rehearsing festive moments of thanksgiving and praise over the course of the earthly and spiritual journey of the covenant people of God under two very different economies of redemptive grace.

What is this something else that narrative theology proffers? To be accurate, the approach of narrative theology is not altogether new. And that should not surprise us in the least. We have already acknowledged the importance of narrative in the sacred scriptures. The Bible as God's story of redemption is also God's interpretation of his acts in blessing and in curse. Geerhardus Vos, who taught at Princeton Seminary in the first half of the twentieth century, was the pioneer of the modern movement in Reformed theology known as biblical theology. The roots of this theological discipline extend all the way back to the earliest days of the Reformation, chiefly in the writing of the Reformed tradition's formative theologians, Heinrich Bullinger and John Calvin. This tradition is more commonly termed covenant theology, a theological approach to redemptive revelation that is structured around the divine covenants, from the creation of the world to the climatic event of the death and resurrection of Jesus Christ, in whose blood the new covenant is securely established (unlike the old).

The great apostle Paul was not only the first and greatest of the missionaries of the Christian era, he was also the greatest of church theologians. His firm grasp of the eschatological in-breaking of the kingdom of God with the coming of Christ and his ascension into heaven, coincident with the breaking-down of the barrier between Jew and Gentile, was inextricably linked to his grand, redemptive-historical perspective on the divine-human covenants, beginning with Abraham, father of all the faithful. The Abrahamic covenant marks the signal moment in redemptive history when God promised—*by covenantal oath and ancient ritual*—to be the God of his people. (Of course, as Reformed theologians maintain, the seed of the Abrahamic promise, who is Christ, was already anticipated in the Garden subsequent to the fall of Adam and Eve, in the announcement of the One who would come to destroy the work of the Serpent, placing enmity between the seed of the woman and the seed of Satan.)

The latter part of the twentieth century has produced another variety of biblical theology, namely, narrative theology. Succinctly stated, the difference between Reformed biblical (or covenantal) theology and narrative theology is the role of Christian dogmatics (confessional theology) in the interpretive enterprise. Narrative theologians are attracted to the charm, the power of stories to shape one's perception of himself and the world; they are attracted to the power of stories to arouse human imagination and aspiration. Architects in this school of interpretation include such notables as Gabriel Fackre, those associated with the "Yale school" (Hans Frei, Brevard Childs, George Lindbeck, and Ronald Thiemann) and others like Walter Brueggemann (who represents a post-Bultmannian approach, one which matches the biblical text with a socio-political agenda suited to the modern world). In the evangelical community the leading spokesman today has been the late Stanley Grenz of Carey Theological College in Vancouver. In the area of Christian ethics the work of Stanley Hauerwas speaks for this new interpretative method. Principles of ethical behavior are drawn from the Christian story, notably, the life of Christ, not abstract principles (as in early Christian ethicism which allegedly reflects Greek and Platonic ideals). Notable also are the ethical theories of Alastair MacIntyre and John Millbank.[1]

What all these modern interpreters have in common is disdain for dogmatic theology, or what they invariably see as rigid, confessional orthodoxy derived from the outmoded, scholastic Age of Reason (what is, in my judgment, nothing less than a distortion and inversion of the historical development of churchly interpretation). The modern age, as a true child of the Enlightenment, still strives to be free of the shackles of dogmatic rigidity, free from the illusion which (as some view it) holds out to the interpreter of the Bible the prospect of attaining a system of doctrine that is truly comprehensive, coherent, and consistent. Reason in the narrative school gives way to emotion, to the power and allure of stories to shape and inspire our thought and action. Accent is placed upon the recital and remembrance of God's creative and redemptive acts. Such recital is regarded as a (purely) communal, religious activity. Theological reflection, we are told, finds its base in stories retold in each succeeding generation. Here is the crucial point: this communal, interpretive retelling *is* theology—and by virtue of its allegiance to the canonical writings of the Old and New Testaments, *Christian* theology. The church's theological reflection—from ancient times to the present—is developmental or evolutionary. Out of this process of remembrance and retelling arises a sacred vocabulary peculiar to the Christian community.

To be fair, there is not a straight line of development from the Enlightenment to the modern day, to the rise of narrative theology. Pure, unadulterated reason (the god of liberalism) has now given way to reason informed by passion, supremely, the passion of Christ's death, resurrection, and ascension as set forth in the biblical story. This is, after all, the postmodernist age in which the fellowship of the saints finds itself, not the age of naked reason. Ours is the age of reason impelled by (religious) emotion. On the one hand, there is growing acknowledgment of the bankruptcy of Enlightenment reason, the inadequacy and failure of all attempts at theological foundationalism (whether based on dogmas of reason or revelation). On the other hand, there is the search for communal accountability and meaning in this dark, strange, evil world—all the more post September eleventh. Narrative theology, in my judgment, is a surrogate for genuine biblical (covenantal) theology. Nonfoundationalism insists there is no comprehensive, unifying structure in redemptive revelation, just as there is no meaningful, universal pattern for comprehending and evaluating human belief and behavior (once called "natural law," rightly formulated). We only have stories to tell—some good, some bad. We remember Abraham and Moses, Jesus and Paul. We remember the Spanish inquisition, the Holocaust, and September eleventh. Religion, no longer the opiate of the people, is seen to be the people's only hope and salvation, the one elusive way to make sense of the world around us—elusive, but the only way of approach to meaning.

Of course, what is principally at stake in this new theological enterprise we call narrative theology is the authority and sufficiency of Scripture, the living Word of God. The dogma of the true church of Christ remains unfettered: Scripture is the infallible, inerrant revelation of God to humankind. It alone sounds forth the saving word of grace and promise to sinners with absolute, divine authority—God being the supreme author of the canonical writings. Martin Luther was unquestionably correct in his teaching concerning the formal and material principles of the Protestant Reformation—Scripture as the eternal Word of God and justification by faith alone as the way of personal salvation. Krister Stendahl's talk of Luther's wounded, introspective conscience is wide of the mark; his caricature of Luther does possess the makings of an intriguing fable, however.

Long before the contemporary obsession for theological "creativity," the need to say something new (what is distinct from genuine progress in the church's *understanding* of the Bible in the history of doctrine), stands the modest attempt(s) of Reformed interpreters to be "reformed and reforming according to the Word of God." Implicit in this Reformation slogan descriptive of the Calvinistic branch of orthodox Christian theology is unqualified commitment and submission to the teachings of Scripture. Any change in theological statement or self-awareness will arise from Word and Spirit, not philosophical musings or prevailing culture (whatever subordinate role they play). Reformed biblical theology, as an extension of classical covenant theology, offers contemporary exegetes, preachers, and students of the Bible the essential vista from which to view the history of redemptive revelation. Reformed theologians, more than others, have followed more closely in the trail of the apostle Paul, both in terms of his grasp of redemptive history and his understanding of the application of redemption in the present, eschatological age of the Spirit (union with the risen Christ).

Within evangelicalism the principal contender alongside Reformed covenant theology for presenting a coherent, comprehensive interpretation of the Bible is modern-day dispensationalism. Consider, however, the remarkable changes that have taken place within the last few decades, the shift from early Schofieldism to progressive dispensationalism. We may well argue the point, but it is clear to me that Reformed teaching has helped clear the way for needed reformulation of dispensational theology. The critical, decisive issue still remains: How do we understand the continuity of God's redemptive purpose with respect to the history of God's covenant with Israel and with her true, spiritual heirs subsequent to Pentecost, what Reformed theology identifies as the single, unfolding "Covenant of

Grace" spanning the entire period from the Fall to the Consummation? Specifically, what is the place of ethnic Israel in the millennial age, wherever one chooses to locate the "millennium"? What is the place of ethnic Israel in the Age to Come? My purpose in this article is not to engage this dialogue among evangelicals, but to commend the distinctive contributions of Geerhardus Vos and Meredith G. Kline as modern-day exponents of traditional Reformed covenant theology. What is most characteristic in their work is the significance and role given to the Mosaic theocracy in the economy of redemption. What is "new" in their work is new only in the sense of a deeper, fuller grasp of the continuity/discontinuity between the two testaments, a subject that lies at the heart of both covenant and dispensational theology. Parenthetically, let me say that theological discourse is necessarily dialogical. Without a doubt, many "evangelical-Reformed" interpreters today have some very basic, biblical doctrine to (re)learn from our dispensational friends, most notably, as regards the importance of the biblico-theological antithesis between the "Law" and the "Gospel" (on which I have written at great length). Certainly, there is no room for pride of place in biblical exposition from the standpoint of the history of Christian interpretation (Evangelical Protestantism stands united in upholding the law/gospel antithesis, essential in the doctrine of soteric justification).

In the formative years of Westminster Seminary three theologians were principally responsible for laying the foundations of the Westminster school, teaching that would change radically in later years. Cornelius Van Til and John Murray were both deeply influenced by the Dutch-American dogmatician and Old Testament scholar, Geerhardus Vos, founder of Reformed biblical theology as a distinct theological discipline. Of course, Vos did not teach at the fledgling seminary, but remained at Princeton. It is now clear that he would have fared better in the theological world of his day and ours had he moved across the Delaware River and planted his mark on American presbyterianism for the sake of future generations. Regrettably, that did not happen, and American presbyterianism and international Calvinism have suffered for it. With respect to Princeton's faculty as a whole, Vos' teachings were lost—or never grasped—at the time Westminster was founded. Vos' work found its home at Westminster, and nowhere else. In my reading of Van Til and Murray, it was Van Til, not Murray, who truly imbibed Vossian theology. In addition to sharing ethnic roots in the Netherlands, the writings of Vos and Van Til are theologically dense and difficult to read as well as comprehend. This circumstance generated strong head winds for the new seminary. Westminster truly had its theological work cut out for it right at the start. Though Van Til is chiefly remembered as a theistic presuppositionalist, what is perceived to be an oddity in the world of classical evangelical-Reformed apologetics, this titan gave Westminster Seminary her distinctive theological character and her unique place in historic Calvinism. The two most important ingredients in Van Til's work are Reformed covenant theology and Christian theism.

By the 1960s a succeeding generation of seminary students after the founding of Westminster would come to learn, or reject, Vossian theology under Professor Kline, Westminster's other brilliant Old Testament scholar and theologian. At this same time the seeds of destruction—the undoing of Vossian theology—were being laid. Norman Shepherd had joined the faculty, having been selected by Murray as his successor in the theology department. Along comes Richard Gaffin in the New Testament department, only to become in later years Westminster's senior systematician. Whereas Shepherd was dismissed from the seminary for doctrinal deviation, Gaffin remained to pursue the same course adopted by Shepherd and several others as early as the late 1960s. Today, the Westminster school houses two claimants to the theological legacy of Vos, one orthodox and the other neoorthodox—the former in the line of Francis Turretin and Herman Bavinck, the other in the line of G. C. Berkouwer and Karl Barth.[2]

A focal issue in dispute at Westminster—a dispute that erupted in the 1970s and continues on to the present—is the interpretation of the Mosaic covenant as *in some sense* a covenant of works. The very concept of a "covenant of works," a commonplace in historic Reformed theology, has of late fallen on very bad times. Complicating matters is the situation in which the current Westminster faculties labor in Philadelphia and in Escondido. There are those on the faculty who regard Shepherd's theology as heretical and those who do not. The ramifications of this dispute in the Reformed world are exceedingly wide and deep.[3] Westminster's controversy brings all the more into sharper focus the growing and contentious debate between traditional Protestant interpreters and those aligned with the New Perspective on Paul and the law. At Westminster the principle antagonists have been made to appear to be Kline and Gaffin.[4] Where Gaffin contradictorily (and misleadingly) stands for Shepherd and against the New Perspective, Kline in no uncertain terms denounces the teaching of both as anathema.[5]

My studies at Westminster coincided with the Shepherd controversy. Doctoral work, following attainment of the master of divinity degree and masters in New Testament, was begun under Norman Shepherd. Even prior to the last program of study, my interest and passion for covenant theology on campus quickened renewed, open discussion of covenant theology in and outside the classroom. During those years Meredith Kline was invited to serve as visiting professor from Gordon-Conwell Seminary, where he had been teaching since 1968. Only later would I come to understand better the circumstance at Westminster in the 1960s. It appears from available writings and conversations with faculty that John Murray's recasting of covenant theology was not widely known or understood. Certain features were discussed and debated. Murray, Old Testament professor and colleague E. J. Young, and others opposed Kline's interpretation of Scripture on several points, most notably, observance of the (creational-)sabbath ordinance in the old and new dispensations, the days of Genesis, and the Mosaic covenant as a legal disposition (as a republication of the original covenant of works in Eden suited to the postlapsum situation). Murray's objection to the covenant-of-works concept was barely understood or comprehended. It did not come into the full light of day until Robert Strimple, another of Westminster's systematicians, brought it out into the open in faculty and student discussions during the mid-1970s.

We now know that Kline's take on the Adamic covenant and the Mosaic covenant as a republication (of sorts) of the creation covenant is representative of mainstream, historic Reformed thinking. The pedigree for Murray's view is found in one strand of Puritan theology, what became the dominant opinion in later Puritanism (after 1648). As I argued in my 1980 dissertation, the key to interpretation of the Mosaic covenant is the doctrine of the first covenant with Adam, the Covenant of Works in its original purity and uniqueness. Adam was created perfect in knowledge, righteousness, and holiness, able to keep covenant with God and to sustain his justified status on the basis of perfect, personal obedience (Adam's representative, federal obedience would have served as the meritorious grounds of humankind's confirmation in righteousness after successful probation). By taking Murray's view of the original Adamic administration one step further, Shepherd and Gaffin have abandoned the Protestant law/gospel contrast altogether, substituting for it the Barthian notion of "law in grace." Collateral support for this novel theological deviation at Westminster now comes from the biblical department's attraction to the New Perspective.

It is clear where my sympathies lie in this yet unresolved seminary dispute. Throughout most of my years of study at Westminster, I enjoyed the singular privilege and opportunity of transporting Professor Kline from the Philadelphia airport to the seminary campus, home for dinner, and back to the airport for his return flight. What a full day of theological stimulation and mentoring it proved to be for me—I too was in flight! From this high altitude I want to close this essay by highlighting the distinctive vista afforded the covenant theologian as he/she canvasses the theological terrain of redemptive history—and that from the biblical-theological perspective of Geerhardus Vos and Meredith Kline.

The creation of humankind in the image of God—humankind federally represented in the person of Adam—had a specific purpose, an eschatological goal. By means of probationary testing, humankind would move from one state of perfection (founded upon the integrity of Adam's creation in the image of God) to a higher state of perfection, namely, confirmation in righteousness, and this prior to the final state of glorification which would have come at the close of history as originally designed by God. The sovereign, all-encompassing decree of God, however, issued in the fall of Adam, making necessary the institution of a second covenant, the "Covenant of Grace," for the redemption of sinners. Behind the historical Covenant of Grace, which is not coextensive with the salvation of God's elect (redemptive covenant is broader than election), stands the "Covenant of Redemption," the covenant between the Father and the Son in eternity, the arrangement or pact which made provision for the accomplishment and application of redemption on the basis of the atoning work of Christ and through the effectual operation of the Spirit in historical time for the elect, and for them alone. The efficacy of the Spirit's work was applicable throughout the entire course of redemptive history, before and after the atoning work of Christ on the cross.

Adamic probation is inexplicable apart from the institution of the Covenant of Works with Adam as federal head of humanity. Divine blessing and approbation—the reward of the covenant—was a matter of *meritorious* accomplishment on the part of Adam (hence, the justification of sinners saved by grace rests upon the *meritorious* obedience of Christ, the Second Adam). The full, clear message of God's free grace in justification was something to be revealed progressively over time—in the historical unfolding of redemptive revelation. The election of theocratic Israel (what is national election—not decretive election, *i.e.,* election unto salvation) would serve the tutelary purpose of instructing the ancient people of God in the way of salvation. The old, Mosaic economy stands as a parenthesis in the history of redemption. The law, which came four hundred years after the Abrahamic promise, reintroduced the principle of works-inheritance—this time in the earthly, temporal sphere of physical life in the land of Canaan. (Salvation is and remains always by grace through faith. It is not a matter of works-righteousness.) Biblical typology and covenant theology are mutually interpretive; the one is incomplete and ultimately incomprehensible without the other. Vossian covenant theology in its mature statement is Kline's distinctive contribution. It took a period of several decades before Kline—in study of Scripture and in conversation with Westminster faculty and students—would arrive at a clearer understanding of the biblical text.[6]

The story of redemption, set forth in the gospels and the epistles, the canonical writings of the new covenant, documents the fulfillment of the ancient promise delivered to ancient, theocratic Israel under the old dispensation of law. The Mosaic economy is part and parcel of the ongoing administration of the Covenant of Grace that has gradually unfolded in salvation history—from seed to full flowering. Covenant theology is the handmaid to typological, as opposed to allegorical, interpretation of the Bible. Who among us would question God's lordship over history and salvation? God has carved out his story in the life and experience of theocratic Israel. In the story book world in which Israel lived, observing or breaking the covenant obligations was awarded temporal prosperity or calamity in the land of Canaan respectively. That ancient picture-world of symbols and types ceased with the (semi-)eschatological realization of the ancient promise. Shadow has given decisive way to reality—with no turning back. The new covenant people of God now worship in Spirit, in the eschatological realities associated with the arrival of the kingdom of Christ. We no longer worship in an earthly temple, on a holy mount. New Jerusalem is the true, heavenly sanctuary, the place where even now the saints are gathered in the Spirit, in resurrection life and power (John 4:21-24). We are seated with Christ in the heavenlies, in anticipation of the consummation of history, the new heavens and new earth, and in anticipation of the redemption of our bodies (Col 3:1-4; Rom 8:19-23). What a vista from the heavenly mountain!

## NOTES

[This paper was first read at the April 2005 Eastern regional meeting of the Evangelical Theological Society (Souderton, Pa.)]

[1] For a representative sampling, see the following works: Walter Brueggemann, *The Covenanted Self: Explorations in Law and Covenant* (Minneapolis: Fortress, 1999) accenting Buber's "dialectical presence of God," and *An Introduction to the Old Testament: The Canon and Christian Imagination* (Louisville: Westminster John Knox, 2003) which exploits "imaginative remembering;" Brevard Childs, *Biblical Theology of the Old and New Testaments: Theological Reflection on the Christian Bible* (Minneapolis: Fortress, 1992); Gabriel Facke, *The Christian Story: A Narrative Interpretation of Basic Christian Doctrine* (third edition; Grand Rapids: Eerdmans, 1996) and *The Doctrine of Revelation: A Narrative Interpretation* (Grand Rapids: Eerdmans, 1997); Hans W. Frei's classic study, *The Eclipse of Biblical Narrative:*

*Notes*

*A Study in Eighteenth and Nineteenth Century Hermeneutics* (New Haven: Yale University, 1974), and his *Types of Christian Theology* (New Haven: Yale University, 1992); Stanley Grenz, *Theology for the Community of God* (Grand Rapids: Eerdmans, 2000); Stanley Hauerwas, *A Community of Character: Toward a Constructive Christian Social Ethic* (Notre Dame: Notre Dame University, 1981), and *Christian Among the Virtues: Theological Conversations with Ancient and Modern Ethics* (Notre Dame: University of Notre Dame, 1997); George A. Lindbeck, *The Nature of Doctrine: Religion and Theology in a Postliberal Age* (Philadelphia: Westminster, 1984); Alastair MacIntyre, *After Virtue: A Study in Moral Theory* (second edition; Notre Dame: Notre Dame University, 1984); John Milbank, *Radical Orthodoxy: A New Theology* (London: Routledge, 1999), and *Theology and Social Theory: Beyond Secular Reason* (Oxford: Blackwell, 1993); and Ronald Thiemann, *Revelation and Theology: The Gospel as Narrated Promise* (Notre Dame: University of Notre Dame, 1985).

[2] This was not the publicly-announced grounds of Shepherd's dismissal. The reason disseminated widely in the media at the time was expediency, not doctrine; this course of action—or sleight of hand—was taken in the hopes of minimizing the impact of Shepherd's dismissal from the seminary. See further Mark W. Karlberg, *Covenant Theology in Reformed Perspective: Collected Essays and Book Reviews in Historical, Biblical, and Systematic Theology* (Eugene, OR: Wipf and Stock, 2000), available online at www.twoagepress.org, and its sequel, *Gospel Grace: The Modern-day Controversy* (Eugene, Ore.: Wipf and Stock, 2003); O. Palmer Robertson, *The Current Justification Controversy* (Unico, Tenn.: Trinity Foundation, 2003); and A. Donald MacLeod, *W. Stanford Reid: An Evangelical Calvinist in the Academy* (Montreal: McGill-Queen's University, 2004). Chapter 15 of MacLeod's book (pages 257–79) chronicles Reid's role in the Shepherd controversy.

[3] See the collection of faculty essays in *The Pattern of Sound Doctrine: Systematic Theology at the Westminster Seminaries,* ed. D. VanDrunen (Phillipsburg: Presbyterian and Reformed, 2004).

[4] Gaffin helped instigate the long-held charge, now openly raised in the seminary's *Journal*, that Kline's interpretation of the Mosaic covenant is dispensational and non-Reformed (which, in Westminster parlance, means heretical!). See Patrick Ramsey, "In Defense of Moses: A Confessional Critique of Kline and Karlberg," *WTJ* 66 (Fall 2004) 373–400.

[5] Vos was unequivocal on the importance of the doctrine of the Covenant of Works in biblical theology, a Reformed-theological staple. Shepherd flatly denies it; Gaffin radically reinterprets it. Just one degree more evasive and deceptive in formulation than his chief spokesperson and former colleague, Gaffin now freely employs the traditional terminology of the Covenant of Works, but undercuts its meaning. By jettisoning the classic Protestant law/gospel antithesis as a speculative and peculiarly Lutheran dogma, Gaffin eviscerates the message of the Protestant reformation, Lutheran and Reformed. The implications of this radical reinterpretation of the doctrine of the covenants register itself elsewhere in the system of doctrine, notably in formulations of the doctrine of justification—by faith *and* works, so teach Shepherd, Gaffin, and the New Perspective crowd. When we come to the exposition of the Mosaic covenant, matters become far more complex in the history of Reformed interpretation. The ambivalence registered in Puritan-Reformed theology of the mid-seventeenth century has been carried over into the modern period. How precisely to formulate the doctrine of the Mosaic covenant as an administration of the ongoing Covenant of Grace, while retaining its peculiar legal cast, remains one of the most perplexing issues in Reformed theology specifically, and in evangelical theology more generally.

[6] Whereas *Kingdom Prologue: Genesis Foundations for a Covenantal Worldview* (Overland Park, Ks.: Two Age, 2000) is Kline's *magnum opus*, his study entitled *Glory in our Midst*

(Overland Park, Ks.: Two Age, 2001) provides unique insight into the institution and phenomenon of biblical prophecy. The culmination of Kline's prophetico-covenantal interpretation of Scripture is laid out in his latest book *God, Heaven and Har Magedon* (Eugene, Ore.: Wipf and Stock, 2006), the capstone of his life's work and reflection on the Scriptures from the perspective of covenant eschatology. No one in the history of Reformed interpretation has exploited the biblical doctrine of the covenants as richly, insightfully, and comprehensively as Professor Kline.

# THREE

# Westminster Seminary

*A Fractured Foundation—A Divided House*

WESTMINSTER SEMINARY, founded in 1929 by prominent American Presbyterian and New Testament scholar-apologist J. Gresham Machen, has from the beginning sought to maintain ties to Old School Presbyterianism (nurtured by Princeton Seminary in the nineteenth and early twentieth centuries) and to British and Continental Reformed theology, notably, English Puritanism as enshrined in the confessional documents known as the Westminster standards. These documents comprise the Confession of Faith and the Larger and Shorter Catechisms, completed in the years 1646 and 1647. The theology of the Westminster standards is the epitome of Reformed teaching at the close of the Protestant Reformation era. These confessional writings embody the fullest, most comprehensive expression of Calvinistic teaching, and they continue to exercise wide influence among Presbyterian and Reformed bodies the world over. Little of any significant doctrinal consequence has occurred since the writing of these summaries of Christian doctrine and life. It is all the more surprising that Westminster Seminary today is bitterly divided over the basic and pivotal Protestant-Reformed doctrine of justification by faith alone, the doctrine Martin Luther rightly identified as the standing article of the Christian church. It is the gospel of sovereign grace that is at stake in the now three-decade-old controversy.

The theological climate at Westminster Seminary, an institution independent of any official ecclesiastical affiliation, has changed dramatically since its founding years when the school enjoyed the closest of ties to the Orthodox Presbyterian Church, formed in 1936. Under the presidency of Edmund P. Clowney, Westminster's first and most competent president, the school began efforts to reach out to a broader ecclesiastical constituency. Clowney himself had grown tired of the OPC and labored to merge the denomination with other American denominations now flourishing in North America, denominations likewise committed to the Reformed faith and creeds.[1] Above all, Clowney was interested in reaching the widest possible audience for the spread of the Reformed faith, both in the academic and ecclesiastical arenas, even if that meant compromising on some of the distinctives of Old School Presbyterianism and Van Tillian apologetics.[2] Clowney found his aspirations jeopardized when the controversy over the views of Norman Shepherd, then professor of systematic theology, ruptured the seminary community, undermining its testimony both at home and abroad. Personal disappointment and ambition explain, in part, Clowney's initial reluctance to deal openly and forthrightly with the doctrinal errors associated with Shepherd and his other supporters on the faculty.

The dominant, ecclesiastical presence currently impacting the mission and outreach of Westminster Seminary in Philadelphia is the Presbyterian Church in America. The situation is quite different at Westminster Seminary California. There, professors who are also ministers in the OPC continue to labor in the tradition of the original founders of the seminary and denomination. More recently, the fledgling United Reformed Church, largely a break-off from the Christian Reformed Church, has made attempts to reform ecclesiastical life in accordance with the teachings of the Reformed confessions. The URC, a denomination well represented on the California faculty, was established as an alternative to other American Reformed churches. Whatever the reasons for yet another Reformed denomination, the united testimony of the Reformed churches languishes today. Divisions (whether justified in their given circumstance or not) inevitably hinder the church catholic from attaining that unity of the faith essential for vitality and strength in Christian mission and witness. Of course, there are many reasons for this crisis. It is not so much the proliferation of denominations *per se* that is the greatest problem, but rather the failure in our day to work together in witness of the doctrinal basics, most notably, the doctrine of justification by faith alone and the doctrine of Scripture (including its proper interpretation within the Reformed system of doctrine). In the modern-day contest, even the science of biblical hermeneutics is up for grabs.[3] Although it is highly unlikely for the Calvinistic churches to formulate a new doctrinal creed for our times, it is most unfortunate that churches true to historic Reformed orthodoxy cannot come together unified in their stand against the present onslaught respecting the standing article of the Christian church. Numerous (lesser) disputes have likewise rendered the churches ineffectual in the wider arena where theological heterodoxy respecting fundamentals of the Christian faith is commonplace.

## Gathering Storm-Clouds

Given developments noted in the above historical sketch, many issues have helped to shape the present theological and ecclesiastical landscape. In the immediate picture, what is of greatest consequence is the change that has taken place in the systematics department at Westminster. Revered, longtime systematician John Murray had an inordinate influence in the early years of the seminary, up to the time of his retirement in 1966 when he returned to Scotland. (Murray's Scotch-Presbyterian heritage and brogue added to both his appeal and his indoctrination of students in Westminster Calvinism. He was a living embodiment of Puritan faith and piety. The Murray-mystique lives on.) Unknown to Murray, however, was the planning of a radical redirection for the seminary, one well underway in the mid- to late-1960s. This reformulation of Westminster theology came about chiefly with the addition of Norman Shepherd, Richard Gaffin, and John Frame to the faculty. In numerous other writings I have commented on this theological change. Here it is sufficient to say that it was Shepherd and Gaffin who reshaped Reformed biblical theology (which is nothing other than the mature expression of historic covenant theology). Shepherd and Gaffin filtered the teachings of Princeton's eminent dogmatician, Geerhardus Vos, through the lens of twentieth-century revisionist Dutch-Reformed theology in the line of G. C. Berkouwer and Herman Ridderbos.[4] John Frame set an altogether different course by his introduction of multiperspectivalism as a surrogate hermeneutic, one methodologically nonReformed. Frame remains convinced that his approach is necessary for modern-day biblical interpretation, for theological rapprochement among Protestants needlessly fighting one another, and for ecumenical realignment.[5]

To our surprise and amazement, the formative work of J. Gresham Machen and Cornelius Van Til—most notably, the latter's distinctive apologetico-dogmatic method—had either been abandoned or redirected by the faculty that succeeded Murray in the systematics department.[6] (Gaffin would later assume the senior position in the department after serving many years in New Testament, his chief interest being Pauline studies.) Joining the ranks of the Westminster theologians, eager to advance the new theological programme at the seminary (especially under the presidency of Samuel Logan), were systematicians Sinclair Ferguson (who oddly came to Westminster as Shepherd's replacement after his dismissal from the seminary), David McWilliams, and Timothy Trumper. (The latter two served only a short time before moving on.) Adjunct professors supportive of the new theology and agenda include Robert Letham and Peter Lillback (now Westminster's president and professor of historical theology). The latest addition to the systematics department at the Philadelphia school is Lane Tipton, who labors with Gaffin in the articulation of a new understanding of Reformed theology. Central in their effort is a reformulation of the doctrine of union with Christ, one that includes a reevaluation of the relationship between the benefits accruing from spiritual union, benefits such as election, justification, and adoption. (Their formulations accent the eschatological, provisional nature of benefits received in union with Christ.)

The legacy of Robert Strimple, reportedly Murray's "best student," lay in teaching Murray's theology with utmost precision and exactitude. The most important difference between Strimple and his mentor, however, was the former's exception to Murray's interpretation of the Adamic order. Happily, Strimple, unlike Murray, retained within the system of Reformed teaching the doctrine of the original *covenant of works* made by God with Adam at creation. This doctrine was rightly viewed as vital and essential in biblical, Calvinistic theology, the theology of the Westminster Assembly. In this, Strimple displayed far greater theological discernment than his master. To his credit, Strimple's teaching career has helped preserve Reformed orthodoxy at Westminster West. Upon his retirement in 2001 his post has been occupied by David VanDrunen (now named the Robert Strimple chair). Others currently serving in the systematics department in California are Michael Horton and Scott Clark. Together these theologians are attempting to carry on the witness and work of Old Westminster, nowhere more aggressively than in regards to the doctrine of justification, the covenants, and election—doctrine now widely disputed in contemporary evangelicalism at large. Since the days of the Shepherd-Gaffin controversy and the founding of Westminster West, the California school has proven, for the most part, to be a seminary-in-exile. At the same time, however, difficulties and disputes plaguing the East have spilled over to the West. In recent years some encouraging progress has been made at Westminster California in the defense of historic Calvinism.[7] Special mention should also be made of Robert Godfrey, Westminster West's current president, who with Strimple stood in opposition to the teaching of Shepherd. (Strimple was Westminster West's first president.)

# Catastrophe Hits

Prior to the eruption of the Shepherd controversy on the seminary campus, Strimple addressed the church and seminary community with the words

"Do not lie to one another" (1974).[8] These words of counsel and exhortation were appropriate and necessary to those troubling the church—and that would surely include Norman Shepherd and his supporters. Whether or not Strimple had the emerging dispute in mind, truth-telling is surely one of the distinguishing marks of the church. From the beginning of the Shepherd controversy there has been gross misrepresentation and dissolution on the part of Shepherd and his defense-team. Where did Shepherd actually stand on the theological issues in debate? What was the (changing) content of his classroom instruction being questioned on the floor of Philadelphia Presbytery (OPC) in the mid-1970s? Questions were flying, and answers were in short supply—even in halls of the theological seminary.

Parts of this history have been recounted elsewhere.[9] Here we note that it was failure to be open and direct with faculty, students, seminary and church community that was the most grievous flaw in President Clowney's handling of the dispute. One other factor was miscalculation—none more so than the false hope that Shepherd's most ardent defender and supporter, Richard Gaffin, would eventually come to his senses. In point of fact, we would later come to realize that Gaffin was co-author, if not father, of the New Westminster Theology. Shepherd, it turns out, was and remains the front man for the movement, its chief spokesperson.[10]

Needless to say, Shepherd's dismissal from the seminary did little to resolve the dispute. Retirement from active ministry in the Christian Reformed Church in 1998 (which denomination Shepherd joined after leaving Westminster), occasioned renewed effort on his part to engage the controversial and divisive issues, now more aggressively and confrontationally.[11] All the while Gaffin carefully orchestrates the seminary and OPC maneuverings. Westminster's theological revisionists "await a new consensus on the core doctrines of the Reformation: for [them], the old consensus no longer bears weight."[12] Joining today's chorus are proponents of the New Perspective on Paul and the law and the group known as the Federal Visionists.[13]

The occasion of honoring retiring systematician Robert Strimple has brought together faculty on the West and the East in the composition of essays for the Strimple *festschrift*, recently released by Presbyterian and Reformed Publishers, entitled *The Pattern of Sound Doctrine: Systematic Theology at the Westminster Seminaries*.[14] Polite, yet searching, this collection of articles reveals the tension and conflict now deeply impacting the two schools. Of all the disputes, none is more urgent or more important than the battle over the biblical, Reformed doctrine of election, justification, and the covenants. Second in importance is the question regarding the place and importance of the Reformed confessions. What authority and weight should they have in the church and in the seminary? The Strimple *festschrift* raises more questions than it answers. The road ahead for Westminster—and for the Calvinistic churches indoctrinated in her competing theologies—is highly uncertain.

The philosophico-dogmatic issue lying at the very heart of the Westminster school of theology—a school in search of her own, distinct identity within international Calvinism—is, "scientifically" speaking, *pre-dogmatic* in the discipline (or science) of theology. Westminster's focal concern is one that falls within the locus of what is called theological *prolegomenon*. There are two aspects to this theological concern: (1) a description of the relationship between systematic theology (or confessional Reformed dogmatics) and biblical theology, what is the biblico-exegetical approach to the interpretation of the canonical text of Scripture, Old and New Testaments, one that elucidates the history of redemptive revelation; and (2) the role of (Van Tillian) presuppositionalism in theological discourse. Simply put, the chief preoccupation of the faculty of Westminster Seminary has been—and remains—the proper method of interpretation, that is, theological methodology. In his essay on the role and impact of John Murray in helping to develop the distinctive theological approach of the newly founded institution, Clowney speaks of the "Westminster Seminary movement."[15] VanDrunen, representative of the new crop of Westminster systematicians, looks back over the history of the seminary only to find an "emerging tradition," one that is still in the process of discovering and defining herself.[16] In a nutshell, Westminster today remains uncertain of first-principles, matters relating to theological *prolegomena*. It does not get more basic than this.

Darryl Hart and Michael Horton address directly the relationship between the two sister disciplines, biblical theology (the redemptive-historical approach to biblical revelation and interpretation) and systematics (the restatement of biblical doctrine in terms of a theological system, one that is at once confessional and dogmatic). It is their conviction that Westminster has not succeeded in bringing together these two important disciplines in fruitful harmony. (Adding to what is explicitly said in the *festschrift*, some among the faculty question whether it is even possible to reconcile the two satisfactorily, at least in terms of the practice of traditional dogmatics, *à la* Old School Presbyterianism.) Hart portrays Old Princeton as priding itself in its "unoriginal Calvinism." This posture is in sharp contrast to what Hart sees as Westminster's urge for creativity, the desire to say something truly new. The question to be asked here is this: Was the seminary in its founding days speaking on behalf of Old Princeton, or was she consciously wishing to be different, to be creative? More precisely, when and where does the change from unoriginal Calvinism to theological creativity occur in the Old Princeton-Westminster tradition? And what role did Geerhardus Vos play, if any, in this shift?

To answer these questions we need to consider in some closer detail those issues that members of the two faculties see as central to the theological work of the seminary, issues that define her unique identity. For Hart, one of the troubling novelties is the introduction of Framian multiperspectivalism and its accompanying "biblicism," according to which the words of Scripture stand apart from theological interpretation. The latter Frame sees as uniquely the creation of the church. (Hence, while churchly theology confounds, Scripture enlightens. The assumption here is that biblical words are transparent, while theology is opaque. What would the Protestant reformers think of this? The answer should be self-evident. Confident that Frame will miss it, the answer is *Nonsense!*) The young Tim Trumper, under the prompting of Gaffin, set out to reinvigorate Westminster Calvinism by promoting Westminster's new theological orientation, identified as "constructive Calvinism," in contrast to stodgy "traditional Calvinism." Securing a faculty at Westminster East sympathetic to this programme and agenda on the heels of Shepherd's dismissal made the earlier aspirations of Shepherd, Gaffin, and Frame once more feasible. As a result, writes Hart,

> systematics lost its regal standing and has vied especially with biblical theology for supremacy. The methods of systematics no longer provide the coherence they once did at Old Princeton. Hence, creativity and constructive Calvinism have become virtues in the Westminster tradition in the way that unoriginality was the hallmark of the Princeton theology.[17]

Quoting G. E. Wright, one of the eminent spokespersons for the broader biblical theology movement (encompassing the school of neoorthodoxy), Horton repeats the charge: "theology must always beware of the scholastic tendency to become unhistorical." He then opines: "What is perhaps surprising is how frequently such sentiments are expressed today even in confessional (even Westminster Seminary) circles."[18] Gaffin, for one, is very sympathetic to the views of Wright (G. E. and N. T.). Horton himself favors theological interpretation that engages the "dynamic play of the [biblical] narrative."[19] In doing so, claims Horton, we are led to "a reinvigorated and revised covenant theology," what is a new take on scholastic, federal orthodoxy.[20] What is the sense of Horton's reservations against the position of G. E. Wright and others like him? More explanation is needed.

VanDrunen, Horton's colleague at Westminster West, sees matters quite differently. (Do VanDrunen and Horton recognize their difference in method and approach?) There is no more urgent task at Westminster, pleads VanDrunen, than the reclamation of historic covenant theology, one which upholds the pivotal doctrine of the Covenant of Works within its dogmatico-confessional teaching. "Though the existence of a system of theology has been affirmed at Westminster in the past only with some ambiguity," writes VanDrunen, "I argue that its defense must be taken up with renewed vigor in the next generation."[21] Something is missing; something is awry at Westminster. A case is made that Gaffin has moved one step away from Murray, two steps away from Hodge.[22] This is not to suggest that there are not problems in Murray's "recasting" of traditional covenant theology. Surely there are, as VanDrunen himself is well aware. Most perplexing is VanDrunen's commendation of Horton's proposal for a revision of covenant theology along lines quite different from that advocated by VanDrunen himself (as I read the two of them). Agreeably, Horton's case for covenant as theological *prolegomenon* is well taken. But much more is at stake in Horton's (dramatic) reading of Scripture. Chiefly, what is at stake is an eschatologico-biblico-theological interpretation of Scripture that undermines the Reformed orthodox understanding of redemption accomplished and applied. It is here that Gaffin's work must be judged a failure. Do Horton and VanDrunen agree or disagree in their assessment of Gaffin's theology on Paul and the law? Though Gaffin takes some exception to N. T. Wright's formulation, it is far from adequate. More is at stake than the doctrine of the imputation of Christ's active and passive obedience (in just so many words); the larger dispute relates to the classic law/gospel antithesis and how that informs our interpretation of Scripture.[23] Without this crucial theological construct we cannot interpret aright the doctrine of justification and the covenants. Nor can we establish the biblical doctrine of the imputation of Christ's righteousness.

Of all the contributors to the *festschrift*, only Gaffin and Clowney totally ignore recent debate and division within the seminaries over issues that remain highly controversial. That may say something about these two opponents in the Shepherd controversy. The estrangement between the two over the dismissal of Shepherd never healed.[24] (Clowney died in March of 2005.) In this volume Gaffin addresses the subject of the meaning and clarity of human language for the purpose of conveying divine truth (either in Scripture or in church theology).[25] In contrast to the view of Frame, Gaffin writes: "Our language is not innately ambiguous. Human language does not inherently veil and confuse as it seeks to communicate and disclose meaning."[26] Gaffin's remarks concerning the inspiration and interpretation of Scripture are brief, but helpful, especially for the Reformed church today as she seeks to rethink the traditional doctrine of Scipture.[27] Perspectivalism and Reformed hermeneutics surely result in competing theologies. Where Gaffin and Frame differ in one respect, they agree on another, specifically, the need to reformulate traditional covenant theology. Strange bed-fellows, to say the least.

Godfrey questions the "sympathetic-critical" posture assumed by Gaffin, Trumper, and Frame. And the confessional dilemma is directly tied to the Shepherd dispute. Godfrey remarks: "The controversy surrounding Shepherd's theology of justification helps to focus for us the relationship of Westminster theology to the Reformed confessions. It shows us that for some who belong to the Westminster school of theology, there is a weakness in understanding both the role and the content of the confessions in the life of the Reformed churches."[28] Uncertainty rules the day at Westminster. The school has lost her mission and her ability to lead and minister effectively in the furtherance of historic Calvinism. A new day has come. The guardians of orthodoxy have changed their line of defense. Westminster West and East stand at the crossroads.

How do other faculty view the seminary scene? Historian Clair Davis compares the difference in homiletical-theological approach between Clowney and Jay Adams with that between Johannus Coccieus and Gisbert Voetius (two prominent disputants in Reformed scholasticism of a former era). This comparison, however, obscures the tension that has surfaced at Westminster in the late twentieth and early twenty-first centuries. Adam's complaint, with some justification, is that the *practice* of biblical theology, the art of preaching, has resulted in esoteric teaching in the hands of amateurs. Biblical-theological or redemptive-historical preaching has fallen into excess, becoming a discipline with subtle, hidden meaning for the initiates of Westminster's newly-discovered art. Davis admits that this conflict is yet to be "resolved and coordinated at Westminster."[29] Adams states plainly: "In my opinion, the proper balance between systematics and the rest of the seminary disciplines must be restored."[30] While Godfrey denounces the Shepherd theology, Davis embraces it as being "very congenial" to the gospel-work of the seminary. "Shepherd expressed biblical creativity [there's that c-word again!] and a heart-desire for a Reformed faith that would be not just described, but vigorously proclaimed."[31] How reliable Davis has proven to be over the course of his tenure at Westminster can be seen in his statement concerning the reason for Shepherd's dismissal: "The Westminster board determined to dismiss Shepherd for the good of the institution, though they had not specified error in his teaching. Though not a satisfactory resolution for anyone, it did provide a response, however ambiguous, to an apparently ambiguous theology." The historical revisionist concludes on an optimistic note: "The lengthy theological reflection carried on throughout the Westminster community on these issues may yet be of help to the church. Further confusion can be diminished, we hope." The truth is, Shepherd was dismissed for views found by the Board of Trustees to be contrary to the teaching of Scripture and the Reformed confessions—hence the eighteen-page "Reason and Specifications."[32]

## Storm's Aftermath: Stability or Peril in International Calvinism?

From any measurement the storm has inflicted incalculable damage. The new theology has impacted churches in both the Calvinistic and the broader evangelical traditions in virtually every corner of the globe, and that for years to come. The New Perspective on Paul on the Mosaic law and the theology of the Federal Visionists are only two variations on a common theme. Older varieties include the Barth-Torrance school, the neo-Calvinist school (Herman Dooyeweerd and Gordon Spykman as representative), and the related, but distinct new Dutch theology of Berkouwer and Ridderbos. All aim to reformulate—along radical lines—the theology of the Protestant Reformation, overturning the classic Protestant understanding of the antithesis between the Law and the Gospel and reassessing the role of "tradition" in biblical interpretation.

Curiously, the "mainline" American-Reformed seminaries claiming to stand in the tradition of historic Reformed orthodoxy—Covenant, Reformed, Calvin, and Westminster in Philadelphia—have skillfully avoided any official (or unofficial) critique of the Shepherd heresy. As for analyses of the New Perspective, some have recently ventured out to address this aspect of the contemporary dispute. Bryan Chapell, president of Covenant Seminary, offers a very weak analysis in "An Explanation of the New Perspective on Paul for Friends of Covenant Theological Seminary."[33] Other seminaries (mostly smaller and less influential)—such as Greenville, Knox, Mid-America, Protestant-Reformed, and Westminster in California—have offered strongly negative evaluations of the Shepherd theology, the New Perspective, and the Federal Vision. (At the same time most, but not all, have exercised reserve with respect to Gaffin's views, views that are virtually identical to those of Shepherd.) Nat Belz, in his report to the churches, "Federal Vision Controversy Simmers," published in the PCA denominational magazine, asserts: "Clearly, there is substantive disagreement which must be settled as to what accords with holy Scripture and the Westminster Standards."[34] The PCA has also established a website with resources for study of the Shepherd controversy. Despite these feeble efforts, the PCA and the OPC have shown ambiguity and indecisiveness. This circumstance furnishes the chief explanation for the present lethargy and malaise in the Reformed churches.[35]

Equally disturbing are the efforts at Protestant-Catholic realignment, based on a superficial appeal to the early ecumenical creeds of the Christian church. The objective is to withstand the inroads of modernism (and post-modernism). Turning back the clock, however, will not work. Catholic and Protestant traditions read the early creeds differently regarding many elements of Christian doctrine. In the newly published book co-authored by Mark A. Noll and Carolyn Nystrom, *Is the Reformation Over? An Evangelical Assessment of Contemporary Roman Catholicism*,[36] the argument is advanced that times have changed significantly. Concerning perceived agreement among two former theological rivals, they highlight the consensus now reached on the basics of Christian doctrine and salvation. In particular, they note:

> It is the same for justification by faith, about which many Catholics and evangelicals now believe approximately the same thing. . . . Thus, on the substance of what is actually taught about God's saving work in the world, if not always on the exact terminology used to describe that saving work, many evangelicals and Catholics believe something close to the same thing. If it is true, as once was repeated frequently by Protestants conscious of their anchorage in Martin Luther or John Calvin that *iustificatio articulus stantis vel cadentis ecclesias* (justification is the article on which the church stands or falls), then the Reformation is over.[37]

Astonishing and troubling as it is, Westminster Seminary has, in fact, played a pivotal role in bringing about this modern-day call for reconciliation between evangelical Protestants and Catholics. Though the seminary would disavow any responsibility for, or concord with, this growing movement among the Christian churches, the Shepherd-Gaffin theology has fostered a reformulation and reassessment of Christian theology such as we see taking place today, a theology amenable to both sides of the former Great Divide—notably in its understanding of the doctrine of justification (by faith and works) and in its repudiation of the forensic understanding of justification and covenant. The modern revisionist doctrine leaves virtually intact the Thomistic conception of "congruent merit" as descriptive of the value of human virtue/obedience with regard to the reception (or earning) of the reward promised by God in his covenant(s), what is viewed as a purely "gracious" arrangement from Creation to Consummation. What is lost here is the classic Reformed-Protestant law/gospel antithesis.

These are increasingly desperate and trying times for the Reformed faith. Heresy and corruption have infiltrated the church and the courts of the church. The lack of strong leadership contributes in a major way to the present crisis. We stand at the edge of a new epoch—a new millennium—in the history of biblical Christianity. Whether we consider the rise of postmodern or post-Christian theologies now rampant among today's churches and theological institutions, or whether we consider the state of Reformed theology more specifically, we are seeing in many places the undoing of the Protestant Reformation.[38] Relativistic interpretations of the Bible and Protestant-Reformed theology are being accommodated to the new methodological approach. All theology, we are told, is contextual; the crafting of theology is relative to one's historical and cultural place. Christian interpretation can never come to a definitive statement on truth. (Dogmatic theology is a thing of the past.) In short, Scripture is no longer regarded as perspicuous. For if it were, Bible interpreters would comprehend (at the finite level) the truth of God as revealed in Scripture through the illumination of the Holy Spirit. But post-fundamentalism tells us that is no longer within our grasp. Truth is not something we can "possess" (contrary to Scripture's admonition to "guard what has been entrusted" to the saints; see 1 Tim 6:20 and numerous, related passages). We are told that we can only look forward to ever-changing restatements and reformulations of biblical truth—tentative apprehensions of truth suitable to the times in which we live out our faith.[39]

To the contrary, I remain convinced that the sixteenth-century Protestant reformers had it right. The written, inspired revelation in the Bible is the truth of God—truth made known to those who have ears to hear. The effects of hurricane Katrina have been devastating; but the effects of the theological fire-storm raging within the Reformed communities are far greater. For those who would promote the teaching of Shepherd, Gaffin, Frame, and others in the New Westminster school, God have mercy. The Westminster faculty has been peddling heresy to pliable, trusting, unsuspecting students for over thirty years, students who have come to Westminster expecting to learn sound, biblical teaching.[40] Cleanup has been slow and beleaguered by the failure of too many ministers, elders, and teachers within the seminary community to act courageously and decisively. Nothing less than unfeigned, public renunciation of teaching destructive of the Gospel is demanded of the institution. Without question, the number of those committed to the teachings of historic Protestant-Reformed orthodoxy is diminishing with great rapidity as we enter this "post-Christian" millennium of church theology.[41] What is desperately needed is a new reformation—a fresh in-breaking of the light of God's Word, pure and unadulterated.

## *Addendum: A Response to the 2006 OPC Study Report on Justification*
### *(in the "Agenda" of the Seventy-Third General Assembly)*

Whatever good is to be found in this critique of deviant teaching in contemporary Reformed federalism is lost on the Report's final product, *theological ambiguity and indecisiveness*. The Report attempts to conjure up Richard Gaffin's illusion that today's principal controversialist, Norman Shepherd (Gaffin's longstanding spokesperson for New School Westminster), has modified his position—most importantly with respect to his denial of the imputation of Christ's active obedience in justification. Only two distinctive viewpoints are given full attention in the Report: the New Perspective on Paul and the Federal Vision. Shepherd's teachings are treated as part of this dual Reformed-theological mutation, or rather, deformation. As I noted previously (in note 32), "Evaluation of the Shepherd theology has been barred by the [2004] General Assembly commissioning this study." And it is the Shepherd theology that has had the greatest impact on the OPC and the Westminster Seminaries.

There is reluctance to identify erroneous teaching on justification by faith (*sola fide*) and sacramental efficacy—among other teachings—as "heretical." Rather, the comfort level of the Report is to speak of such teachings as "aberrant." On the one hand, the Report makes a case for the meritorious character of the obedience required of the First and Second Adams as federal heads. On the other hand, the Report also permits the view that "grace" informs the Covenant of Works. In so doing, the Report undermines the idea of "strict" merit—which indicates that the reward for obedience in the Covenant of Works is a matter of divine justice (not unmerited grace—"reward" over and beyond the creature's just desert). It also undermines the unique role of faith in soteric justification, faith being the alone "instrument" in the believer's procurement of justification. Professor Meredith Kline's objection to applying the term "grace" to the prelapsarian covenant—a correct position to be taken—is regarded in the Report as a peculiarity in Reformed thinking, out of step with mainstream teaching as reflected in the theology of Turretin, among many other stalwarts of the faith. (The implication is that Kline's thinking is likewise "aberrant"—but for different reasons.) No attempt is made in the Report to come to grips with problems inherent to federal Reformed scholasticism. Until those problems are directly addressed and resolved, theological confusion and misformulation will continue to prevail.

Given the posture adopted in the Report, it is a mystery how it can boldly declare that "Law and grace are incompatible in the context of justification" (lines 494–95). *This is the heart of the theological dispute:* When the Report allows nonmeritorious "grace" to inform the first covenant with Adam, that very supposition (wholly speculative, not biblical, in origin) jeopardizes the meritorious accomplishment of the Second Adam in the Covenant of Redemption. The classic Protestant-Reformed antithesis between law and grace is just that: *antithetical.* Introducing the notion of *nonmeritorious reward* (what is an oxomoron) clouds the issues and obscures the Gospel of sovereign, electing grace in the justification of sinners. Only in terms of adherence to the classic theological contrast between law and (gospel-)grace can discussions move beyond mere semantics. Theological language and terminology are consequential; they are meaningful. Reformed theology that is genuinely reformed and reforming cannot have it both ways. What position do the framers of this Report wish to take? Doutbless, both framers and supporters of the Report think they have weathered the storm by achieving a workable, compromise statement. Perhaps—but only for a time. In truth, the two antithetical views cannot stand side by side. Until we all understand that, there will be no peace in the house of Westminster. Consensus through compromise has no place in the House that God is building. Regrettably, the end result of the Report is to encourage ongoing covenant confusion and theological ambiguity. In so doing, it has undermined its own usefulness and fidelity to Scripture.

One last note: disciples of Gaffin now feel badly betrayed. Since Gaffin served on this study committee as one of its members, it is assumed that his views have changed and that he personally affirms the view adopted in the Report favoring Reformed orthodoxy (this is a mistaken reading of Gaffin, however). Gaffin's problem is both theological and moral. Deception and ambiguity continue to function as his *modus operandi.* Forced into a corner, Gaffin has nevertheless made sure that the Report gives him the necessary leeway—the necessary qualification or escape hatch—to modify and reshape the views laid out in the Report to suit his own thinking. Hiding under the compromise statement adopted in the Report, Gaffin makes no attempt at open recantation, no move to renounce doctrinal error. Some conjecture that Gaffin is double-minded, others that he is cowardly in his (supposed) abandonment of teaching distinctive of the Shepherd-Gaffin school he helped fashion. Such conjectures will be bandied about for years to come. What is demanded of Gaffin and his cohorts—including the Westminster Seminaries—is full, unambiguous, uncompromising renunciation of deviant (heretical) teaching that has dominated the life and witness of the institution(s) for more than three decades.

[For another response to this Report, see Rich Lusk, "A Reply to 'The OPC Justification Report' on Union and Imputation (With Special Reference to the Views of Richard B. Gaffin)," posted at www.trinity-pres.net/essays/opc-report-response.php. On a humorous note, the OPC study report has been named by some members of the OPC as "the Report that cannot be discussed"—or so it was thought.]

## NOTES

[This paper was first read at the November 2005 national meeting of the Evangelical Theological Society (Valley Forge, Pa.)]

[1] Several histories of the Orthodox Presbyterian Church and the Presbyterian Church in America are now available. Other denominations represented on the seminary faculty have included the Church of England (Anglican), the Church of Scotland (Presbyterian), the Christian Reformed, and the General Baptist. Of special mention is *Pressing Toward the Mark: Essays Commemorating Fifty Years of the Orthodox Presbyterian Church*, edited by C. G. Dennison and R. C. Gamble (Philadelphia: The Committee for the Historian of the OPC, 1986).

[2] See Greg L. Bahnsen, "Machen, Van Til, and the Apologetical Tradition of the OPC," in *Pressing Toward the Mark* 259–94. John Frame's appointment meant the repackaging of Van Til.

[3] The battle over biblical interpretation has taken a new direction with the rise of post-fundamentalism. Illustrative of this new orientation is John R. Franke's *The Character of Theology: A Postconservative Evangelical Approach* (Grand Rapids: Baker, 2005). Of lesser import, but no less divisive, are those who contend that literalistic interpretation of the "days" of creation in Genesis 1 is the only acceptable view in Reformed orthodoxy.

[4] Consult Mark W. Karlberg, *Covenant Theology in Reformed Perspective: Collected Essays and Book Reviews in Historical, Biblical, and Systematic Theology* (Eugene, Ore.: Wipf and Stock, 2000). Available online at www.twoagepress.org. Its sequel, *Gospel Grace: The Modern-day Controversy* (Eugene, Ore.: Wipf and Stock, 2003); and *The Changing of the Guard: Westminster Theological Seminary in Philadelphia* (Unicoi, Tenn.: The Trinity Foundation, 2001), available online at www.trinityfoundation.org, and also included in *Gospel Grace*. Peter Golding follows this traditional Calvinistic line of interpretation in *Covenant*

*Theology: The Key of Theology in Reformed Thought and Tradition* (Ross-shire: Focus, 2004).

[5] For a critique of Frame's work, see my essay "On the Theological Correlation of Divine and Human Language: A Review Article," *JETS* 32 (1989) 99–105; and "John Frame and the Recasting of Van Tilian Apologetics: A Review Article," *Mid-America Journal of Theology* 9 (1993) 279–96 (which appeared in the Spring of 1998). Frame presents his case for ecumenism in *Evangelical Reunion: Denominations and the One Body of Christ* (Grand Rapids: Baker, 1991). New directions in hermeneutics have also taken place in the biblical department at Westminster (in the work of the late Raymond Dillard, Peter Enns, Doug Green, and Moisés Silva, among others) and the practical department (in the work of the late Harvie Conn). Most recently, see Peter Enns, *Inspiration and Incarnation* (Grand Rapids: Baker, 2005), a work incisively reviewed by Brenton C. Ferry in *New Horizons* 26 (October 2005) 23–24. Enns offers a reactionary, evasive retort in *New Horizons* 26 (November 2005) 22, while in the same issue Ferry maintains his position critical of Enns (22–23).

[6] See especially John M. Frame, "Machen's Warrior Children," in *Alister E. McGrath and Evangelical Theology: A Dynamic Engagement,* ed. S. W. Chung (Grand Rapids: Baker, 2003) 113–46. Compare the comments made by John R. Muether in "Machen Memoir: Fifty Years Later," in *New Horizons* 25.5 (May 2004) 11–12. Iain H. Murray in *Evangelicalism Divided: A Record of Crucial Change in the Years 1950–2000* (Carlisle: The Banner of Truth Trust, 2000) assesses the theological erosion that has taken place within evangelicalism, including Reformed-Protestantism. Like theologian David Wells, Murray gives a very bleak picture. Regarding Wells' insightful critiques, Murray rightly comments: "Perhaps no modern author has written more powerfully on this subject" (256, n. 1). Although Murray is not afraid to offer his criticisms of many prominent individuals, he has turned his eyes away from the theological deviation that has transformed Westminster Seminary, proving himself unwilling to decry the inroads of the Barth-Torrance school in the work of Sinclair Ferguson, Carl Trueman, and others. Clearly, for many it is a different matter when the crisis hits close to home.

[7] One positive development, Frame left Westminster West to teach at Reformed Seminary in Orlando. This was good for Westminster West, bad for Reformed Seminary, though Reformed obviously does not see it this way. (Legend has it that President Godfrey did cartwheels down the hallways of the seminary on news of Frame's leaving. Hurrah!)

[8] *The Presbyterian Guardian* 44 (1975) 88–89. It was first given as a chapel-talk at Westminster Seminary in the summer of 1974.

[9] Accounts of the seminary's handling of the controversy are found in O. Palmer Robertson, *The Current Justification Controversy* (Unicoi, Tenn.: Trinity Foundation, 2003); in A. Donald MacLeod, *W. Stanford Reid: An Evangelical Calvinist in the Academy* (Montreal: McGill-Gween, 2004), especially chapter 15; and in my *Gospel Grace.* Although Samuel Logan's presidency was terminated by the Board of Trustees, conflict within the faculty still lingers, with division over the New Perspective and related teachings. The new Chairman of the Board, John White, is stridently pro-Shepherd. New to the equation is the role to be played by Proclamation Presbyterian Church (Bryn Mawr, Pa.), where the newly-appointed President Peter Lillback continues to serve as senior pastor. The session of the church has taken the seminary under its wings as her adopted child. Even after being informed of the doctrinal controversy raging in the Westminster community, the elders have affirmed their full support for Lillback and the seminary faculty, having decided the case without any study or cross-examination (personal correspondence with the author over the period of time from April to September of 2005). One of the prominent ruling elders on the session is John M. Templeton, Jr., son of the wealthy financier, investor, and philanthropist. The son

now heads up the Templeton Foundation, which has as its principal interest furtherance of the relationship between science and religion. Senior writer Tony Carnes in "The $1 Billion Handoff: Sir John Templeton's born-again son takes control of the famous foundation—but there are strings attached," (*Christianity Today* 49.9 [September 2005] 88–91) points out the difference in religious perspective between the father and son—the former being a universalist, the son a born-again evangelical. Both are described as "sticklers for detail." One would have thought that the concern for detail would have been applied by the son to the situation now facing the congregation of Proclamation Church. But that has not been the case.

Gaffin, Trueman, and Ferguson all differ with aspects of the New Perspective. But in the final analysis it amounts to a distinction without a difference. Ferguson, representative of the three, has acknowledged that he agrees with the Barth-Torrance school on this one point, namely, the continuity between law and gospel (*law in grace*). Gaffin stands as the chief architect in the theology of New Westminster. Many in the Reformed community attempt to "reorthodize" his position in order to bring his views in line with historic Calvinism. These individuals are unwilling to question or engage Gaffin as Westminster's senior systematician. One matter is certain in Gaffin's mind: "Meredith Kline's views [on covenant theology] will not be taught at Westminster [in Philadelphia]." It is not enough that Gaffin insinuates that Kline's view is dispensational and anti-confessional (in which case virtually the entire Reformed tradition is in error), but he fears above all that his own interpretation may justly receive a fatal blow by the exposition of Scripture in the hands of faithful interpreters. In the case of Gaffin and others, aversion to the doctrine of the Mosaic covenant of works betrays an aversion to the doctrine of the Adamic covenant of works at creation, including the classic Protestant law/gospel antithesis. Murray's views on the covenants are the exception in the history of Reformed interpretation. Murray's reservation concerning the Covenant of Works doctrine has been exploited by many at Westminster for the wrong reasons. Gaffin and his colleague Lane Tipton differ with Shepherd somewhat in his denial of the active obedience of Christ. This also marks a minor, insignificant difference. Gaffin relies heavily upon Turretin's misformulation of the covenant-of-works idea in regards to the concept of "merit," ignoring what is basic and foundational in Turretin's covenant theology, the law/gospel antithesis. A recent issue of *Reformation and Renewal Journal* 14 (2005) devotes itself to the promotion of the Shepherd/New Perspective theology (with the exception of the essay by I. John Hesselink who argues in defense of Reformation theology). Concerning the relationship between law and gospel, Andrew Sandlin concludes that "Barth is essentially right" (21). Compare also, A. T. B. McGowan, "Justification and the Ordo Salutis," in *Foundations* (Spring 2004) 6–18. McGowan embraces the theology of New School Westminster.

Through the penmanship of Patrick Ramsey in the essay "In Defense of Moses: A Confessional Critique of Kline and Karlberg" (*WTJ* 66 [2004] 373–400), Gaffin attempts to undermine Kline's theology, viewing it as contrary to the teaching of Reformed orthodoxy as formulated in the Westminster standards. The author, an OPC minister in London, Kentucky and graduate of Greenville Presbyterian Theological Seminary (student of Morton Smith), misunderstands and misstates the Kline-Karlberg position, while at the same time misreads Reformed theology. Ramsey's critique of Kline and Karlberg and his interpretation of the Reformed tradition regarding the doctrine of the Mosaic covenant are analogous in substance (if not in detail) to that of Gaffin. Publication of this essay in the *Westminster Journal* was designed to raise doubts over Kline's orthodoxy—and it amounts to a feeble attempt to turn the tables of controversy. Curiously, there is no mention by Ramsey of the Shepherd dispute. Brenton C. Ferry provides a helpful response in "Cross-Examining Moses' Defense: An Answer to Ramsey's Critique of Kline and Karlberg (*WTJ* 67 [2005] 163–68). As I

*Notes*

wrote in my April 2005 ETS paper, "A focal issue in dispute at Westminster—a dispute that erupted in the 1970s and continues on to the present—is the interpretation of the Mosaic covenant as *in some sense* a covenant of works. The very concept of a 'covenant of works,' a commonplace in historic Reformed theology, has of late fallen on very bad times." ("New Vistas in Old Testament Narrative: Geerhardus Vos and Meredith G. Kline as Exemplary Reformed Interpreters," 5; published here as Chapter Two.)

[10] As the front man, Shepherd has unfairly carried the brunt of criticism. Westminster Seminary in Philadelphia is the primary source of the doctrinal deviation found in our American-Reformed churches today. The seminary refuses to renounce the Shepherd(-Gaffin) heresy. MacLeod recounts: "Shepherd had intended to spend the entire year of his sabbatical at the Free University of Amsterdam, studying the doctrine of union with Christ in sixteenth-century Reformed thinking" (*W. Stanford Reid: An Evangelical Calvinist in the Academy*, 265). Shepherd's plans and circumstance having changed, Gaffin took up the task of reformulating the doctrine of union with Christ from the perspective of Pauline eschatology. Gaffin and Tipton continue to work out the implications of this reformulation for biblico-systematic theology, while at the same time reinterpreting Calvin's theology (contra the theology of Luther). Gaffin's ideas were first introduced in his 1969 doctoral dissertation which was "thoroughly rewritten for publication but with only minor alterations in substance," appearing as *The Centrality of the Resurrection: A Study in Paul's Soteriology* (Baker Biblical Monograph; Grand Rapids: Baker, 1978) 9; the book has since been retitled, *Resurrection and Redemption*.

Gaffin's antipathy for the "legal mindset" attributed to scholastic Reformed orthodoxy (federal theology) in its formulation of the Covenant of Works, justification by faith, and the imputation of Christ's righteousness (among other elements of doctrine) is drawn from neoorthodoxy's critique of post-Reformation theology. Gaffin substitutes a realistic conception of union with Christ, one that moves beyond the formulations of Reformed orthodoxy by obscuring or dissolving the distinctive benefits of redemption accomplished by Christ and applied by his Spirit in regeneration (*i.e.*, union with Christ). At the same time, Gaffin's interpretation grossly distorts the teachings of federal theology. It is certainly fair to say that contemporary scholarship has rightly identified a weakness in federal theology's exposition of the *ordo salutis* (the "order" in the application of salvation). Missing in the federalist interpretation is an adequate discussion of the relationship between *ordo* and *historia salutis*. To be sure, there are historical and contextual factors that account for this circumstance. Many critics, however, have gone too far in their negative assessments of federalism, contending that the theological formulations of scholastic Reformed orthodoxy have jeopardized the soteriological import of Christ's death and resurrection. Most unfairly, these critics have accused federal theology of creating a "legal fiction" in its understanding of the believer's state of justification. They contend that federal theology—with its "bipolar" construction of justification and sanctification—has torn apart the benefits accruing to the believer's union with Christ, converting them virtually into separate, discrete, and unrelated aspects of soteriology. (That's what they say, wrongly.)

A sampling of recent writings by graduates of Westminster include: Kevin Woongsan Kang, "Justified by Faith in Christ: Jonathan Edwards' Doctrine of Justification in Light of Union with Christ" (Ph.D. dissertation, Westminster Theological Seminary, 2003); Jeffrey C. Waddington, "Jonathan Edwards's 'Ambiguous and Somewhat Precarious' Doctrine of Justification," *WTJ* 66 (2004) 357–72; Howard Griffith, "High Priest in Heaven: The Intercession of the Exalted Christ in Reformed Theology, Analysis and Critique" (Ph.D. dissertation, Westminster Seminary, 2004); and Benjamin T. Inman, "God Covenanted in Christ: The unifying role of theology proper in the systematic theology of Francis Turretin"

(Ph.D. dissertation, Westminster Theological Seminary, 2004) all adopting the Gaffin reading of Pauline eschatology and Reformation theology. Each of these treatments is marred to one degree or another by confusing and misleading formulations, some blatantly false. Each has contributed in some measure to the corruption of Reformed teaching. Critical assessments of federal theology—in conjunction with startling reformulations of traditional doctrine concerning mystical union and the theology of the sacraments—is found in William Borden Evans, "Union with the Second Adam" (Th.M. thesis, Westminster Theological Seminary, 1986), and in his "Imputation and Impartation: The Problem of Union with Christ in Nineteenth-Century America Reformed Theology" (Ph.D. dissertation, Vanderbilt University, 1996). This line of interpretation is pursued by D. G. Hart in *John Williamson Nevin: High-Church Calvinist*, America Reformed Biographies, ed. D. G. Hart and S. M. Lucas (Phillipsburg: Presbyterian and Reformed, 2005). Compare my review of Keith A Mathison's *Given For You: Reclaiming Calvin's Doctrine of the Lord's Supper* (Phillipsburg: Presbyterian and Reformed, 2002) in Appendix E. One of the most recent critiques of Shepherd (in light of Calvin's teaching) is found in Samuel E. Waldron, "John Calvin versus Norman Shepherd on *Sola Fide*," in *Reformed Baptist Theological Review* 2 (2005) 87–106. Consult also, Guy Prentiss Waters, *Federal Vision and Covenant Theology: A Comparative Analysis* (Phillipsburg: Presbyterian and Reformed, 2006). Gradually, the New Westminster school has imbibed notions from modern-day scholarship that are highly detrimental to Reformed orthodoxy.

[11] In a calculating move, Shepherd joined the Christian Reformed Church in order to thwart the effort of those who were in the process of leveling of charges against him in the OPC's Presbytery of Philadelphia. Two of Shepherd's most recent writings appear in *Backbone of the Bible: Covenant in Contemporary Perspective*, ed. P. Andrew Sandlin (Nacogdoches, Tx.: Covenant, 2004) which I have reviewed in *TrinJ* 26 NS (2005) 149–50 (see Appendix A).

[12] My review of *Backbone of the Bible* cited above, *TrinJ*, 150. Richard A. Muller's rethinking of covenant theology explains why he accepted Lillback's revision of Calvin's teaching on the covenants, *The Binding of God: Calvin's Role in the Development of Covenant Theology*, Texts and Studies in Reformation and Post-Reformation Thought, gen. ed. R. A. Muller (Grand Rapids: Baker, 2001) in the series he edits for Baker Book House. See further, my "Current Theological Trends in Reformed Seminaries: The Dilemma in Ministerial Education," the Eastern regional meeting of the Evangelical Theological Society in Lancaster, Pa. (April 3, 1998) available at www.tren.com.

[13] Consult the study report of the Reformed Church in the United States, www.rcus.org/synod-report-Shep3.htm; David J. Engelsma, "Covenantal Universalism: New Form of an Old Attack on Sovereign Grace," Part 1, in *Standard Bearer* (April 15, 2004) 316–19; and Engelsma, "The Account of a Fallen Seminary and a 'Falling' Church," in *Standard Bearer* (April 15, 2004) 320–21.

[14] Phillipsburg: Presbyterian and Reformed, 2004. Allan Fisher's arrival as editor at Presbyterian & Reformed Publications opened the door for published criticisms of the Shepherd theology—a first in the history of Presbyterian and Reformed. Before very long, however, internal theological conflict led to his resignation (August 2005). David J. Engelsma, in his book review of *The Pattern of Sound Doctrine* in the *Protestant Reformed Theological Journal* (38 [2005] 96–101), writes: "The title of this book is puzzling. The content demonstrates that the Westminster seminaries in Pennsylvania and in California are gravely ill and that the ailment is precisely their failure to hold the pattern of sound doctrine. Basic to the failure is the low esteem for systematic theology at the seminaries" (96). He reiterates: "The

pattern of sound doctrine is seriously distorted at Westminster" (97). Engelsma rightly sees that more than systematic formulation (confessional dogmatics) is jeopardized in the New Westminster school. "The other result of minimizing systematic Reformed theology, solidly based on the creeds, if not phasing it out altogether, is, as Godfrey contends, the certain arising of heretical teaching and the toleration of heresy when it appears" (99).

[15] *Pattern of Sound Doctrine* 34. I fail to see any such "movement" in the formation and early theological development of Westminster Seminary. What I see is the desire to preserve historic Calvinism and to expound the Reformed system of doctrine more consistently and faithfully in accordance with the formal and material principles of Scripture—Scripture as self-authenticating and self-interpreting, and the gospel of justification by faith alone. Westminster at the beginning stood committed to the reformational principle, "reformed and reforming according to the Word of God." To be sure, the newly-developing discipline of biblical theology (à la Vos) was to have a important place in the interpretation of Scripture. And equally certain, Vos belongs to the tradition of Old Princeton, not the New Westminster School.

[16] *Ibid.*, 219.

[17] *Ibid.*, 25–26.

[18] *Ibid.*, 51.

[19] *Ibid.*, 66.

[20] *Ibid.*, 67. See my book review of Michael S. Horton's *Covenant and Eschatology*, in *TrinJ* 24 NS (2003) 125–29, republished in *Gospel Grace* 287–94. Gaffin commends biblical theology, in distinction from systematic theology, for its "nonspeculative, exegetically based character" ("A New Paradigm in Theology?" in *WTJ* 56 [1994] 380). Russell D. Moore in *The Kingdom of Christ: The New Evangelical Perspective* (Wheaton: Crossway, 2004) observes: "The inaugurated eschatology proposed by many modified covenantalists differs sharply from the traditional Reformed understanding of the final matters of Christian theology, often due to interaction with the broader fields of biblical scholarship. Perhaps most representative of this trend has been Westminster Seminary theologian Richard Gaffin, Jr." (46). Quoting from Gaffin's work, Moore adds that this Kingdom perspective mandates an "already/not yet" framework, one that "has been undermined unintentionally by covenant theology's traditional treatment of eschatology as 'last things'" (47). "[A]n inaugurated eschatology is capable of 'making clearer (what traditional Reformed theology has largely missed) the eschatological dimension of the Christian life and the present existence of the church, grounded in the fact that not only the justification but the regeneration/renewal already experienced by believers at the core of their being is nothing less than eschatological in nature (for example, "new creation," 2 Cor 5:17; "raised with Christ," Eph 2:5-6)'" (47). Endorsing Gaffin's formulation of covenant theology, Moore concludes: "It is by no means simply a continuation of Princeton fundamentalism. This is because, Gaffin asserts, B. B. Warfield was unable to account for the uniquely eschatological nature of the Kingdom (especially the work of the Spirit) that pervades the New Testament, especially the Synoptic Gospels and the Pauline epistles. Accordingly, modified covenantalists argue that the growing embrace by the heirs of Warfield of an inaugurationist understanding of the presence of the Kingdom is an advance toward a more biblical Kingdom theology" (49). See also Moore, "What Hath Dallas to Do With Westminster? The Kingdom Concept in Contemporary Evangelical Theology," *Criswell Theological Review*, NS 2 (2004) 35–49. I have reviewed Moore's book in *JETS* 48 (2005) 410–15, republished here as Appendix C.

[21] *Pattern of Sound Doctrine* 196.

## Notes

[22] *Ibid.*, 199. VanDrunen perceptively identifies two differences: (1) Gaffin's departure from Murray on the question of the inter-relationship between biblical theology and systematics (Gaffin sees the latter as jeopardizing the historicity—and historical flow—of divine revelation in the Bible); and (2) Gaffin's departure from Murray and Charles Hodge on the classic Protestant-Reformed law/gospel antithesis. Included here is Gaffin's rejection of Hodge's position regarding the works-principle operative in the Mosaic administration of the Covenant of Grace.

[23] Although Horton and VanDrunen oppose the Shepherd theology, they differ in their articulation of covenant theology. VanDrunen's critique of Shepherd is found in *Katekomen* 14 (2002) 23–26, reprinted in *The Outlook* 53 (March 2003) 5–8. See also the forthcoming collection of essays of faculty members of Westminster West in *Covenant and Justification: A Westminster Seminary California Faculty Symposium*, ed. R. Scott Clark (Phillipsburg: Presbyterian and Reformed, 2006), drawn from the seminary conference held in the Spring of 2004. For those who know the history of the seminary controversy, Shepherd emphatically stated that his dismissal from Westminster did not remove his theology—the New Theology—from the school. Truer words were never spoken by Shepherd.

For a representative statement of orthodox Lutheran teaching affirming the law/gospel contrast, see Ralph A. Bohlmann, *Principles of Biblical Interpretation in the Lutheran Confessions* (revised edition; St. Louis, Mo.: Concordia, 1983). He provides a concise and helpful list of principles of interpretation on pages 144–45.

[24] For Gaffin, Clowney committed the treasonable offense when he turned against Shepherd and called for his dismissal. The rest is history.

[25] See note 5 above.

[26] *Pattern of Sound Doctrine* 191.

[27] See the combative exchange between Franke, Trueman, and Gaffin in *Westminster Theological Journal* (Fall 2003).

[28] *Pattern of Sound Doctrine* 140. Application of the term "grace" to the prelapsarian epoch in the teaching of the orthodox Reformed scholastics (like Francis Turretin and, later, Herman Bavinck) did not dissolve the foundational law/gospel antithesis, which contrasts different ways to the eschatological goal (by way of probationary testing)—the first by works, the second by saving grace. The position of O. Palmer Robertson retains lingering remnants of scholastic (mis)formulation and is illustrative of the thinking of many contemporary Reformed expositors. In defense of the Reformed doctrine of the twofold covenants, the Covenant of Works and the Covenant of Grace, Robertson rightly notes: "It emphasizes properly the absolute necessity of recognizing a pre-fall relationship between God and man which required perfect obedience as the meritorious ground of blessing" (*The Christ of the Covenants* [Grand Rapids: Baker, 1980] 55). (This is the clear implication of the classic Protestant-Reformed law/gospel contrast.) On the next page, however, Robertson errs in saying, "To speak of a covenant of 'works' in contrast with a covenant of 'grace' appears to suggest that grace was not operative in the covenant of works. As a matter of fact, the totality of God's relationship with man is a matter of grace. Although 'grace' *may* not have been operative in the sense of a merciful relationship despite sin, the creation bond between God and man indeed was gracious" (italics mine). The issue here is more than semantics. The case need not be restated here; see the argument presented in my *Gospel Grace: The Modern-day Controversy*.

[29] *Ibid.*, 283.

[30] *Ibid.*, 268.

[31] *Ibid.*, 289.

[32] "Reason and Specifications Supporting the Action of the Board of Trustees in Removing Professor Shepherd (Approved by the Executive Committee of the Board, February 26, 1982)," published in John W. Robbins' *A Companion to the Current Justification Controversy* (Unicoi, Tenn.: Trinity Foundation, 2003). Under threat of legal action, the Board of Trustees was obliged to furnish a substantive reason for dismissing a tenured professor. Finding itself on the horns of a dilemma—seeing itself unable to denounce Shepherd's teaching as heretical (without such a judgment by a majority of the faculty or the trustees or by an ecclesiastical court of the church) and needing appropriate grounds for his dismissal—the Board gave as its "official" reason for Shepherd's removal the need to distance the seminary from ongoing controversy (*i.e.*, political expediency), while making clear at the same time that Shepherd's theology was considered by the Board to have deviated from the Bible and confessional Reformed teaching (a strange and awkward position for the Board to have assumed). The theological critique of Shepherd's theology convinced Shepherd to abandon his threat of a legal suit against the seminary (see note 11 above). An effort was made by the seminary to submerge the Board's findings as much as possible. The still-unresolved Shepherd dispute has contributed in large measure to the desire of Westminster West to distance herself more and more from the Philadelphia faculty. In addition to the recent name change, see the statement of clarification "Did you know?" in *Evangelium: A Quarterly Publication of Westminster Seminary California* 3.4 (Sept/Oct 2005) 11. Of course, much more still needs to be done and said in opposing the heterodoxy of Westminster in Philadelphia. Westminster West's attempts at defending the teaching of historic Reformed theology have seemingly made little impact among the Reformed churches. Her critique of the contemporary scene is blurred, the force of argument blunted, by acceptance or tolerance of Gaffin's formulations of the controverted doctrine. (Currently, Gaffin serves on the special seven-member committee to report to the 2006 General Assembly of the Orthodox Presbyterian Church. Evaluation of the Shepherd theology has been barred by the General Assembly commissioning this study.) In the past President Robert Godfrey has correctly spoken of the ills of Westminster in Philadelphia as theological *and* moral. See notes 35 and 40 below.

[33] See www.covenantseminary.edu/resource. Chapell (and the PCA more widely) fails to see the gravity of the issues. He does anticipate, however, that the debates will be around for a long time to come. On that he is right.

[34] *ByFaith* 2 (March/April 2005) 15.

[35] The 2005 General Assembly of the OPC granted the special seven-member committee another year before reporting on its evaluation of the New Perspective and related teachings (VanDrunen serves as chairman). However strong the committee's opposition to the New Perspective might be (in so many words), it is nullified by widespread adoption of the Shepherd theology within the OPC.

The website of Westminster Theological Seminary (August 2005) posts a statement on justification, adopted by the Faculty and Board at the May 2005 meeting of the Trustees. Once again, the seminary voices affirmation for the doctrine of "justification by faith alone," as it has done consistently throughout the long history of the seminary controversy—a doctrine affirmed by Shepherd himself! The question is, What is meant by that phrase? The seminary in this statement makes mention of "some apparent confusion" within the Reformed community regarding the doctrine of justification. Is the confusion "apparent" or real? Simply put: this official statement of Westminster Seminary is just one more smokescreen. Deception and misstatement still rule the day at Westminster. A similar false statement was sent from the OPC General Assembly to the 2005 PCA General Assembly, as well as other to ecclesiastical bodies. In the meantime, the seminary has granted Gaffin a sabbatical for the 2005 Fall semester; Tipton has been given approval to teach an additional, elective course in the Fall semester on the topic of covenant theology—presumably in an effort to address the "apparent confusion."

[36] Grand Rapids: Baker, 2005.

[37] *Ibid.*, 232

[38] See Chapter Three, "Paul, the Law, and Contemporary Theology: The Undoing of the Protestant Reformation," in my *Gospel Grace* 93–121.

[39] Note here the work of Stanley Grenz and John Franke. The latter's recent release, *The Character of Theology*, has been endorsed by Robert Webber, James Smith, Roger Olson, Brian McLaren, and Peter Enns (back cover of the book). The heart of Franke's argument is this: "The contextual nature of theology suggests the companion notion of theology as a second-order discipline and highlights its character as an interpretive enterprise. As such, the doctrinal, theological, and confessional formulations of theologians and particular communities are the products of human reflection on the primary stories, teachings, symbols, and practices of the Christian church. Therefore, these formulations must be distinguished from these 'first-order' commitments of the Christian faith. For example, theological constructions and doctrines are always subservient to the content of Scripture and therefore must be held more lightly. In addition, the second-order nature of theology has entailed the development of conceptual vocabularies and sophisticated forms of argument that can appear to be far removed from idioms of Scripture. . . . The content of this theological meta-discourse should always be viewed as second-order, interpretive venture subject to further clarification, insight, and correction" (104). By way of further amplification Franke adds that "the task of theology in its various historical, cultural, ecclesial, and confessional contexts and expressions is to offer its particular witness to the Christian faith as an ecumenical enterprise for the purpose of contributing to the common task of the church to clarify the teaching of the one faith. . . . [T]he task of theology is critical and constructive reflection on the beliefs and practices of the Christian church. It suggests a model for theology that is inherently reforming in its openness to the Word of God and the multicultural Christian witness of the historical and global church and in keeping with the nature of theology as an ongoing, second-order, contextual discipline" (118).

What does this say about Scripture as the Word of God? Franke explains: "The assertion that our final authority is the Spirit speaking in and through Scripture means that Christian belief and practice cannot be determined merely by appeal either to the exegesis of Scripture carried out apart from the life of the believer and the believing community or to any 'word from the Spirit' that stands in contradiction to biblical exegesis. The reading and interpretation of the text is for the purpose of listening to the voice of the Spirit, who speaks in and through Scripture to the church in the present" (131–32). What is Franke's distinction between the "primary teachings of the Bible" and churchly theology? Embracing the views of Stanley Hauerwas, Franke contends that "theological constructions and doctrines 'are not the upshot of the stories; they are not the meaning or heart of the stories.' Instead, they should be understood as tools whose purpose is to assist the community in hearing the Spirit's voice and 'to help us tell the story better.' Put another way, the task of theology is not an attempt to identify and codify the true meaning of the text in a series of systematically arranged assertions that then function as the only proper interpretive grid through which to read the Bible. Such an approach is characteristic among those who hold confessional statements in an absolutist fashion and claim that such statements teach the 'system' of doctrine contained in Scripture. The danger here is that such a procedure can hinder the ability to read the text and to listen to the Spirit in new ways. Theology should always lead us back to the Bible. Its goal is to place the Christian community in a position to be receptive to the voice of the Spirit speaking in and through the biblical text to refashion the world after the eschatological mission and purposes of God. In light of this, the principle that the text of Scripture takes primacy over theological construction provides the basic parameter for understanding the interface between exegesis and theological reflection. If our working presupposition is not that the text exists primarily for the sake of theology but that theology serves the reading of the text, then we can no longer follow the commonly held view that the logical flow of Christian thought moves from biblical studies to a form of systematic theology. From this perspective, biblical scholars deliver to theologians the authentic biblical teachings in their unsystematic multiplicity, and theologians, in turn, bring these materials together into a systematic statement of what purports to be the doctrinal system taught in the Bible" (135).

The upshot of all this is that Franke drives a false wedge between Bible teaching (the "content of Scripture") and church theology. Consequently on this view, confessional Reformed dogmatics is relativized/contextualized in such a way that theology is no more than a speculative, rationalistic enterprise in need of ongoing reformulation (but to what end?). Franke naively views exegesis as *pre-theological* reflection on what the Bible teaches. Were there any doubts where Franke is going in his thinking, we quote the following: "Viewed from the historical perspective, the Bible is the product of the community of faith that produced it. The compilation of Scripture occurred within the context of the faith community, and the biblical documents represent the self-understanding of the community in which they were developed" (151). Not even Scripture is shielded from a historico-cultural hermeneutic that ends up in a relativistic sea of change. "What unifies this relationship between Scripture and the communal tradition of the church," writes Franke, "is the work of the Spirit. It is the Spirit who stands behind both the development and the formation of the community as well as the production of the biblical documents and their coming together into a single canon as that community's authoritative text. The community found these documents to be the vehicle through which they were addressed by the Spirit of God. The illuminating work of the Spirit brought forth these writings from the context of the community in accordance with the witness of that community. This work of illumination did not cease with the closing of the canon. Rather, it continues as the Spirit attunes the contemporary community of faith to understand Scripture and to apply it afresh to its own context in accordance with the intentions of the Spirit" (152). For a sharply contrasting interpretation, see my "Doctrinal Development in Scripture and Tradition: A Reformed Assessment of the Church's Theological Task," *CTJ* 30 (1995) 401–18 (republished in *Covenant Theology in Reformed Perspective* 341–55).

[40] "The legacy of Westminster Theological Seminary is indisputable," remarks Lillback. "The Westminster Confession, the foundational creed of the Seminary, forms the basis of both the Presbyterian Church in America and the Orthodox Presbyterian Church as well as churches in many countries worldwide. Its faculty, both past and present, is world-renowned. Its excellent scholarship is thoroughly acknowledged, its publications read globally. By any standard, it is the crown jewel in Reformed theological instruction. My vision is that God might not only preserve this heritage but that through our faithful and cooperative commitment, he might graciously broaden its impact for the glory of our God and for the advancement of the Kingdom of Christ," posted on Westminster's website (April 2005). Similarly, Sam Logan has depicted the seminary as the "doyen" of Reformed schools throughout the world.

The headline story announcing Lillback's appointment as President of Westminster in the April twenty-nineth issue of the *English Churchman* reads: "Faith and works heretic to lead Westminster Philadelphia." Regrettably, it is a story not well known in most places. Not only does deception and deceit reign at the seminary, but pride and theological elitism mar the school's ability to evaluate clearly, objectively, and honestly her work and witness to Scripture and the Calvinistic faith. Equally regrettable is the stalemate that has taken hold in the Reformed world. Illustrative is the OPC's and the PCA's Presbytery of Philadelphia: By and large, the vast majority of members of these presbyteries—as elsewhere throughout the OPC and PCA—have resolutely supported Gaffin, chief architect of the New Westminster Theology, and shielded him from his critics. Apathy, intimidation, fear of recrimination have all been major factors in giving shape to the current state of affairs in the Reformed communion.

[41] For the fourth and last in a series of devastating exposés of the church in the world and the world in the church, see David F. Wells, *Above All Earthly Pow'rs: Christ in a Postmodern World* (Grand Rapids: Eerdmans, 2005). This masterful, insightful work analyses the cultural-ecclesiastical milieu of the church today. No where in "Reformed-evangelical" Protestantism is theological deviation and outright doctrinal perversion more evident than in the denial or restatement of the biblical doctrine of justification by faith alone, once regarded as article of faith on which the church stood or fell. The Spring 2005 issue of the *Criswell Theological Review* (NS, vol. 2) is devoted to the subject of the New Perspective on Paul. In the opening editorial R. Alan Streett speaks of "a swirling doctrinal controversy so emotionally charged that scholars everywhere are being forced to take sides in the debate." To be sure, this crisis in theology has overtaken the evangelical community. "The debate," Streett adds, "seems to be reaching a critical point" (1). He points out that some conservative seminaries and schools are now barring those who espouse the New Perspective, some faculty already having been fired. Decisive action such as this is both commendable and necessary for the purity, peace, and well-being of the church of Christ. The Shepherd heresy promoted at Westminster Seminary is merely one variation of the New Perspective on Paul and the law. Included in the same issue of the *Criswell Review* is "The New Perspective on Paul: A Select and Annotated Bibliography" by Jay E. Smith to help readers sort through the voluminous, burgeoning literature, which shows no signs of abating (91–111).

Professor Sinclair Ferguson—for the second time—has resigned from full-time teaching at Westminster, accepting the call to serve as senior pastor of First Presbyterian Church, Columbia, South Carolina. The Associate Reformed Presbyterian Church, of which this congregation is a member, eagerly embraces the New Theology described here in this paper. Assuredly, the Westminster controversy has dogged Ferguson in the classroom and in the pulpit—and will continue to do so, until he abandons his ties to the Torrance-Shepherd-Gaffin school. Without hesitation, the New Perspective should be barred from classrooms and pulpits.

## FOUR

# Paul Elliott's Christianity and Neo-Liberalism

*Drama in the Orthodox Presbyterian Church*

## Setting the Stage

On the contemporary scene it has become popular to portray the church's call to theological self-understanding (more exactly, her witness and life) as dramatic performance, consisting in the retelling—and reliving—of the Christian Story.[1] The Story begins with the biblical record of the inspired acts and teachings of God and continues along the church's historical trajectory that brings us into the present. Theology is the drama of living out biblical teaching in the succession of generations of those who call upon the name of the Lord in faith and humble contrition. Assuming this point of view, for the sake of the cast presented in this play, the theological controversy now preoccupying the attention of Reformed churches—those standing in the tradition of the Westminster standards and the other historic Reformed creeds—is pure drama.

At stake in this dispute is the correct interpretation of Scripture and the confessions. Modern-day revisionists contend that the church's earlier interpreters, up to and including the Protestant reformers of the sixteenth and seventeenth centuries, missed or misconstrued what was fundamental in the interpretation and proclamation of the Gospel. No one will deny that the Scriptures require careful exegetico-theological exposition, exposition that draws upon the entire gamut of intellectual study among a multiplicity of academic and practical disciplines. No small task on any reckoning. Study of the history of Christian doctrine, however, provides a significant degree of control and guidance in the church's ongoing task in elucidating the text of Scripture. Contemporary Christian doctrine builds upon the insights of the past—learning from its strengths and weaknesses, gleaning from faithful restatements of what the Bible teaches and disposing of error (great and small). The New Perspective on Paul and related movements in contemporary biblical-theological interpretation have called for a radically new understanding of the foundational doctrine in Christian faith and life, the doctrine of justification by faith (apart from the works of the law). The drama playing itself out in the Orthodox Presbyterian Church is merely one stage production in modern church-theater.

Paul M. Elliott in *Christianity and Neo-Liberalism: The Spiritual Crisis in the Orthodox Presbyterian Church and Beyond* offers his analysis and critique of the plight of one, small Reformed denomination, one that is influential far beyond her size.[2] In the course of argument, the author gives some attention to trends in evangelical Protestantism more broadly. The title of the book is intended to recall the work of J. Gresham Machen, tireless and courageous defender of biblical Christianity, founder of the OPC in the opening half of the twentieth century. Machen's masterful and insightful diatribe, entitled *Christianity and Liberalism,* was an account of the growing cleavage between two religions, both claiming rights to the title of Christianity.[3] The nature and ramifications of the doctrinal controversy addressed in Elliott's book has only gradually come to light in recent years, and that from several sources. The history of the dispute in the OPC is a story that needs to be told. Neither Elliott nor the present actor/writer engages the issues dispassionately. Both have had significant roles to play in what has become the latest act in the drama known as Calvinism.[4] One can only continue to hope and pray that, like the phoenix rising from the ashes, the OPC and the Reformed churches of our day may yet regain a sure footing in the truth of the Gospel and in the Word of God—without feign or compromise.

# Act One

## *The Formative Years*

Denominations are born with the best of intentions. Whether each and every denomination is justified in its formation is a question we need not address here. Given the rapidly deteriorating conditions in the northern Presbyterian church in the early years of the twentieth century, Machen had little alternative than to start over again with a group of pastors and lay people committed to the fundamentals of the Christian religion, the Reformed faith, and Presbyterian church government. The circumstances that Machen faced gave him and his followers no other recourse. Unfortunately, the formative years of the new denomination, what was to be called the Orthodox Presbyterian Church, were far from peaceful and smooth, even among its constituents. Division over differing understandings of Calvinist teaching and church polity, including ecumenical relations with other evangelical Protestant bodies, worked against a strong, vibrant witness for (Reformed) Christianity in its struggles against modernism. Nineteenth-century liberal teaching, the rise of neoorthodoxy associated with the writings of Karl Barth and Reinhold Niebuhr, the existentialism of Rudolf Bultmann, and other mutations of Protestant theological heterodoxy were gaining supremacy in the leading academic institutions of the day, even those that formerly were conservative strongholds.

Machen's first, notable achievement was the founding of Westminster Theological Seminary in Philadelphia, conveyer of Old-Princeton Calvinism. The systematicians serving on the young faculty at the beginning were John Murray and Cornelius Van Til. Though Machen was principally known as a New Testament scholar, he clearly had command of the Reformed faith as a system of doctrine. The new denomination and seminary, working in tandem, were not only committed to the systematic presentation of the teaching of the Bible, they were also intent on coherence and consistency in doctrine and in practice. Faithfulness (or "precision") in doctrinal formulation and earnest, conscientious application of Calvinism in the practical life of the church provided justification for the new enterprise in Reformed education, training, and witness.

This objective, good as it was, did tend to nurture an attitude of elitism and exclusivism among members of the OPC. Though very small in number since its beginnings, the new denomination had hopes of expanding significantly, given the deplorable condition of American presbyterianism in those dark, ominous days. Numerical growth, however, was not to be. What the denomination and seminary lacked in numbers was more than compensated in theological acumen. But a sense of superiority quickly set in—pride in the rightness of her cause and in her self-sacrifice—virtues that were seen as means to galvanize, solidify, encourage, and console the faithful remnant who had abandoned property and prestige for the foolishness of the Gospel. There is much that is commendable about the formation and development of the OPC in the opening decades of its existence. The positive achievements, however, ought not to blind us to the negative features. Westminster Seminary would become the chief source for the inculcation of theological pride and exclusivism within the OPC (and in other pockets of the Reformed world). This personality-trait led to the notion that the seminary and the denomination, widely perceived as the bastions of Reformed orthodoxy, are above criticism. Hence, the thinking is that the Westminster Seminary/OPC interpretation of confessional Calvinism is not to be questioned or challenged. At present, OPC leaders are on a campaign to exhort congregations and members to be subject to the courts of the church (as they lead astray and abuse church-power). The destructive outcome of this high opinion and self-esteem has become all too apparent in accounts of the current theological controversy.

As the intellectual incubus for the fledging denomination, how did Westminster view her peculiar niche in the broader theological world? From the beginning, the seminary faculty was largely focused on matters *propadeutic* and *pre-theoretical* (or presuppositional). In an earlier article I wrote:

> The philosophico-dogmatic issue lying at the very heart of the Westminster school of theology—a school in search of her own, distinct identity within international Calvinism—is, "scientifically" speaking, *pre-dogmatic* in the discipline (or science) of theology. Westminster's focal concern is one that falls within the locus of what is called theological *prolegomenon*. There are two aspects to this theological concern: (1) a description of the relationship between systematic theology (or confessional Reformed dogmatics) and biblical theology, what is the biblico-exegetical approach to the interpretation of the canonical text of Scripture, Old and New Testaments, one that elucidates the history of redemptive revelation; and (2) the role of (Van Tillian) presuppositionalism in theological discourse. Simply put, the chief preoccupation of the faculty of Westminster Seminary has been—and remains—the proper method of interpretation, that is, theological methodology.[5]

Whereas Murray provided (in most instances) the careful, meticulous exegetico-dogmatic justification for the theology of the Westminster standards, largely as a restatement and enlargement upon Scottish and English Calvinism, Van Til pressed for the necessity of an apologetic that was thoroughly consistent with Reformed covenant theology.[6] It was the latter systematician who proved decisive for the peculiar task assumed by the seminary faculty as a whole (though always with a measure of debate and disagreement). Hence, it was Van Til, not Murray, who became known as "Mr. Westminster."[7] Theistic presuppositionalism thus distinguishes the Westminster Seminary hermeneutic—distinctive of Old Westminster, in contrast to the multiperspectival hermeneutic that now prevails at New Westminster.[8] Theistic presuppositionalism is nothing other than the traditional Protestant-Reformed hermeneutic, the principle of *sola scriptura,* in its most consistent expression. The hermeneutical methodology is circular, presupposing at every point in the interpretive process the veracity and reliability of the written Word of God as infallible (and inerrant). Simply put, the Scriptures are self-interpreting and self-authenticating; we think God's thoughts after him.

The Van Til-Murray legacy persisted until the middle of the 1960s, when change was introduced (however subtly) by the addition of Norman Shepherd, Richard Gaffin, Jr., and John Frame to the faculty.[9] This redirection of the seminary would prevail in the years that were to come. An account and evaluation of this radical change is the substance of Elliott's book, *Christianity and Neo-Liberalism*.

# Act Two

## *The Theological and Moral Dilemma*

The scene changes dramatically: Orthodoxy meets heterodoxy in the OPC. The *festschrift* written and assembled in honor of Westminster West's chief systematician, Professor Robert Strimple, who taught since the opening years of Westminster in southern California until his retirement in 2001, serves as a primary vehicle for the airing of serious disagreements now found among the two faculties.[10] Surprisingly, Elliott makes no mention of this 2004 publication.[11] On more than one occasion Robert Godfrey, current president of Westminster West, has spoken of the Shepherd controversy as "a theological and moral problem for the seminary." Overseeing the work of the seminary, while seeking to defend historic Reformed orthodoxy, has proven to be a very difficult challenge in the face of ongoing dissension and dissembling. The fate of the OPC lies in the hands of the Westminster Seminaries, even though the OPC now occupies a meager presence in terms of present faculty alignments. To be sure, ramifications of the present-day debates are felt among other Reformed-ecclesiastical bodies.

The substance of what follows in the Second and Third Acts of the OPC drama is a commentary and evaluation of the Robbins-Elliott critique of the theological controversy regarding the biblical doctrine of justification by faith (and related doctrines). The dispute over the teaching of Norman Shepherd that surfaced in the mid-1970s has been chronicled in several recent publications, including this account by Elliott. We need not rehearse this history again in any detail. Rather, we address the main argument of Elliott (and John Robbins) as laid out in *Christianity and Neo-Liberalism*. After an overview of the plight of evangelical Reformed-Protestantism generally, Elliott states: "The Orthodox Presbyterian Church is now in such a spiritual crisis, and the crisis has spread well beyond it. The crisis centers on the conflict between authentic Biblical Christianity and an Antichristian counterfeit" (12). He adds:

> The cancer of liberalism—or to put it in twenty-first century terms, neo-liberalism—has grown and spread, slowly and subtly for at least three decades in the OPC. *Neo-liberalism is the denial of fundamentals of authentic Biblical Christianity by reputedly conservative churchmen, who simultaneously claim that they remain completely faithful to Scripture and to the doctrinal standards of their churches.* Neo-liberals pretend to be what they are not, and profess to believe what they do not.
>
> Neo-liberalism principally manifests itself in the denial of the full inerrancy, infallibility, and authority of Scripture, and denial of the Gospel doctrine of justification by faith (mere belief) in Christ alone. But from those two fundamental errors, the cancer of neo-liberalism spreads to corrupt sound teaching on other foundational truths. [12]

The root of modern-day Reformed heterodoxy at Westminster is what Elliott calls "neo-liberalism," its chief and fatal defect being the hermeneutical methodology adopted by its teachers and interpreters of the Bible. A word here about theological interpretation: Every student of the Bible, whatever his or her level of intellectual rigor, is engaged in *theological interpretation*. What we are hearing much more often nowadays in Reformed academia—following the trend in its secular counterpart—is the necessity to come to grips with multiple interpretations of the Bible by expositors (of every theological stripe). Here again, the new, reigning *modus operandi* is theological multiperspectivalism in its various guises and hues. But to the contrary, there is only one, faithful interpretation of the biblical text (with multiple *applications*). The reason this is so derives ultimately from the formal principle of Scripture, the principle that the Bible as the inscripturated Word of God is unified and consistent in all its parts (we have in view here the doctrine of Scripture in its fullness). According to Calvin, the church's interpretive work is a matter of the interplay between Word and Spirit. The Holy Spirit alone brings illumination and true understanding. It is the self-attesting Christ who speaks in the pages of Scripture. From the standpoint of the economy of redemption, the Spirit is the Lord Christ. He is the one who not only redeems and regenerates, but also illumines the mind to receive the things of the Lord. There is undivided unity in the work of redemption accomplished and applied. Proper interpretation of the Word of God is acquired by the church in the course of the history of biblical exposition, to a greater or lesser degree, as God sovereignly brings his Word to bear upon his people. Needless to say, no single interpreter has a complete grasp of the teaching of Scripture, nor is the confessional church infallible in her doctrine (i.e, dogma, including ethical teachings). But to the extent that the church confesses what is the teaching of the Bible, to that extent church doctrine is to be believed and obeyed.[12]

Here is where Orthodox Presbyterians encounter the dilemma of their own making: History and rhetoric suggest that the OPC is impeccably orthodox in her confession and practice. Elliott notes:

> Most people in the Christian community at large, as well as in the OPC itself, mistakenly believe that the OPC and WTS remain bulwarks of conservative theology. They assume that both still follow the path charted by their leading founder, J. Gresham Machen, who was guided by the principle that "the Bible forbids a man to substitute any human authority for the Word of God." Few in the OPC, or in the Christian church at large, understand that the OPC and WTS have long since taken a different path, the part of neo-liberalism, and that this has led the OPC to its spiritual crisis. In some cases, this misunderstanding results from lack of information, in other cases, from misinformation. But in still other cases, as we shall see, it stems from disinformation—that is, misinformation deliberately disseminated by church leaders to conceal the facts and history of the crisis. [15]

More than being a matter of "misinformation" or "disinformation," the OPC's perception of herself today—in the heat of controversy—is more the result of calculated deception on the part of the seminary. Elliott's historical sketch is helpful in drawing out this character flaw in the OPC. Less convincing, however, is the comparison drawn by the author between the liberalism of the early twentieth-century and the neo-liberalism of today. Elliott's analysis, in my judgment, falls short. Nevertheless, some real similarities with respect to theological subterfuge and ecclesiastical maneuverings have emerged in the life of the OPC over the course of the last three or four decades. Leaders and members of the OPC have learned bad theology; they have acquired bad habits.[13]

The theological issues are complex, as they are fundamental in the system of Reformed doctrine. Four criticisms of the Robbins-Elliot critique of the early OPC/Old Westminster tradition must be noted: (1) it misunderstands the integral bond between historic Reformed covenant theology and the rise and development of biblical theology in the modern period (in the tradition of Geerhardus Vos and Meredith G. Kline);[14] (2) it mistakenly contends that the *only* exegesis of Romans 2:13 consistent with Protestant-Reformed orthodoxy is one which sees here the enunciation of the *hypothetical* works-principle of divine inheritance, whereby eternal life is granted to the "doers of the law," human righteousness being the ground of salvation (this opinion not only overreaches, it entails a misreading of the biblical text in question);[15] (3) it falsely links the perspectivalism of John Frame and his student/colleague Vern Poythress to the theological hermeneutic of Cornelius Van Til (the two interpretive methods, multi-perspectivalism and theistic presuppositionalism, are worlds apart);[16] and (4) it holds a defective view of the role and significance of the Reformed confessions, including proper understanding of creedal subscription (the Robbins-Elliott critique of the OPC's study report on the days of creation is illustrative of this problem).[17]

Turning to the focal issue of the controversy in the OPC and in the Westminster Seminaries (the doctrine of justification by faith alone), Elliott observes: "The history of the advance of another gospel in the OPC largely coincides with the history of its failure to condemn the false teachings of Norman Shepherd—and the OPC's conspiracy of silence on the matter, which has only begun to be broken in the past few years" (126). Elliott provides his readers a summary of the events leading up the dramatic turnabout at Westminster, what resulted in the termination of Shepherd's teaching position. To Elliott's account we add the following detail: It was not until the summer and fall of 1981, after the release of the May 4, 1981 letter to "Friends of the Reformed Faith," that President Edmund Clowney began in earnest to read and comprehend what it was that Shepherd had been teaching. Hearing the tapes of Shepherd's class-lectures on the Holy Spirit and the Sandy Cove camp-lessons delivered in the summer of 1981 ("Life in Covenant with God"), and reading my article published in the pages of *The Westminster Theological Journal* (Fall 1980), Clowney made a 180-degree turn. Shepherd's days were now numbered; the heresy could no longer be contained or concealed.[18] (The *WTJ* article was a distillation of my Westminster doctoral dissertation on the subject of Reformed covenant theology begun under Shepherd.) Regrettably, misinformation and dissembling would still mar the labors of Clowney and impede the work and witness of the seminary in the years to come. Given these circumstances, progress of a sort had nevertheless been made; Shepherd was on his way out.

The history of the controversy and the present situation in which the Board now found itself led the Board to dismiss Shepherd initially on grounds of expediency, rather than doctrinal error. Above all other considerations, the seminary found itself needing to distance itself from Shepherd's teaching in order to preserve its theological reputation, its enrollment, and its finances. It was only the ensuing threat of litigation on the part of Shepherd that made it necessary for the Board to provide adequate justification for its decision in firing Shepherd, a tenured professor. Hence, the writing of "Reason and Specifications Supporting the Action of the Board of Trustees in Removing Professor Shepherd, February 26, 1982." Expediency would not play here; only substantive theological error (*i.e.*, doctrinal "heresy"[19]) would suffice. The eighteen-page document did achieve its twofold objective: (1) laying out a detailed statement of the theological grounds for Shepherd's dismissal; and (2) ameliorating this doctrinal judgment by making expediency the "official" reason. Anticipating difficult days ahead, the Board adopted a very shrewd and clever position, but one that was subversive and morally dishonest.[20] The public was misinformed in several reports and statements made in the Christian media. Students and supporters of Westminster were likewise misled and deceived.

# Act Three

### *The Babylonian Captivity of the Seminary and the OPC*

Many attempts at discussion and entreaty were made throughout the course of the Shepherd dispute and in the years immediately following Shepherd's dismissal, all to no avail. Within the seminary some effort was made to engage further discussion of covenant theology, specifically, the differences in formulation between two of the seminary's leading theologians, Meredith Kline (representative of classic Reformed teaching) and Richard Gaffin (representative of the new revisionist thinking). The forum for this was the Covenant Roundtable, which dissolved after its first sit-down meeting in March of 1994 (prior dialogue was conducted through correspondence).[21]

During the years after Shepherd's dismissal the faculty and administration (under the presidency of George Fuller and Samuel Logan) worked to secure a faculty that was unified and committed to the new theological programme. Faculty members were given free reign to pursue their own interests and ideas wherever they might take them. This has been the result: The biblical department has opened the gates to critical interpretation of the Bible and looks favorably upon the New Perspective; the systematics department continues to advance the (Gaffin-)Shepherd theology; the practical department seeks to implement the methodology of theological contextualization pioneered at the seminary by Harvie Conn; and the church history department attempts to situate New Westminster in the stream of historic-revisionist Calvinism, otherwise known as "constructive Calvinism."[22] (Faculty members opposed to Shepherd's teaching moved on to other seminaries, Robert Knudsen being the one exception.)

Numerous efforts have also made to denigrate and ridicule the views of Shepherd's opponents, to malign their character, and to impute sinister motives in their criticisms of the seminary. Some in the Presbytery of Philadelphia (OPC) had hoped to obtain disciplinary action against the signers of the May 1981 letter, but failed in that effort. Elliott records:

> The Presbytery held an adjourned meeting in June 1982 to take up unfinished business form the May meeting. That business included a neo-liberal effort to instigate judicial charges against signers of the May 4, 1981, letter to "Friends of the Reformed Faith" which had pulled aside the cloak long covering the evil taking place at Westminster Seminary. Like the Seminary board, the Presbytery was poised to "shoot the messengers"—to discipline godly watchmen who had sounded the alarm, rather than disciplining the heretics in their midst. [141–42]

Likewise, the trial of John Kinnaird in Philadelphia Presbytery, leading up to the deliberations of the 2003 General Assembly, was something of a replay of the Shepherd hearings of the late 1970s and early 1980s (with Gaffin again taking the lead role). In the end, notes Elliott, "[n]ot only was Kinnaird acquitted, the General Assembly also declared that those who found him guilty were the ones in error" (176).[23]

Dissension over the action taken by the General Assembly resulted in a compromise measure the following year, formation of a seven-member committee to study and report back to the Assembly concerning the church's position on the doctrine of justification by faith in light of views currently being taught among Reformed-evangelical churches. After one extension, the committee is due to report to the June 2006 meeting of the General Assembly. Enough has already been said in various places to question the integrity and effectiveness of this New Measure, one destined to obscure and confuse the issues. Given the history of the controversy and Gaffin's appointment to this committee, freedom of expression (diversity in the interpretation of Scripture, *i.e.*, multiperspectivalism), will no doubt prevail.

Both the Westminster Seminaries and the OPC are now of the age when the temptation to preserve the institutions at any cost begins to be felt increasingly, more so with each new generation. The quest for authority, power, and control in the church is alluring, especially when thought to be in hand's reach. At the close of 2005, Westminster Seminary in Philadelphia announced receiving a very large amount of donor money (presumably as a validation and confirmation of her theological leadership).[24] Alongside a slowly-growing endowment, extensions in the United States, Great Britain, and Korea, a greater voice in secular academic circles (such as the Society of Biblical Literature), and the availability of cyber-technology for global communications, Westminster is positioned to reach an increasingly wider audience.[25] It has every intention of doing so, bearing a new torch and sword.

## Retrospective: *A Soliloquy*

The curtain rises one final time: On the darkly lit stage appears one actor.[26] The audience is told that his allegiance is, in the first place, to the Playwright's original script, faithfulness to the inscripturated Word of God. His primary commitment, therefore, is not to the established institutions—either the wayward seminary, or the errant denominations claiming to speak for the Scriptures and historic Reformed orthodoxy. From first-hand knowledge of the theological controversy, he testifies that there is no one who bears more responsibility for the plight of the OPC and the Westminster Seminaries than Professor Gaffin. Our focal concern in this drama of life and death in the churches is this systematician's theological formulation of the doctrine of justification by faith alone. Readers of *Christianity and Neo-Liberalism* have been rightly informed that Gaffin's new perspective on Paul—Gaffin's contextual, redemptive-historical reading of the apostle Paul (over against the situation of the church in the old, Mosaic economy)—bears similarity to the New Perspective of E. P. Sanders, James D. G. Dunn, and N. T. Wright, among other spokespersons who might well be named.[27] Elliott is correct in linking the mature views of Gaffin to his doctoral dissertation completed under Norman Shepherd in 1969.[28] Gaffin's interpretation of the Pauline doctrine of union with Christ informs his doctrine of justification and sanctification, two of the many "benefits" accruing to the believer by virtue of saving faith.

The conclusion to which Gaffin is drawn, in the words of Elliott, is this: "'[J]ustification' is both 'constitutive,' 'transforming,' and 'forensic.' This is the view of both Roman Catholic theologians and Karl Barth" (151 n. 14). Christ's justification, to which the apostle Paul refers in Romans

4:25, is not only determinative of the justification of those united to Christ through faith, it is *paradigmatic*. Quoting Gaffin: "The constitutive, transforming action of the resurrection is specifically forensic in character. It is Christ's justification" (151). Viewing the application of redemption as a "single act of God," Gaffin explains the many benefits of redemption applied in terms of their oneness (the many and the one). Union with Christ is the joining of the believer to Christ and his Spirit—the union of the individual to Christ, the Head, and the church, the Body. Christ being formed in us, believers are justified by the obedience of faith. In Gaffin's view, justification is constitutive and transformative (what is proper to sanctification, in distinction from justification). According to the teaching of historic Reformed orthodoxy, good works are *evidential* of the believer's justification.

What is particularly striking about Gaffin's view of the application of redemption, summed up in his doctrine of union with Christ, is the emphasis placed upon the eschatological *and* provisional. Justification, Gaffin tells us, occurs "in the mode of perseverance." The divine act of justification bears the eschatological imprint of the "already" and the "not yet." Accordingly, justification is neither truly fixed, *i.e.*, once-for-all, nor truly constitutive. Gaffin's formulation confounds two benefits, justification and sanctification, which believers enjoy in union with Christ. According to the Gaffin-Shepherd formulation, individual election to salvation is losable, mirroring the experience of ancient, theocratic Israel.[29] Pentecost marks a radical change in the progress and economy of redemption. The Christian, we are told, is united to the exalted, glorified Christ, viewed as a wholly new-covenant experience, one not proleptically enjoyed by the saints of old. Elliott notes the following:

> In response to a question at the 2005 Auburn Avenue Pastors Conference, Gaffin admitted that his teaching implies a different method of salvation for Old Testament versus New Testament saints. He said that it would be "redemptive-historically anachronistic to say that an old covenant believer like Abraham or David" was "united with Christ, because the Christ who is in view, and union with Christ, is specifically the exalted Christ, the redemptive-historical Christ if you will, the Christ who is what He is now by virtue of His death and resurrection, and He did not exist . . . in the situation of Abraham or David. [149–50]

Even if we were to conceal from view all the evidence provided in Gaffin's own words, and even if we were to set aside the fact that Gaffin is the co-author, if not father, of the theology of New Westminster, the question remains to be answered: Why has Westminster's senior systematician not seen the deep errors in Shepherd's formulations? To be sure, Gaffin in his writings does exhibit more restraint than did Shepherd in the early years.[30] The result, however, is teaching that is only more subtle and more misleading. Where does all this leave the OPC denomination and her sister institution(s), the Westminster Seminaries? The answer remains uncertain, although present indications would strongly suggest that the Orthodox Presbyterian Church is proving to be a felled experiment in American Presbyterianism.[31] The seminaries and the denomination can still reverse their course; but conflict can only be resolved in obedience to the Word of God. What is required is proper interpretation of the Scriptures (as opposed to interpretation that is false and misleading). Although the author of *Christianity and Neo-Liberalism* and his publisher, John Robbins, are to be commended for pursuing the cause of truth, they miss the mark as able, insightful theater critics. It is incumbent upon other actors in this drama to speak. The next act of the ongoing play has not yet been written.[32]

## NOTES

*Backstage*

[This paper was first read at the March 2006 Eastern regional meeting of the Evangelical Theological Society (Philadelphia, Pa.)]

[1] Michael S. Horton in *Covenant and Eschatology: The Divine Drama* (Louisville: Westminster John Knox, 2002) and Kevin J. Vanhoozer in *The Drama of Doctrine: A Canonical-Linguistic Approach to Christian Theology* (Louisville: Westminster John Knox, 2005) attempt to portray theology—first and second order—in terms of the church's dramatic performance of the Word. Horton writes as a historian of doctrine, Vanhoozer as a philosopher of language and literature.

[2] Paul M. Elliott, *Christianity and Neo-Liberalism: The Spiritual Crisis in the Orthodox Presbyterian Church and Beyond* (Unico: The Trinity Foundation, 2005). The extent to which Eliott's publisher, John Robbins, had a hand in the writing of this book, the reader is not told. In any case, it is apparent that Elliott's work replies heavily upon the analysis and critique of Robbins advanced in several of his own publications issued by The Trinity Foundation. Elliott informs us that his research is based on "conversations and correspondence with men who participated in many of those meetings (debating Shepherd's teaching)" (127 n. 5). Despite its shortcomings, Elliott's book is must reading. There are those who cannot understand how serious theological deviation could have taken place at Westminster. Others are pleased to see that the seminary has come of age, having moved away from narrow confessionalism by adopting a revisionist/multiperspectivalist interpretation of the creedal standards of the church. Accordingly, confessional church doctrine is merely tentative, provisional, and relative in nature—a product of its times.

[3] J. Gresham Machen, *Christianity and Liberalism* (Grand Rapids: Eerdmans, 1923).

*Notes*

⁴ See my *Gospel Grace: The Modern-day Controversy* (Eugene, Ore.: Wipf and Stock, 2003). Contrast Peter A. Lillback's revisionist account of Calvinism in *The Binding of God: Calvin's Role in the Development of Covenant Theology*, Texts and Studies in Reformation and Post-Reformation Thought, gen. ed. R. A. Muller (Grand Rapids: Baker, 2001).

⁵ See Chapter Three. With respect to the doctrinal controversies, Elliott draws a sharp line between the faculties of Westminster East and West. In a footnote he correctly indicates that Westminster Theological Seminary in Philadelphia is "[n]ot to be confused with Westminster Seminary California (WSC), which has its roots in WTS Philadelphia but has become separate and independent" (14 n. 3). It needs to be said, however, that Westminster West has not been fully insulated against false teaching, as in the case of John Frame and others who have served on the California faculty. Furthermore, Westminster West has found it difficult walking the tight-rope—vigorously opposing Shepherd's formulations, while approving Gaffin's theology of justification, election, and the covenants. Although Gaffin has maintained his support for the teachings of Norman Shepherd and John Kinniard, having openly acknowledged that their views are (substantively) his views, Westminster West has turned a blind eye, overlooking Gaffin's passionate defense of Shepherd and Kinnaird (perhaps with some degree of bewilderment).

⁶ For a thumb-nail sketch and analysis of Murray's covenant theology, see my essay "Paul's Letter to the Romans in the *New International Commentary on the New Testament* and in Contemporary Reformed Thought," *EvQ* 71 (1999) 3–24; republished in *Covenant Theology in Reformed Perspective: Collected Essays and Book Reviews in Historical, Biblical, and Systematic Theology* (Eugene, Ore.: Wipf and Stock, 2000) 227–45 (available online at www.twoagepress.org).

⁷ Today, it is systematician Richard Gaffin who covets the mantle that was once Van Til's. Gaffin's views, analogous in substance to the New Perspective on Paul and the law, has won the endorsement of the current seminary faculty—with a measure of debate and disagreement.

⁸ See my critiques of John Frame and Vern Poythress in the essays "On the Theological Correlation of Divine and Human Language: A Review Article," *JETS* 32 (1989) 99–105; and "John Frame and the Recasting of Van Tilian Apologetics: A Review Article," in *Mid-America Journal of Theology* 9 (1993) 279–96.

⁹ Consult further the paper cited in endnote 5 above.

¹⁰ Though retired, Strimple "continues to be a venerable presence on the Westminster California campus, dispensing solicited and wise advice to faculty," in *The Pattern of Sound Doctrine: Systematic Theology at the Westminster Seminaries*, ed. David VanDrunen (Phillipsburg: Presbyterian and Reformed, 2004) xi. In point of fact, it was Strimple's counsel and urging that prevailed upon the faculty of Westminster Seminary California to abstain from public, open criticism of Gaffin in his support, defense, and propagation of the Shepherd theology. Rather than attempt to refute or engage Gaffin's critics, these "Middle-men" have chosen to ignore and suppress the evidence. (No one on the WSC faculty heeded Professor Meredith G. Kline's concerns regarding Gaffin's heterodox views, expressed on numerous occasions.) Criticism of the Shepherd theology by faculty of Westminster West is nullified—or denuded—by approval of Gaffin's formulation. One cannot have it both ways. Neither is distortion of the truth, including the history of the seminary controversy, ever justified.

Criticism of teachings emanating from Westminster's Old Testament department (notably in the work of Doug Green and Peter Enns), as well as ongoing criticism of the Shepherd theology, the New Perspective on Paul, the Federal Visionists, and Frame's multiperspectivalism, shows no signs of diminishing. This offers some encouragement for the future of evangelical-Reformed Christianity. (See the recent prevarication and dissembling of President Peter Lillback in his exchange with Miss Martha McElwain, posted on the website of The Trinity Foundation, the February/March 2006 issue of *Trinity Review* [www.trinityfoundation.org].)

[11] *The Pattern of Sound Doctrine.* Missing also is reference to, and interaction with, my exposé *Gospel Grace: The Modern-day Controversy* (Eugene, Ore.: Wipf and Stock, 2003).

[12] See my "Doctrinal Development in Scripture and Tradition: A Reformed Assessment of the Church's Theological Task," *Calvin Theological Journal* 30 (1995) 401–18; republished in *Covenant Theology in Reformed Perspective* 341–55. Elliott questions the objective of the OPC to "[induct] Orthodox Presbyterian ministerial candidates into a culture of interpretation," by shaping a "a community of interpretation" (79, original italicized). The issue here, however, is proper training in the *accurate* interpretation of the Bible by the community of faith. That is to say, there is a right and a wrong practice of "indoctrination."

[13] Elliott notes: "Using the word 'neo-liberalism' in the same sentence with the name 'Orthodox Presbyterian Church' violates a widely accepted but false paradigm held by the vast majority in the OPC. They believe that their denomination remains a bastion of conservative theology. They reject the idea that liberalism of any description could have gained a foothold in the OPC, much less have come to seriously corrupt it" (36). Granting this point, Elliott's assessment of what he sees at work in the OPC, namely, the "hermeneutic of trust," is not altogether helpful in his discussion of the denomination's present woes. Elliott's interpretation of the days of creation distorts the nature, history, and significance of the dispute over the doctrine of justification by faith (and related doctrines) in the OPC. Much greater care and understanding are required in the analysis of confessional Reformed orthodoxy and the theology of Old Westminster.

[14] See my "Reformed Theology as the Theology of the Covenants: The Contributions of Meredith G. Kline to Reformed Systematics," in *Creator, Redeemer, Consummator: A Festschrift for Meredith G. Kline,* eds. H. Griffith and J. R. Muether (Greenville, SC: Reformed Academic, 2000); republished in *Covenant Theology in Reformed Perspective* 357–77. Michael Horton builds on the Kline-Karlberg formulation in his *God of Promise: Introducing Covenant Theology* (Grand Rapids: Baker, 2006). For my review of this book, see Appendix B.

Elliott contends: "The paleo-liberals' opposition to systematic theology is reflected today in the so-called Biblical Theology movement. This movement's adherents include many neo-liberals in the OPC, PCA, and at Westminster Seminary in Philadelphia, and even some conservatives" (108). Geerhardus Vos, father of biblical theology as a distinctive discipline within the Reformed encyclopedia, was one of the leading dogmaticians of his day. It is necessary to distinguish Reformed biblical theology in the line of classic Reformed federalism from the neo-Dutch school represented in the writings of Herman Ridderbos, Richard Gaffin, and others. Compare further, Appendix C.

[15] Elliot reasons: "Perhaps the example *par excellence* of the [OPC Philadelphia] Presbytery's confused thinking was its handling of Thesis Twenty, a keystone of Shepherd's heresy of justification by faith-plus-works—his radically wrong interpretation of *Romans* 2:13." Quoting Shepherd: "The Pauline affirmation in *Romans* 2:13, 'the doers of the Law will be justified,' is not to be understood hypothetically in the sense that there are no person who fall into that class, but in the sense that faithful disciples of the Lord Jesus Christ will be justified (compare *Luke* 8:21; *James* 1:22-25)" (135–36). This Pauline text, in my view, delineates two groups of individuals, those who are the inheritors of the kingdom of Christ and those who are outside the gates of the kingdom (those whom Scripture identifies as the reprobate). This

*Notes*

biblical text does not tell us *how* the doers of the law are constituted and made righteousness (in Christ), *i.e.*, how they are justified, sanctified, and glorified. We learn the answer to that question later in the Epistle to the Romans (and elsewhere in the Scriptures). Certainly it is the case that Shepherd misconstrues this Pauline text, contending the expression "the doers of the law" is to be understood to teach that the law-keepers are the ones who keep the law *as the way of salvation* (*i.e.*, as the "instrumental" means of justification). Here Shepherd reads his own, erroneous view of justification into Romans 2:13.

To reiterate an important teaching of Scripture, those who are justified and sanctified in Christ are the "doers of the law." Only they fulfill the law of righteousness (compare, for example, Rom 8:1ff.). The godly saints are righteous not on the ground of their works ("the obedience of faith"), but solely on the ground of Christ's obedience federally imputed to the elect, those for whom Christ died and made reconciliation and atonement. To do justice to the teaching of Scripture, it is necessary to acknowledge *two aspects* of soteric justification, the constitutive and the demonstrative. Good works are evidential of justification; without good works there is no justification (see, for example, Heb 12:13). (This does not mean that justification in grounded upon the believer's obedience.) Many of Shepherd's critics fail to recognize sufficiently this point of doctrine. In analogous fashion, there are two aspects of sanctification, the definitive and the progressive. See Karlberg, "Justification in Redemptive History," *WTJ* 43 (1981) 213–46; republished in *Covenant Theology in Reformed Perspective* 157–80.

[16] The Robbins-Elliott critique falsely equates the new methodology of Framian perspectivalism with analogical reasoning, what has been commonplace in traditional Reformed-theological exposition, eloquently set forth in the twentieth-century Reformed dogmatics of Herman Bavinck, another figure whom Robbins and Elliott wrongfully attack. They denounce the classic Reformed view as "pagan." In his numerous writings, Robbins has engaged the long-standing dispute over the views of Gordon Clark, Robbin's mentor, and Cornelius Van Til, "Mr. Westminster." Following Robbins's lead, Elliott calls for a univocal interpretation of the truth of God revealed in the Scriptures (as opposed to analogical interpretation). The view entertained by Robbins and Elliott not only blurs the Creator/creature distinction, it confounds the metaphysical being and epistemological determination of the infinite, omniscient, self-existent God with that of the finite, dependent creature made from the dust of the ground. Elliott boldly asserts that human knowledge of divine truth "is complete, and it is univocal" (294). That is to say, man knows God's thought exactly as God knows his thoughts. Were man to possess this kind of knowledge, knowledge unique to the supreme Being, he would have to be deified. Here lies "pagan" doctrine.

To be sure, the knowledge of the truth of God granted to those who are regenerated and renewed in the likeness of Christ, whose minds are illumined by the Spirit of Christ, is—as Van Til argues—true and complete (as far as it goes in the created order). According to scholastic terminology, God's truth is *archetypal*; truth known in the human mind is *ectypal* (both before and after the Fall). Knowledge in the mind of God and knowledge in the mind of man are not identical.

[17] Specifically, Elliott's understanding of the *animus imponentis* ("the intention of the imposing body") is historically inaccurate and theologically untenable, for two reasons. Firstly, the creeds and confessions of the church are subordinate standards in the church (Scripture is the primary norm for faith and practice). Secondly, the manner in which the church courts have interpreted and handled the secondary norms determines the role and significance of creedal subscription in the life and witness of the church. The notion of "strict subscriptionism," which Robbins and Elliott appear to advocate, is unscriptural. This is to say nothing about Elliott's demand for a literalistic interpretation of the days of creation,

which on a proper, exegetico-theological reading of Scripture, is ruled out. (Responding to the theological crisis in the OPC, Elliott has been instrumental in the formation a new denomination, the Evangelical Reformed Presbyterian Church, one requiring the literalistic reading of the days of creation.) All this to say, the creeds of the church are neither infallible, nor inerrant. Determining in light of Scripture what is doctrinally major and minor in the confessions is part of the ongoing work of the church. The theological task is not over; the last chapter in the history of doctrine has not been written.

[18] The turning point in the Shepherd controversy at Westminster was the distribution of the "Letter to Friends of the Reformed Faith" (1981). In a subsequent (unpublished) paper I was asked to critique Shepherd's theology for the benefit of those given the task of writing the document entitled "Reason and Specifications Supporting the Action of the Board of Trustees in Removing Professor Shepherd, February 26, 1982."

[19] Elliott writes: "Today in the OPC, as elsewhere in the Reformed and larger evangelical world, there is great resistance to the use of the term 'heresy'" (112). Elliott makes reference to remarks by James S. Gidley in the pages of *New Horizons,* reprimanding those engaged in heresy-hunting within the OPC. Gidley's admonition is part of the current campaign within the OPC (and the seminary) to undermine and silence the opposition voices. Vanhoozer explains: "Heresy, a particularly virulent strain of false teaching, is worse than occasional theological error. After all, it is virtually impossible for finite human knowers, even saints, not to be in error about some things. Heresy is not merely an instance of imprecision or ignorance; it is altogether more destructive, both in regard to truth and in regard to its effects on those who hold it (*The Drama of Doctrine* 423).

[20] The faculty of Westminster has inherited new rules by which to play, resulting in the spread of half-truths and deception. No where is this more telling than in attempts to "reorthodox" the theology of Professor Gaffin.

[21] My first published criticism of Gaffin's formulation on covenant and justification appeared in a review of Don B. Garlington's *Faith, Obedience and Perseverance* [*TrinJ*] 18 NS (1997) 254–58] followed by my essay "The Search for an Evangelical Consensus on Paul and the Law" [*JETS* 40 (1997) 563–79] both republished in *Covenant Theology in Reformed Perspective,* 263–67 and 209–26 respectively.

[22] The term "historic-revisionist" is an oxymoron, but one appropriate to the theology and hermeneutic of New Westminster (wanting it both ways). See my *Gospel Grace,* chapter 8, esp. 255–64. Tim J. R. Trumper's recent apology for Westminster's "constructive Calvinism" is found in "A Fresh Exposition of Adoption: II. Some Implications," *Scottish Bulletin of Evangelical Theology* 23 (2005) 194–215. Although Trumper shows some ambivalence and uncertainty regarding what he would like to tell to his readers, at the same time he again vigorously promotes the views of his mentor and former teaching colleague, Richard Gaffin. Both Trumper and Gaffin eschew the label "revisionist" for their work, but their theologizing is well deserving of it. In this essay Trumper accents the distinctive characteristics of New School Westminster in the following manner: (1) by reasserting disdain for "the naively uncritical spirit of [traditional] orthodox Calvinism" and opting for Gaffin's "sympathetic-critical attitude" (*ibid.,* 195 n. 7). (2) by seeing "the kernel of truth found in neo-orthodox criticisms of Westminster Calvinism [as] an opportunity for biblical renewal" (*ibid.*); (3) by commending the multiperspectivalism of Frame and Poythress; (4) by rejecting the Reformed doctrine of the Covenant of Works (dismissing present-day controversy on this point of doctrine as needlessly contentious); (5) by viewing the *classic* Protestant Law/Gospel antithesis as a peculiarly "Lutheran" construct, portending "that even if a covenant of works survives the maturation of a Reformed biblical theology, it will not continue

to dominate federal theology as it does presently in the minds of some" (*ibid.*, 204); and (6) by answering the charge that the traditional Reformed doctrine of justification creates a "legal fiction" (here Trumper commends the renovative or transformationist perspective on justification by faith [*ibid.*, 211 n. 59]). More than once in this essay, Trumper sees "the current [theological] climate of change" (*ibid.*, 206) as indicative of God's present action "shedding more light upon his Word." Even if the New Westminster theology were to find growing, popular support among contemporary "evangelicals," would that prove its advocates right? May not God be working to preserve his truth among those standing in defense of Reformation teaching, even though their number is small? One final comment: Trumper is deficient in his understanding of progression and retrogression in the history of doctrinal formulation. Whatever imbalance can be found in the federalist doctrine of justification (and union with Christ), polemics—then as now—demands focus upon the forensic (or more precisely, the constitutive) aspect of God's justifying act in salvation, what is pivotal in the doctrine of the Christian life.

On another battlefront, mounting criticism of Peter Enns' work highlights the unsettled position within the OPC concerning reception of higher-critical views of the Bible. Enns' most recent critics speaking out in the pages of *New Horizons* are J. V. Fesko and James W. Scott (27 [February 2006] 21–22). Commending Enn's book, Tremper Longman asserts that those enlightened by modern (revisionist)) biblical interpretation can "safely ignore" those denouncing views set forth by Enns in this book (this Longman says, surprisingly, in the pages of *Modern Reformation* 14.6 [November/December 2005] 34). With respect to the writings of faculty, students, and graduates of the school, Elliott comments: "One wonders if the two-thirds of OPC ministers who are Westminster Theological Seminary graduates ever read their *alma mater's* journal, or the books being produced by its faculty [and students, I add]. If they do, the lack of outrage would indicate that Westminster has been so effective 'in inducting Orthodox Presbyterian ministerial candidates into a culture of interpretation' that it has become difficult if not impossible for many of these men to see the problem" (106–07).

Biblical Theological Seminary (Hatfield, Pa.) has announced new directions for its school. The leading faculty spokesperson for this change is systematician John R. Franke. (See his new study, *The Character of Theology: A Postconservative Evangelical Approach* [Grand Rapids: Baker, 2005]). In "How the Vision Impacts My Teaching" (available on the seminary's website, December 2005) Franke's colleague, R. Todd Mangum, indicates his openness to the transformationist interpretation of justification (the view associated with the Shepherd-Gaffin school, the New Perspective, and others), and looks with a critical eye to the teaching of orthodox Protestant scholasticism, notably, Reformed federalism.

[23] Elliott notes how "[today's leaders in the OPC] have labeled men who have called for a return to authentic Biblical Christianity in the OPC as unethical, intolerant, mean-spirited, unfaithful to their ordination vows, spiritual adulterers, and worse" (22)—and in violation of the Ninth Commandment. This is nothing other than the rhetoric of self-defense, self-preservation, ridicule, and deceit. The practice of ignoring O. Palmer Robertson's history in *The Current Justification Controversy* is indicative of Westminster's ongoing denial and obfuscation.

Included among the signers of the May 1981 letter was Meredith G. Kline. Even today, members of the Presbytery of New Jersey (OPC) seek occasion to try Kline for his views on the Mosaic law. See the recent essay by Patrick Ramsey, "In Defense of Moses: A Confessional Critique of Kline and Karlberg," *WTJ* 66 (2004) 373–400, and my comments in chapter 3, endnote 9. Previously, Kline's article entitled "Covenant Theology under Attack" (in its original form) was rejected for publication in *New Horizons* for having explicitly named Norman Shepherd and his erroneous teaching. The original article was subsequently printed and distributed to the ministers of the OPC by Park Woods Orthodox Presbyterian Church (Overland Park, Ks.). Likewise, the pages of *The Westminster Theological Journal* were closed to Kline, unless he were to submit to editorial censorship, specifically, deletion of critical remarks concerning Shepherd's theology. Years later in a review article by Robert Letham (*WTJ* 65 [2003] 385), permission was granted to make a passing, negative comment regarding the Shepherd-Gaffin theology, subtle and disingenuous though it was on the part of Letham. (Correspondence initiated by Letham with me proved unproductive.) More recently, Presbyterian and Reformed Publishing has issued books highly critical of the Shepherd theology. However, given the latest developments at Presbyterian and Reformed, the direction for future publications remains very much in the air.

[24] This was announced on Westminster's January 2006 website. The seminary's closer alignment with Proclamation Presbyterian Church, an affluent congregation pastored by the seminary's president, Peter Lillback, may hold the greatest financial prospect for the seminary since its beginnings in 1929. John Templeton, one of the ruling elders at Proclamation, is highly supportive of Lillback and his new leadership at the seminary (see Chapter 3, endnote 9).

[25] Elliott observes: "Dr. Peter Lillback has attracted a growing audience in his roles as a conservative activist on social issues and as a leader in educating Americans about the nation's Christian heritage" (297). Unquestionably, Westminster's new president in Philadelphia has gained a name for himself in the promotion and defense of the Christian origins of America. Like D. James Kennedy's *Center for Reclaiming America for Christ*, the Providence Forum, where Lillback also serves as President, encourages political activism among the churches, *while* adopting a quasi-theonomic understanding of Christian faith in the formation of public, social policy. Both Kennedy and Lillback regard the Ten Commandments as God's moral blueprint for society, contending that the unique American politico-religious experiment is founded upon Judeao-Christian principles (past and present). Following the vision of Puritan John Winthrop, America is viewed as "a light on the hill," having a distinctive Christian mission in the New World—and beyond. (Their views reflect a postmillennial interpretation of Bible prophecy.) No doubt, the broader Christian audience sees this as a change for the better at Westminster, a theological institution long seen to stand outside the mainstream of evangelical thinking. Michael S. Horton's "How the Kingdom Comes" (*Christianity Today* 60 [January 2006] 42–46) makes for a refreshing read. The author counters Kuyperian imperialism is all its guises.

[26] The troupe-performer is Karlberg, soliloquizing in defense of historic Reformed orthodoxy, contra the teachings of New School Westminster.

[27] Nicholas Perrin offers a strong rebuttal to Guy Prentiss Waters' *Justification and the New Perspectives on Paul: A Review and Response* (Phillipsburg: Presbyterian and Reformed, 2004) in his review article "A Reformed Perspective on the New Perspective," *WTJ* 67 (2005) 381–89. Curiously, Gary Johnson and Guy Waters, coeditors of a forthcoming volume seeking to defend the Reformation doctrine of justification by faith against all its detractors, refused—on behalf of the "Middle-men"—to accept my submission if I did not delete criticism of Richard Gaffin's position, one substantively identical to that of Norman Shepherd and advocates of the New Perspective. (I had been invited to write on the topic of "The Significance and Basis of the Covenant of Works: Exegetical and Theological Factors.") In their own writings Johnson and Waters have linked the teachings of Shepherd to that of the New Perspective. Waters has commented: "What theological and practical consequences is the adoption of NPP having within Reformed Christianity? This, sadly, is not a theoretical

question. We may point to the writings of Norman Shepherd and the resolutions passed by the session of Auburn Avenue Presbyterian Church [PCA]" (*Justification and the New Perspectives on Paul* 204). Yet, I am faulted for drawing the same link, and for refusing to look the other way with regard to Gaffin's heterodox formulations. Today's increasingly hostile theological climate leads only to further division and discord. One of the most recent attempts to advance Shepherd's teaching is found in Paul A. Rainbow's *The Way of Salvation: The Role of Christian Obedience in Justification* (Carlisle: Paternoster, 2005), which I have not yet seen.

[28] Only at this point in the history of the theological controversy at Westminster Seminary can the gaps and ambiguities in Gaffin's doctoral study, *Resurrection and Redemption*, be explained. The Robbins-Elliott critique of this work by Gaffin is partial and inconclusive in some important respects. More significantly, Robbins and Elliott misread theologians like Bavinck, Vos, and Van Til (among others) in light of Gaffin's reshaping of the Westminster School and in light of their own commitment to the philosophy and theology of Gordon Clark. Their resulting critique is distorted.

[29] See Chapter 3, endnote 10. Israel's national election is different from decretive election, individual election to salvation. Theocratic election in the old economy is temporal and typological. Informing the Mosaic law-administration of God's redemptive covenant is the peculiar operation of the works-inheritance principle, functioning alongside the faith-inheritance principle (whereby eternal salvation is secured exclusively on the ground of the righteousness of God in Christ, the Messiah who was to come, God's sacrificial Lamb).

[30] Shepherd's early restraint must not be thought to have ameliorated or tempered his teachings then under critical review. Specifically, Shepherd's now-explicit rejection of the doctrine of the active obedience of Christ as the meritorious ground of the believer's justification (alongside Christ's passive obedience) was implicit from the very start. See "Reason and Specifications."

[31] The reason for the downfall of Westminster Seminary is theological and moral failure, something not anticipated or contemplated by the former historian of the OPC, Charles G. Dennison. See his studies in *History for a Pilgrim People: The Historical Writings of Charles G. Dennison* (Willow Grove, Pa.: The Committee for the Historian of the Orthodox Presbyterian Church, 2002). Curious are the observations made by historians D. G. Hart and John R. Muether in "Turning Points in American Presbyterian History—Part 12: 1973: The Presbyterian Church in America," in *New Horizons* 27.2 (February 2006) 19–20. With good reason, the authors question the extent to which the Presbyterian Church in America is a *Presbyterian* denomination, admonishing the PCA for turning its back on its Reformed-theological heritage in favor of "word and deed ministry" (as promoted in the pages of *World* magazine, and elsewhere). In so doing, contend Hart and Muether, the PCA has eclipsed the doctrine of the "spirituality of the church," a distinctive teaching in old Southern Presbyterianism. Quick to see defects in the PCA, Hart and Muether have remained silent on the defects of the OPC, specifically, propagation of the heretical doctrine of justification by faith and deeds. See Karlberg, *The Changing of the Guard* 37 n. 28. As Elliott rightly points out, there remains a "conspiracy of silence" among large numbers of Westminster's constituency and supporters.

[32] We can expect to hear again from Shepherd himself, no doubt after receiving his next cue from Professor Gaffin, Westminster's dramaturge. Shepherd enters and exists the stage at fortuitous moments in the drama. In a moment of candor—and speaking on behalf of fairness—Frame had suggested that Gaffin should also have been dismissed from the faculty of Westminster along with Shepherd (not that Frame himself differs theologically with either

of them). That Gaffin was not dismissed, however, finds its explanation in what Frame sees as his "Gaffinesque" manner of teaching, teaching that is only one degree more subtle and obscure than Shepherd's had been in the early years of the controversy. See Karlberg, *The Changing of the Guard* 35 n. 26.

## FIVE

# Westminster and Washington

*Church and State in American Calvinism*

WITHIN INTERNATIONAL Calvinism one of the long-standing issues still left unresolved concerns the relationship between the church and the state, two institutions ordained by God—the first for the governance of those confessing the name of God as Lord and Redeemer, and the second for the governance of human societies. As distinct institutions, they appear on the world scene after the transgression of our first parents in the Garden of Eden, the site of God's presence and revelation (the Word). Originally, God's rule over humankind is theocratic. The distinction (and separation) between ecclesiastical and political realms does not pertain here. Theocracy is peculiar to the original government of humankind at creation (although theocracy is reintroduced—with modification—at the time of the reconstitution of the Israelite people as a holy nation). This theological understanding of church and state, however, takes us ahead of our discussion. First we must come to grips with the diversity of Reformed-Protestant thinking on this subject.

## The American Experience

Our focus in this paper is the American scene, beginning with the arrival of the Pilgrims and Puritans to the New World. These individuals were desirous in founding a nation that would succeed religiously and politically, where England failed. The American colonies were either an experiment in religious toleration or in religious exclusivism. There were those who wished to form a distinctly Christian society, one essentially theocratic in its outworking. The subsequent rise of deism, however, greatly impacted the formation and government of the American peoples as a free, diverse nation. Unique among political documents in world history was the Constitution of the United States. Democracy reached a new plateau in the newly founded nation, a form of government that would become the model for other reforming and developing nations.

By the nineteenth century, after the adoption of the United States constitution, the age of expansion across the North American continent and the Industrial Revolution brought about new challenges and conflicts which helped to erode the earlier Puritan aspiration to establish the new nation as a Christian theocracy. More than anything else, Americans were becoming less preoccupied with Old World Calvinism, both with regard to its doctrinal self-understanding and its ethos. With the rapid watering-down of the distinctives of the Calvinist tradition, including its comprehensive "world-and-life view" of all things temporal and eternal, an eclectic version of Protestant evangelicalism came to the ascendancy, especially through the efforts of the nineteenth-century revivalists. Arminians and Calvinists either viewed themselves as rival opponents or as co-ambassadors in the ever expanding American wilderness, urban and rural. (The origins of modern-day practice of cobelligerency lie here.)

Princeton Seminary, from its heyday in the late nineteenth century until the opening two decades of the twentieth, offered one interpretation of the relationship between church and state, different from that of the Southern Presbyterians. Reformed thinking was impacted by the issue of slavery and by the outcome of the Civil War. Distinctive among the Southern Presbyterians was the doctrine of the spiritual nature of the church—meaning the detachment of the church from secular, social affairs. (In part, this doctrine had an eye on maintaining the status quo in the American way of life.) Presbyterians in the north showed eagerness to engage the culture and society, all in the effort to exercise influence in American society. The Protestant Episcopal Church, as an offshoot of Reformed Anglicanism, likewise vied for prestige and power in the American political scene. Other mainline denominations similarly followed suit. America was fast becoming a nation of diverse religious bodies, Protestant, Jewish, and Catholic. Aspirations to preserve the Judeo-Christian ethic served to draw the nation together both religiously and politically.

The democratic spirit of the America peoples was severely tested in the latter part of the twentieth century with the advent of pluralism, one that now encompassed all of the world religions. At the same time, secularism proved to be the supreme challenge in what has been termed the "post-Christian era." Historic evangelical and Reformed Protestantism faced new and stronger opposition which demand renewed study of biblical principles and practices. Resurgent evangelicalism on the American political scene reached into the White House, notably under the presidency of Richard Nixon, Jimmy Carter, Ronald Reagan, and the Bushes (father and son). President George W. Bush considers his election to be a "divine calling to change the world" and to recapture the vision of Reagan, who saw America as "a light on the hill" having a unique (Christian) mission in the New World—echoing the politico-religious aspirations of Puritan John Winthrop. At the same time, Presidents Carter and George W. Bush hold a pluralistic understanding of what it means to have faith in God, though both are numbered among the "evangelicals." Given the history of the American experiment, it is preferable to address the relationship between "religion and state," rather than "church and state."[1]

## Westminster Calvinism: Competing Views within Reformed Theology

It is the testing of new ideas that prompts reconsideration of biblical, Reformed teaching on church-state relations. In the tradition of the Westminster divines of the seventeenth century, the civil magistrate was understood to have responsibility for protecting—and advancing—the program and mission of the church.

> The civil magistrate may not assume to himself the administration of the Word and sacraments, or the power of the keys of the kingdom of heaven: yet, he hath authority, and it is his duty, to take order that unity and peace be preserved in the Church, that the truth of God be kept pure and entire, that all blasphemies and heresies be suppressed, all corruptions and abuses in worship and discipline prevented or reformed, and all the ordinances of God duly settle, administered, and observed. For the better effecting whereof, he hath power to call synods, to be present at them, and to provide that whatsoever is transacted in them be according to the mind of God.[2]

This doctrine, however, was modified by the American Presbyterians almost a century and a half later. Greater care was exercised in distinguishing the proper role of government leaders and that of the ministers of the church. Even so, confessional Presbyterians continued to differ in their thinking regarding political theory, especially the role of the church in speaking her voice on social and political matters.

Unquestionably, Reformed federalism played a significant role in the rise of American democracy, specifically, in the articulation of the representative form of government served by various branches of leadership. What made its lasting imprint on American society was the Presbyterian form of government, not the content of religious belief, namely, the Reformed faith. Calvinism would continue to retreat from the mainstream of public discourse, only to be silenced by the dominant voice of secularism in the public square.

Theologians continued to study and discuss the biblical teaching on the origins of the state as a divinely-ordained institution and its relationship to the church as a distinctly religious and confessional body. The views of Calvin and the other magisterial reformers were all formulated in what is known as the age of "Christendom," when it was inconceivable that national identity might be freed of any and all religious association, be it Lutheran, Reformed or Catholic. On the one hand, the example left by the Scottish kirk and by the Dutch Calvinists left no room for alternative points of view. On the other hand, conflicts in the Church of England and the ravaging, terrifying religious wars on the European continent in the centuries following Luther's stand against Roman dogma and practice left nations in religious and political upheaval.

Contrary and divergent teachings on the relationship between church and state characterize the thinking of Evangelical-Reformed Christianity since the time of the Protestant Reformation down to the present. We will return to the modern context for ongoing Protestant-Reformed debate on the subject of church and the state. But first, we consider present-day attempts by Reformed spokespersons to engage—and shape—the American political scene.

## The Political Aspirations of D. James Kennedy and Peter A. Lillback

Both James Kennedy's project, "Reclaiming America for Christ," and the Providence Forum, headed up by Peter Lillback, espouse a quasi-theonomic understanding of Christian faith in the marketplace. According to this view, the Ten Commandments are seen as the moral blueprint for society. (Remnants of morality are preserved, to lesser degree, in the religions of Muhammad, Buddha, Confucius, and others.) It is zeal for the Puritan (and postmillennial) vision for a Christian America that motivates Kennedy and Lillback to call Christians to active engagement in the public arena. Such zeal has also led them to reassess the faith-stance of prominent early Americans, notably, George Washington and Abraham Lincoln.[3]

Luther's doctrine of the two kingdoms, the kingdom of man and the kingdom of Christ, necessitated the involvement of Christians in both realms. This teaching was fully shared by Calvin and the Protestant reformers in general. (The Anabaptist tradition, however, has taught otherwise.) The transmission of Calvinism onto American soil at the very time that deism was on the ascendancy in Europe, as well as in the American colonies, resulted in the loss of conviction and fervor among succeeding generations of English Puritans in the New World. The subtleties of theological and political discourse proved difficult to identify and untangle. Biblical imagery and language were profuse in accounts and portrayals of American life and politics, but they offered no guarantee that Reformed doctrine was being conveyed and preserved in the use of this politico-religious rhetoric. Hence, the case for the Christian origins of America remains highly dubious at best.

More important is the answer to the question regarding what Scripture teaches concerning the proper relationship between church and state. Here we turn to the biblical notion of theocracy and to the distinctive teachings of Reformed covenant theology. Summarily stated, biblical history is distinguished by the progressive unfolding of three successive epochs: creation and the subsequent two dispensations of redemptive covenant, the old and new. The Fall introduced a radical disjunction in the original state of affairs. Not only would two seeds of humanity develop over the course of redemptive history (from the Fall to the Consummation), namely, the seed of the woman (that is, Christ) and the seed of the Serpent, the nature and conduct of human affairs were now either "common" or "holy." Fulfillment of the cultural mandate in the fallen world is a common-grace activity, whereas the gathering of the saints in worship and witness is "holy" activity, the manifestation of saving grace in the hearts and minds of redeemed sinners. The saints are those who have been called out from the world, those who confess that the triune God of the Bible is Lord and Savior.[4]

The original state of creation is a pure theocracy, unmixed and untainted. The site of the theophanic presence of God, what is named the Garden of Eden, would have expanded to include the entire world—had Adam succeeded in keeping covenant with God. The focal test in Adam's time of probation was the subjugation of Satan, including rejection of his false and rival claim for supremacy and obeisance, a challenge to the authority and wisdom of the true Lord of the covenant. Adam's "one act of righteousness" would have resulted in Satan's expulsion from the Garden (what was an encroachment on holy ground) and banishment to eternal perdition. History turned out otherwise. For pedagogical purposes, God reintroduced theocratic rule over ancient Israel by reconstituting this nation as the one favored among all the nations of the world. National, corporate election, not the individual election of each and every Israelite to salvation (life in the eternal kingdom of God), is what distinguishes Israel's status as the chosen people of God in the old economy, what was a parenthesis in redemptive history.

As a result of the Fall, all human beings enter the world as covenant-breakers, by virtue of their federal union with the First Adam. They stand outside the covenant of God—or to be more exact, outside the Covenant of Grace. The original covenant, the Covenant of Works, lies broken and incapable of fulfillment (except in the case of the Second Adam, who by his obedience accomplished salvation for the sake of the elect). The sabbath is a sign of God's covenant; hence, sabbath-keeping belongs only to the people of God, not to those who do not confess the name of God as Lord and King. Sabbath-rest belongs to the people of God, and to them alone. It is an eschatological sign and seal of entrance into the consummate rest of God, life eternal (already enjoyed by the saints in principle, though not yet in fullness). Under the Mosaic economy of redemption, sabbath-keeping included cessation from labor on the seventh day of the week. That component of sabbath-observance has been abrogated with the inauguration of the new covenant.[5] The corporate worship of the saints now fulfills the requirement of sabbath-observance. (Our common-grace activities, including secular vocational work, do not receive the sign of the Covenant of Grace. They do not share in the eschatological hope of the heavenly rest that comes from above. Here, again, we must distinguish between common and holy endeavors in the kingdom of this world and in the kingdom of God respectively.[6])

The Decalogue is a summary of the covenant of law God made with Israel through Moses, mediator of the old covenant. It is the moral blueprint for the people of God, specifically, the reconstituted theocracy (tailored to the particularities of the postlapsarian world). Abrogation of the old covenant and establishment of the new requires some modification and adaptation of the Decalogue to the present dispensation of grace. (This interpretation of the Mosaic law is commonplace in Reformed theology. Dispensationalism, a relatively modern method and theory of interpretation, offers a very different understanding of the law of God under the former and latter dispensations of the Covenant of Grace. Progressive dispensationalism provides some needed correction to earlier teaching.) The main point we are making is this: The Ten Commandments have been given directly and specifically to the covenant people of God, not to the ungodly. Although the Decalogue does embody principles of natural law (known to all humankind through general revelation), the Mosaic legal code pertains exclusively to the redemptive community, the community of faith. God providentially governs the nations by his own sovereign decree and ordinance. Since the Fall, the state is the common-grace institution ordained for the governance of all the nations of the world—the one exception being ancient, theocratic Israel in the period from Moses to Christ. Given this biblical circumstance, the laws of Moses serve as a guide, not a norm, in the formation of public policy.[7]

The error of the Kennedy-Lillback school of thinking is in applying biblical law, namely, the Ten Commandments, to the secular kingdoms of this world—imposing God's law upon the ungodly, those standing outside the community of faith (the covenant community). Without question, the call for social activism and involvement on the part of Christians is proper *in its own sphere*. But the church as an institution, distinct and separate from the state, must not interfere with, meddle into, or attempt to settle the affairs of the secular state. Christians may and do have a voice in the open, public square; Christians and nonChristians alike are called and raised up by God to serve as civil ministers. Ultimately, all morality is derived from God—either directly by special revelation to the covenant people of God, or indirectly through natural law and by means of God's sovereign, providential superintendence of the affairs of the world. Lastly, it must be underscored, the calling of ministers of the Gospel is to preach the Word, not to speak on behalf of the church as political and religious leaders. (Of course, the preaching of the Word will address the wider moral issues and social concerns of the day, but only as the by-product of the exposition of Scripture, the canonical writings of the Old and New Testaments given by God to the covenant community. The early Protestant reformers uniformly identified this wider political "application" of the covenantal and canonical text as the civil use of the law of God.)

## Engaging Russell D. Moore's Political Theory

The complexities and subtleties in treating the subject of the relationship between church and state can best be untangled by placing Reformed doctrine in the broader context of discussion among Protestant evangelicals. Russell Moore's timely and provocative book, *The Kingdom of Christ: The New Evangelical Perspective,* offers the occasion and opportunity to evaluate and assess the teaching of Reformed federalism.[8] Crucial in this discussion are the Reformed doctrines of covenant and eschatology, including the prospect of the future "millennial" kingdom of God on earth announced by the Old Testament prophets. Covenant and eschatology mutually inform one another.[9]

For those committed to the teaching of historic Reformed federalism, the names of Geerhardus Vos and Meredith G. Kline, two modern-day exponents of this theological tradition, are of signal importance in the ongoing elucidation of the biblical doctrine of the covenants.[10] Moore, who stands in a different tradition, looks to Carl F. H. Henry, a theological giant in his own right. Comparing these two interpretive approaches, we may properly identify the views of the latter on the subject of the relationship between church and state as that having closer affinity to a modified Constantinianism, which views one of the church's roles as instructing and advising the state (to one degree or another).[11] With respect to biblical eschatology, Reformed theology in its most consistent expression is amillennial, whereas the position represented by Henry and Moore is premillennial. More significantly, the deviation in theological understanding between these two schools of thought is to be attributed, largely, to the rise of fundamentalism as a distinct breed of Protestant theology impacting the twentieth century (notably, from the middle of the century onwards). Accordingly, writes Moore, "The move toward a Kingdom eschatology does not repudiate the fundamentalist roots of evangelicalism, but in fact implicitly reasserts its roots in both historic Christian orthodoxy and twentieth-century American fundamentalism."[12] Having said that, Moore does identify both negative and positive features of the fundamentalist movement.

From Moore's point of view, social politics are inextricably linked to the redemptive work of Christ. "An evangelical exploration of the present/future kingship of Christ is by its very nature a consideration of political theory since the social and political element is interwoven with biblical Christology."[13] Consequently, the kingdom of God has both civil (*i.e.*, political) and ecclesiastical ramifications: The redemptive-eschatological inbreaking of the kingdom of God impacts the institutions of church and state. Moore looks to the Israelite theocracy (what was actually typological, temporary, and pedagogical) for justification. To be sure, Moore identifies a christological fulfillment in the civil exercise of the law of Christ. He explains that "because the throne of David is occupied and active even now [by virtue of Christ's heavenly session at the right hand of God]," the church can be actively engaged in political and cultural pursuits, as a transforming and redemptive influence.[14] He amplifies:

> Because the Davidic ruler reigns *presently* with justice and wisdom (Ps 72:1-2; Jer 23:5), believers are given an authoritative standard by

which they may condemn political tyranny and domestic abuse of power, even by those who claim evangelical identity. International human rights abuses may be resisted in light of the King who one day will exercise righteous diplomacy between the nations (Isa 2:4). Believers cannot have the option of inaction against judicial abuses since they are presently ruled by One whom the Scriptures describe as judging His subjects with fairness and equity.[15]

The second theologian of major consequence for Moore is G. E. Ladd. It is his formulations of a modified premillennial eschatology, one recognizing both the "already" and the "not yet" with regard to the arrival of the kingdom of God on earth, which Moore finds particularly attractive. "While dispensationalists severed the Kingdom from the present activity of the Messiah, Ladd argued, the amillennialists severed it form the goal of history by relegating the Kingdom to the arena of the human heart, the church, or the supra-temporal heavenly state."[16] Here again, this school of prophetic interpretation fails to acknowledge Israel's theocratic and typological significance under the old economy of redemption.[17]

Finally, this brings us to comment upon the meaning and significance of the federal representation and headship exercised by Adam in the original Covenant of Works, and how that relates to the work of the Second Adam. In this connection we also consider the meaning of humankind's creation in the image of God and the essential qualification of covenantal holiness to restore the creational bond between the Creator and the creature. According to Reformed federalism, Adam had been created in true knowledge, righteousness, and holiness. By virtue of his creation as "son of God" (as image-bearer of God) Adam was in covenant relationship with his Creator. However, Adam did not yet enjoy the highest blessing that would come through obedience (similarly, it was necessary for the Second Adam to "learn obedience" in the procurement of our redemption). At first, Adam was placed on probation. It must be said in no uncertain terms, the Reformed doctrine of probation is not speculative, but thoroughly biblical. Exegetico-theological interpretation requires this understanding of Adam's state and condition at the opening of history.[18]

Transgression of God's command resulted in the breaking of the covenant. But for the grace of God, the history of humankind would have come to an immediate and swift end. ("Grace" is the manifestation of God's redemptive love and provision, something that is neither relevant nor necessary prior to the Fall.) The reestablishment of covenant, now termed the Covenant of Grace, required an entirely new and different basis. Through the representative headship of the Second Adam, redeemed humanity would enjoy fellowship and life everlasting with God on the meritorious grounds of Christ's substitutionary obedience. One of the added benefits of Christ's atonement—its chief purpose being the redemption of the elect—is the introduction of common grace, the enjoyment of temporal blessings by the elect and the reprobate over the course of redemptive history. As already noted, the establishment of the (secular) state as a common-grace institution was necessitated by the abrogation of the covenant at creation and the dissolution of the original theocracy. Before the Fall, all was "holy to the Lord." Adam's failure to pass probation as federal head of the human race and the subsequent remedy supplied by God in the realization of the Covenant of Grace over the course of history leading up to the final Day of Judgment combined to bring two antithetical kingdoms into direct conflict, the kingdom of God and the kingdom of Satan—ultimate victory being assured in Christ.[19]

In this setting of common grace *and* common wrath cultural endeavors would be marked by both pleasure and frustration. The cultural labors of humankind (elect and nonelect) would succeed in measure and limit, according to divine providence. God's image-bearers indiscriminately would enjoy a sense of satisfaction and fulfillment in temporal affairs. All these cultural endeavors—as "common," not "holy," activities—would serve only a limited, temporal purpose, one aiding in the expansion and support of the human race until the close of history. In this same period special grace would effect the historical differentiation between the elect and reprobate. God the Spirit would efficaciously call out his elect, chosen before the foundation of the world. The institution of the church as a covenant community regulated by the canonical Scriptures belongs to the realm of the "holy." The church is distinct and separate from the world. As a spiritual body it is built through the preaching of the Word, not by exercise of the (civil) sword. Moore rightly notes:

> Thus, Louis Berkhof, arguably the most influential America Reformed theologian of the twentieth century, defined the kingdom rule of Christ virtually exclusively in terms of individual, spiritual salvation. . . . [T]he Kingdom of God is defined as "the rule of God established and acknowledged in the hearts of sinners."[20]

As correct as Moore is in making this observation, we contend that Berkhof was absolutely correct in his reading of the Bible, making proper distinction between cult (the worship and witness of the saints) and culture (common-grace endeavors). To be sure, Berkhof speaks for an earlier tradition of covenant theology, not the modern (re)interpretation which Moore identifies as "the developing form of 'new world' amillennialism."²¹ If by "new world" one has in mind this present world, "the world that now is," then we must demur. Neither the political kingdoms of this world nor the cultural accomplishments of humankind (produced by the elect and the nonelect) contribute to the arrival of the (spiritual) kingdom of Christ, already making its presence in the hearts of the sons and daughters of God. It is essential that we consider how the Fall effected man's capacity to image his Creator. The question is this: Does fallen man remain God's image-bearer? And if so, how?

Traditionally, Reformed theologians have distinguished between the image of God in the broader and the narrower senses, the former having reference to man's capacity for intellectual understanding and ethical responsibility (among many other aspects of man's nature) and the latter to man's possession of perfect knowledge, righteousness, and holiness. Though the latter was lost in the Fall, the former remains and constitutes man's ongoing likeness to God. (Renewal in the image of Christ reestablishes the creature's judicial status and ethical capacity to exercise his priestly functions once again, sanctifying the name of God and consecrating all things to his glory. Renewal takes place in union with Christ.) There are good theological reasons for questioning this interpretation of man as image of God. The clue to the biblical concept of the "image of God" lies in the opening chapter of Genesis, where we are told that man was to be created after the image of the Glory-counsel. Man's likeness is presented in terms of the twofold office, that of priest and king (patterned after that of the angels who also had to pass through probation in order to obtain confirmation in righteousness). Humankind after the Fall remains in the image of God so far as it is enabled, by means of common grace (the fruit of the working of the Spirit of God in the world), to exercise its kingly function in fulfillment of the cultural mandate.²²

Adam's progeny are born into the world as covenant-breakers and inheritors of a depraved nature, one incapable of rendering man's endeavors pleasing to God for reconciliation, spiritual fellowship, and life eternal (*i.e.*, salvation). The atonement of Christ, which provided full satisfaction for the requirements of the Covenant of Works by means of his active and passive obedience, conveys a twofold benefit: (1) the salvation of God's elect; and (2) the temporal blessings of common grace in the period from the Fall to the Consummation. In the Reformed system of doctrine, failing to distinguish between the two operations of the Spirit, one common and the other special, more often than not leads to theological misunderstanding concerning the redemptive mission of the church in the world. The church's mission is spiritual, not of this world (in the sense of helping to construct the political and cultural foundations for the kingdom of God on earth). Doubtless, too few Reformed and Protestant theologians have recognized this teaching of Scripture.

To modify his nomenclature, Moore builds a case for his version of "new world millennialism" most directly from his doctrine of Christ. After weaving together several theological strands—drawn from eschatology, soteriology, and ecclesiology—he argues for the ultimate rejuvenation of the cosmos in terms of the redemptive work of Christ and the regenerating and renewing work of his Spirit in spiritual and physical transformation.

Moore states: "The cosmic extent of salvation is seen as the Second Adam offers up to the Father a created order in which He has subdued every enemy (1 Cor 15:24-26), and there is nothing unclean in the garden over which He rules" (Rev 21:1-8).[23] Moore anticipates that the consummation of God's kingdom reign on earth will come about through the efforts of the people of God to establish righteousness in all the land—as far as the waters cover the seas. According to his view, the cultural mandate is fulfilled by Christ in the establishment of his kingdom on earth sometime in the period between the advents, the age of the "millennium." (Just when this "millennium" begins is a mute question.) This, Moore tells us, is the consensus among those holding to the emerging "new evangelical perspective." He observes:

> This [understanding] is true especially in the growing number of Reformed theologians, led in recent years by Anthony Hoekema, who have sought to underscore the active obedience of Jesus in terms of His fulfillment of the cultural mandate given to Adam at creation.[24]

As true as that might be among consensus-thinkers, it stands in conflict with traditional Reformed amillennialism, what remains in my view as the most consistent presentation of biblico-systematic theology that is faithful to the teachings of the Bible.

The covenant theology of the Westminster divines and the political theory of Washington, the seat of the America government, speak to two entirely distinct and different concerns and circumstances. The former is the distillation of God's inscripturated revelation to his covenant people; the latter is expressive of the ever-changing application of natural law in the common-grace sphere of public policy-making. Whatever commonality is found in biblical and social morality is attributed to the manifestation of natural law at work in the hearts of men and women. The laws of nature, impressed by God upon the human conscience, and the covenant of law made with ancient, theocratic Israel in the old dispensation of Moses (summed up in the Ten Commandments) are not only compatible, but they share some degree of affinity. For the Protestant reformers of the sixteenth century and those standing in their tradition, the civil use of the law of Moses continues to have applicability as guide, not norm, in public policymaking. What is required of the corporate body of Christ, the church as a unique institution, is that she render to God the things that belong to God. At the same time, Christians are to render to Caesar (secular government) the things that belong to Caesar.[25] The difficulty for theocrats—of whatever stripe—lies in committing civil rule into the hands of divine providence. Their error is in succumbing to the temptation to normalize and stabilize public moral policy by direct appeal to Scripture and natural law, teaching that can only be explicated by faithful exposition of the Word of God within the community of faith.

## NOTES

[1] Washington National Cathedral, a member of the Anglo-American episcopal communion and the nation's premier house of worship for all peoples and all faiths, serves as a leading political and religious force in America. Within the mainline Presbyterian church (PCUSA), National Presbyterian Church in Washington seeks to exercise similar influence in politics and culture. The amalgamation of different religions within one house of worship is best represented at the nation's Cathedral. National Presbyterian has been distinguished by a significant evangelical contingent within its membership, past and present.

[2] Westminster Confession of Faith 23.3

[3] Contrast the excellent, magisterial study by E. Brooks Holifield, *Theology in America: Christian Thought from the Age of the Puritans to the Civil War* (New Haven: Yale University, 2003). Compare also, Mark A. Noll, *America's God: From Jonathan Edwards to Abraham Lincoln* (New York: Oxford, 2002), and the earlier collaboration, M. A. Noll et al., *The Search for Christian America* (Westchester, Ill.: Crossway, 1983).

As a historical revisionist, Lillback offers a radical reinterpretation of the theology of Luther and Calvin on matters relating to fundamental doctrines in the Protestant-Reformed faith. See *The Binding of God: Calvin's Role in the Development of Covenant Theology,* Texts and Studies in Reformation and Post-Reformation Thought, gen. ed. R. A. Muller (Grand Rapids: Baker, 2001); this study has received mixed reviews, depending on one's theological persuasion.

[4] All of the endeavors of the people of God, individually and corporately, are to be consecrated to God in love and devotion, but all is not "holy" (that is to say, all is not sanctified by covenantal holiness). Common-grace activities undertaken by the saints are consecrated to God, but they do not share in the eschatological promise of consummate blessing. Technology and medicine, for example, are beneficial in this present world-order, but they do not contribute to the eternal state. (The distinction between the holy and the common is analogous to that between the sacred and the secular.) What determines the blessing of

covenantal holiness, whether of temporal or eternal duration, is the ordinance of God. Illustrative of this principle is the sanctification of children in the household of faith, which principle is different from that of decretive election (what is the *proper purpose* of redemptive covenant).

Commenting upon the text in Acts 7:48, G. K. Beale writes: "Stephen's terminology is in line with the rest of the New Testament, where 'handmade' refers to the old creation and 'made without hands' refers to the new creation, most specifically to the resurrection state as the beginning of the new creation" (*The Temple and the Church's Mission: A Biblical Theology of the Dwelling Place of God,* New Studies in Biblical Theology 17; D. A. Carson, series editor (Downers Grove: InterVarsity [2004] 223). The eschatological state is inaugurated by the Spirit who resurrected Christ from the dead. Spiritual regeneration and the renewal of all things are not of this world, but come from above. Sanctified humankind is the divinely produced culture, holy and separate from the mundane.

[5] This change in Sabbath-observance reflects the point made in the preceding endnote that even as confessors of the true and living God our earthly endeavors (*i.e.*, our common-grace activities) do not receive the divine promise of eschatological reward and blessing. Such promise is extended to the saints in their ordered life, witness, and worship of God. Under the old economy, cessation from vocational labor was typological of the eternal rest awaiting the people of God. Before and after the law (*i.e.*, the old, Mosaic covenant), labor in the fallen world—without the enjoyment of the weekly Sabbath-rest—had become part of the common curse, experienced by believer and nonbeliever alike.

[6] I have elaborated on the theology of the covenants in numerous writings; for an overview and summation, see *Gospel Grace,* chapters 1 and 8.

[7] See my essays, "Reformation Politics: The Relevance of Old Testament Ethics in Calvinist Political Theory," *JETS* 29 (1986) 179–91; "Moses and Christ: The Place of Law in Seventeenth-Century Puritanism," *TrinJ* 1O NS (1989) 11–32; and "Covenant and Common Grace: A Review Article," *WTJ* 50 (1988) 323–37. All have been republished in *Covenant Theology in Reformed Perspective: Collected Essays and Book Reviews in Historical, Biblical, and Systematic Theology* (Eugene, Ore.: Wipf and Stock, 2000); the book is available online at www.twoagepress.org. The question of the appropriateness of patriotic music in the context of Christian worship is the subject of my article "Patriotic Music in Worship," *The Outlook* 53 (July/August 2003) 4–5.

[8] Russell D. Moore, *The Kingdom of Christ: The New Evangelical Perspective* (Wheaton: Crossway, 2004). I have previously reviewed this book in *JETS* 48 (2005) 410–15, republished here as Appendix C.

[9] Happily, at many points both Moore and Henry favor Reformed teaching.

[10] Consult further, Mark W. Karlberg, "Reformed Theology as the Theology of the Covenants: The Contributions of Meredith G. Kline to Reformed Systematics," in *Creator, Redeemer, Consummator: A Festschrift for Meredith G. Kline,* eds. H. Griffith and J. R. Muether (Greenville, SC: Reformed Academic, 2000); republished in *Covenant Theology in Reformed Perspective* 357–77; and chapter 2 above ("New Vistas in Old Testament Narrative: Geerhardus Vos and Meredith G. Kline as Exemplary Reformed Interpreters").

[11] Moore writes: "This denial of any Constantinian identification of any secular social order with the eschatological Kingdom of God is perhaps one of the most valuable political contributions of evangelical premillennialism, a strength that the larger evangelical tradition would do well to absorb. With an insistence on a future Christocentric political Kingdom, evangelicals have maintained that all secular political orders are provisional and temporal,

*Notes*

and thus cannot hold ultimate allegiance over the church" (*The Kingdom of Christ* 71). Despite this comment, Moore's political theory is a version of modified Constantianism.

For an alternative position, one following the lines laid out in this essay and previous writings of mine, see the contributions of David VanDrunen and D. G. Hart in *Modern Reformation* 13.5 (September/October 2004). See also David VanDrunen, "Natural Law and Christians in the Public Square," *Modern Reformation* 15.2 (March/April 2006) 12–15. Representative of the spate of books on church and state, special mention goes to Jon Meacham, *American Gospel: God, the Founding Fathers, and the Making of a Nation* (New York: Random House, 2006); and William R. Hutchison, *Religious Pluralism in America: The Contentious History of a Founding Ideal* (New Haven: Yale University, 2003).

12 *The Kingdom of Christ* 54.

13 *Ibid.*, 65.

14 *Ibid.*, 69.

15 *Ibid.*, 70. The mistake in both premillennial and postmillennial readings of Old Testament prophecy concerning Israel's occupancy in the land during the messianic rule of Christ lies in the failure to identify the meaning and significance of ancient Israel's corporate election and the institution of theocratic rule under Moses. Moore faults Charles Hodge for failing to read the relevant Old Testament texts at face value, asserting that he "contrasted a spiritual understanding of the Davidic reign of Christ with the 'carnal' nature of premillennialism, which he dubbed a 'Jewish doctrine' because of the 'essential earthly character of the doctrine'" (*ibid.*, 62). On this teaching, however, Hodge was right. Moore's interpretation of the Bible leads him to conclude: "While amillennialists have pioneered the way for evangelical theology to understand the biblical witness to the present session of Christ at the right hand of the Father in fulfillment of Psalm 110, they have yet to demonstrate convincingly how He is presently exercising the kind of global worldwide dominion that is described in Davidic promise passages such as Psalm 72. If these passages are references to the reign of Christ over the new heavens and new earth (as Hoekema and other 'new creation' covenantalists argue), they must explain more thoroughly from whence come the enemies over which the Davidic King will rule with a rod of iron (Ps 2:9; 110:1-2; Rev 2:26-27; 12:5; 19:15). It would seem therefore that a temporal millennial reign of Christ in the flow of this age's history is part of the messianic hope of Scripture" (*ibid.*, 64–65). Compare Mark W. Karlberg, "The Significance of Israel in Biblical Typology," *JETS* 31 (1988) 257–69; republished in *Covenant Theology in Reformed Perspective* 193–207.

16 *Ibid.*, 32.

17 Moore observes: "It was Ladd's view of the future consummation, however, that Reformed amillennialists likened to a 'new postponement theory' similar to that of the dispensationalists because Ladd's future earthly consummation of the Kingdom denied the essentially spiritual nature of the Kingdom of God" (*ibid.*, 35). Amillennialism, i.e., traditional Reformed covenant theology, affirms the semi-eschatological, Pentecostal existence of the New Testament church, devoid of its theocratic, "earthly" cast. This cast had been shed in the transition from shadow to reality in the history of redemption, a transition effected by the reconciling and atoning work of Christ.

Moore is cognizant of the fact that whatever rapprochement has taken place in recent years has come about as the result of the modification of thinking by former dispensationalists and covenantalists (Some have modified traditional teaching more radically than others). Moore comments: "Remarkably, the move toward a consensus Kingdom theology has come most markedly not from the broad center of the evangelical coalition, as represented by Henry or Ladd, but from the rival streams of dispensationalism and covenant theology themselves" (*ibid.*, 23). See Mark W. Karlberg, "Israel and the Eschaton: A Review Article," *WTJ* 52 (1990) 117–30; republished in *Covenant Theology in Reformed Perspective*, 309–23. With respect to the question regarding the modern state of Israel, Moore laments: "Dispensationalists should have been the ones reminding the rest of the evangelical coalition that the eschatological restoration of Israel is accomplished by the Messiah, not by the United Nations" (*ibid.*, 73). Moore's prospect for "geopolitical stability and peace in the Middle East" is based upon his premillennial interpretation of Scripture.

[18] In his most recent writing on the subject, Rowland S. Ward rejects the Reformed doctrine of probation as speculative in origin ("Why works works: Biblical revelation unfolds from the covenant of works," *Australian Presbyterian*, 579 [March 2006] 11–12). At the same time, he reasserts the idea that divine grace informs all covenants, pre- and postlapsarian. He opposes the biblical notion of merit in the Covenant of Works with the First Adam, though he does see the merit of the substitutionary obedience of the Second Adam in the Covenant of Grace. Ward repeats the error of the Reformed scholastics in holding to the law/gospel antithesis (which is biblical) and the nature-grace synthesis (which is speculative). Ward finds rationalistic speculation in the wrong place. In the same issue of the *Australian Presbyterian* J. Ligon Duncan offers a different take on the doctrine of the covenants ("God's core promise: J. Ligon Duncan III talks to Peter Hastie" 4–10), though his discussion lacks a degree of consistency in formulation. Likewise, William Edgar in *Truth in All its Glory: Commending the Reformed Faith* (Phillipsburg: Presbyterian and Reformed, 2004) rejects the notion of merit in connection with the covenant of works, substituting the notion of a *gratuitous* arrangement. (At the same time he opposes Shepherd's take on justification and Gaffin's take on the *ordo salutis*. Not surprising, Edgar's treatment is meager and evasive on the critical issues in the Westminster dispute.) On the importance of the works-principle in the Covenant of Works and its significance for the doctrine of the active obedience of Christ (and the doctrine of probation), see the helpful and concise essay by Brian L. De Jong, "What Machen Meant," in *New Horizons* 27 (June 2006) 23–24.

Equally important is acknowledgment of the operation of the principle of works-inheritance in the Mosaic economy (specifically, on the symbolico-typological level). Brian Estelle rightly criticizes O. Palmer Robertson for failure in this regard. He remarks: "treatments of the Mosaic covenant could have been strengthened by drawing upon a host of Reformed luminaries from the past—something noticeably missing from his book—who lave explained the operation of a works principle in the Mosaic economy differently than Robertson does" (book review of *The Christ of the Prophets* [Phillipsburg: Presbyterian and Reformed, 2004] in *New Horizons* 27.1 [January 2006] 24).

[19] Moore posits: "If redemption is the restoration of the creation order, not its repudiation, then evangelical theology must take seriously a creation mandate that values human culture as an aspect of human vicegerency over the earth" (*ibid.*, 122).

[20] *Ibid.*, 97. Moore commends the thinking of modified covenantalists like Michael Williams, who noted that "the influence of Augustinian eschatology was not challenged by the early attempts at inaugurated eschatology by theologians such as Vos." Williams does acknowledge that "Vos did 'lay the groundwork for much of later Reformed revisionist thinking in eschatology,' because Vos's 'already/not yet' tension 'was the starting point that allowed later thinkers such as Herman Ridderbos, Oscar Cullmann, Anthony Hoekema, and even the Baptist premillennialist George Ladd, to move beyond Augustinianism and toward a genuinely restorational eschatology'" (*ibid.*, 50).

[21] *Ibid.*, 100.

[22] Just as the Spirit of God was/is at work in creation and recreation, so also he works in the

arenas of common and special grace (postlapsum). These several aspects of the Spirit's work call for a fuller, more comprehensive formulation in the doctrinal locus of pneumatology, much more than has previously been the case in the history of Christian dogmatics. Here, again, I commend the helpful contribution made by Meredith G. Kline in his most recent work, *God, Heaven and Har Magedon: A Covenantal Tale of Cosmos and Telos* (Eugene, Ore.: Wipf and Stock, 2006) with regard to the doctrine of the endoxation of the Spirit. Compare his earlier reflections in *Glory in our Midst* (Overland Park, Ks.: Two Age, 2001).

[23] *Ibid.*, 106.

[24] *Ibid.*, 99. Moore further explains: "This Christological, Kingdom focus guards the New Testament emphasis on the glory of God in salvation, a glory that cannot be understood apart from the identify and mission of Christ in establishing His Kingdom" (*ibid.*, 104). Somehow or other Moore views biblical missiology as being in conflict with the (Reformed) doctrine of the decrees. He amplifies on his position (contra the teaching of covenant theology): "This Christologically focused Kingdom soteriology therefore protects evangelical theology from a resurgent supralapsarianism that defines this glory theocentrically in terms of the supra-temporal glorification and reprobation of individuals" (*ibid.*, 104–05). In my reading of Scripture both the infra- and the supralapsarian perspectives are necessary in explicating the outworking of God's decrees in history. In rejecting "supralapsarianism" (or more precisely, double predestination) Moore emphasizes Christ's present establishment of the Kingdom on earth—amidst all the vicissitudes of human purpose and determination.

A point of clarification: Amillennialism sounds the note of realism, not pessimism. Moore is mistaken when he writes, "In many ways, then, the 'pessimistic' eschatology of fundamentalism [both pre- and amillennial] differed little from its 'pessimistic' soteriology, which saw the cataclysmic intervention of the Spirit of Christ as the only hope for totally depraved individuals" (*ibid.*, 75). Following the position of Robert Saucy, Moore remarks: "Scripture does speak of salvation in strikingly national and political terms, terms which are difficult to apply to the new covenant church as a multi-national Spirit body, and which are impossible to relegate to the eternal state" (*ibid.*, 96). Moore chastises covenant theologians for speaking "too quickly of the church as 'spiritually' replacing Israel. The covenantal land promises are posited too often as typological of the 'spiritual' blessings of forgiveness of sins and eternal heavenly life" (*ibid.*, 119). At issue here is Moore's (mis)reading of the prophetic idiom in the Old Testament. He contends that "The 'new earth' by itself does not adequately explain texts such as Isaiah 65:17-25, which seem to conflate the 'new heavens and the new earth' with an intermediate stage of the kingdom in which death and rebellion are still present" (*ibid.*, 64). We commend the interpretation of Old Testament theologian Meredith G. Kline in place of Moore's literalistic exegesis of biblical prophecy. See especially Kline's *Glory in our Midst* and *God, Heaven and Har Magedon*.

[25] The following three quotations from *The Kingdom of Christ* serve to highlight the chief difference in formulation between the author and present writer regarding the role of culture in the coming eschatological kingdom of heaven:

> (1) "In the emerging 'new earth' understanding of the salvific transformation of the cosmos, human cultural endeavors are not simple temporal concerns, which will be consumed and forgotten in the static, timeless salvation enjoyed at the eschaton. Instead, creation is to be redeemed, albeit not by human effort, but by the cataclysmic coming of Christ, the Messiah, for whose inheritance the universe was created in the first place. . . . Furthermore, the New Testament seems to imply that some cultural human endeavors from within the stream of human history will be sancti-

fied and will continue in the new order of the everlasting Kingdom of God (Rev. 21:26)." [*ibid.,* 122]

(2) "After all, 'culture' is a matter of the Adamic mandate that will continue into the eschaton, while the political structures will not continue into the eternal state but will be evaporated by the Kingdom of Christ (*ibid.,* 123)."

(3) "The politics of the Kingdom enter the present era through the visible demonstration by the church of what it means to live under the eschatological reign of Christ by being a New Society called to 'mirror in microcosm' the messianic rule in the new heavens and new earth (*ibid.,* 36)."

Rhetoric and caricature aside, the cataclysmic coming of Christ in glory and power renders human culture—the product of common grace—wholly ineffectual. Only the spiritual edifice of the body of Christ, the church, remains (see, for example, 1 Cor 3:10-17; Eph 3:14-21; Rev 21:1-4). Abraham, father of all the faithful, was looking "to the city that has foundations, whose architect and builder is God" (Heb 11:10). That city comes down from above. In the New Jerusalem there will be no need for the likes of technology or medicine. The consummate, eternal order renders the temporal, earthly order obsolete. The New Society has no earthly pedigree; it is uniquely and exclusively the House that God has built. What the Spirit of God is now producing is a sanctified "culture"—a people redeemed by grace, a spiritual household, a holy temple in the Spirit.

# Appendix A

## Backbone of the Bible: Covenant in Contemporary Perspective

*Edited by P. Andrew Sandlin*
(Nacogdoches, Tx.: Covenant, 2004)

Here is a book destined to inflict great harm upon the Reformed church at the very depths of her identity as a Reformed-Protestant confessional body, a near fatal strike at the theological core of her doctrine and life fleshed out over the last six centuries of intense, ongoing polemical debate and contention for the biblical faith. This collection of writings, featuring papers read at a symposium held in August 2003 at the annual summer conference of the Southern California Center for Christian Studies, begins with not one, but three opening statements regarding the book's agenda—a "Foreword" by John Frame, a "Preface" by Roger Wagner, and an "Introduction" by the book's editor, Andrew Sandlin. All three vie for first grabs at winning the reader's sympathy and unflinching approval. The last word will need to come from official spokesmen of the various Reformed orthodox denominations (or individual churches, if necessary). That challenge is just now being met—at least in some church quarters—in a way that honors and upholds the Word of the gospel, the Word personified in Jesus Christ, head of the church. Truth will prevail, but the number of stalwart saints may diminish. Such are the times in which we live.

We begin this review by highlighting—with brief commentary—the major lines of attack and the plan of occupation advanced in the seven papers: "Sects in the City [of God]" (Jeffery Ventrella), "The Sensible Covenant" (Randy Booth), "Ethics and Covenant" (Roger Wagner), "Covenant in Redemptive History: 'Gospel and Law' or 'Trust and Obey?'" (Andrew

# Appendix A

Sandlin), "Justification by Faith in Pauline Theology" (Norman Shepherd), "Justification by Works in Reformed Theology" (Norman Shepherd), and "The New Covenant: Membership, Apostasy, & Language," by Jeffrey D. Niell). Pride of place is given to Shepherd, the leading spokesman for the New Covenant Theology. To be accurate, respecting the historical development of federalism from its beginning to the present day, the co-fathers of the modern movement (or deconstruction) within contemporary Reformed theology are Shepherd and his former colleague at Westminster Theological Seminary, Richard B. Gaffin, Jr. Gaffin obtained his doctorate at Westminster under Shepherd in 1969. John Frame has also played a major role in the history of the seminary controversy. (On a historical note: my doctoral studies in the late 1970s were likewise pursued under Shepherd, up to the time he requested to be released from our teacher-student relationship. At the time parting was sorrowful, but the wisest course of action.)

**The lines of attack.** First and foremost, the claim is made that these writers represent the teachings of genuine Calvinism. Those on the other side of the controversy have, they say, distorted Calvin's doctrine of law and grace. Parenthetically, the Shepherd-New Covenant School reads Calvin in the light of the Barthian doctrine of law *in* grace, a wholly divergent theology of grace from that found in Calvin and the Protestant reformers (on that there was unqualified consensus). The point is made more than once that there is a world of difference between biblical terminology (the exact words and terms employed by the biblical writers) and theological terminology (the invention of systematicians, *i.e.,* the church "dogmatists"). Corollary is the idea that Scripture—at critical and controversial points in post-canonical theological debate—actually favors ambiguity over precision. The genius behind this hermeneutical principle, which includes the artificial distinction between "Scripture" and "theology," is Frame, the biblicist (by self-designation). Of course, the New Covenantalists can and do dogmatize their point(s) of view, but that's OK by these writers. Secondly, and of equal necessity, attempts are made at every opportunity—this publication being one of them—to ridicule and castigate opponents of Norman Shepherd. Frame here is at his best. The publisher's inclusion of Frame's "Addendum," what amounts to a weak attempt at an apology to his readers, only adds fuel to the fire. Following on the heels of the previous attack, thirdly, is the effort by these contributors/reformulators to set forth what Frame calls "third alternatives" (viii)—that by way of the distinctive methodological approach concocted by Frame, called theological multiperspectivalism. Fourthly and lastly, the central plank in the Shepherd-New Covenant Theology is the repudiation of what Shepherd's calls the Reformed-Protestant "works/merit paradigm," in favor of a "faith/grace paradigm." Regarding the merit concept, Sandlin interjects: "It is simply a fiction" (70).

**The plan of occupation.** After renouncing the classic Protestant law/gospel antithesis in no uncertain terms, the need for a radical reformulation of "Calvinist" doctrine, one driven by the dictates of a Barthian understanding of the relationship between law and grace, arises and moves to center-stage. Years of heated debate provide the incubus for the drafting of this manifesto, nowhere more evident than in the two essays penned by Shepherd. Polemics serves as the immediate context for doctrinal (re)formulation, just as it has since the beginning of the Protestant Reformation. The only difference is that the spirit of our age has led to the destruction and dismantling of the Protestant-Reformed faith in the hands of Shepherd and his companions. More than anything else, this volume is a promotion and defense of Shepherd's theology. The reader is led to believe that Shepherd better understands the gospel than all who have proceeded in the history of Christian doctrine. Frame pontificates: The formulation of his good friend and former colleague—the one who hired Frame to teach in the systematics/apologetics department at Westminster (as Frame informs his readers)—"is clearly a Biblical, evangelical, and Reformed understanding of the gospel and nothing else" (xi).

To further explicate the New Covenant Theology, we focus in the remaining portion of this review on the latest installment of Shepherd's position, what stands essentially unchanged since the 1970s. (Shepherd was dismissed from Westminster in 1982 for teaching found to be contrary to Scripture and the Westminster standards. For more on this history, see my *Gospel Grace: The Modern-day Controversy* [Eugene, Ore.: Wipf and Stock, 2003], which includes references to relevant documents and writings by other participants in the Westminster controversy.) Shepherd's first essay begins by taking to task the views of R. C. Sproul laid out in his book *Getting the Gospel Right* (1999). Representative of scholastic Reformed federalism, the doctrine advanced by such modern-day theologians as John Dick, Charles Hodge, and Meredith Kline (all of whom are opposed by contributors in this collected writings), Sproul's theology of justification and the covenants is found by Shepherd to be one that bypasses the death of Christ, resulting in a deviant, unscriptural view—a view that substitutes human, autonomous, legal (*i.e.,* meritorious) obedience for the righteousness of Christ. According to Shepherd, the righteousness of Christ imputed to believers is the death and resurrection of Christ, excluding his life of active, meritorious obedience. Shepherd insists that there is no concept of meritorious obedience ("works" opposed to "grace") to be found anywhere in the Bible (except by way of Judaistic perversion of God's call to grace). In denying the imputation of the active obedience of Christ, Shepherd maintains that the ground of life and salvation is the atoning death of Christ, what Reformed theologians have spoken of as the passive, in distinction from the active, obedience of Christ. Is this dispute over one (for some, narrow) point of doctrine pedantic? Not for Shepherd, and not for his critics. The heart of Reformation doctrine is at stake here. (The "irenic, peacemaking" Frame, as he portrays himself, would have us think otherwise.)

Shepherd asserts: Structurally speaking, the traditional Reformed-Protestant and the Roman Catholic views "are exactly the same" (86). "For both, justification is grounded in the merit of good works. The only difference—and it is not an insignificant difference—is that the works are not our own as in Roman Catholicism, but they are the works of Christ imputed to us" (86). Key here is Shepherd's repudiation of the notion of meritorious accomplishment associated with a covenant of works, the covenant which Scripture and Reformed theology teach was made with the First and Second Adams in their federal (representative) capacities. Crucial also is Shepherd's dismissal of the Reformed doctrine of probationary testing, either in the case of Adam or Christ, our substitute. According to Shepherd, all of is grace—no merit or probation in the divine scheme of things.

Shepherd explains: "The imputation of the active obedience of Christ is absolutely essential to an evangelical view based on the works/merit paradigm. Without it, either there is no justification, or justification takes place on the ground of personal (infused and/or performed) righteousness. We are then back with Rome and have rejected the Reformation" (114). Shepherd's allegation that the faith/grace paradigm is the proper intention of the early reformers and creeds is pure fabrication. On this misreading of Reformation theology, see W. Robert Godfrey's direct challenge to Shepherd in the recently-published *festscrift* honoring Godfrey's colleague Robert Strimple, entitled "Westminster Seminary, the Doctrine of Justification, and the Reformed Confessions," in *The Pattern of Sound Doctrine: Systematic Theology at the Westminster Seminaries* (ed. David VanDrunen; Phillipsburg: P&R, 2004). Several contributors to this *festschrift* (which also marks the 75th anniversary of Westminster Seminary's founding) acknowledge the pressing need to address major, critical questions never before asked within the walls of the seminary. We look forward to answers to these questions from Westminster's systematicians in their effort to make sense of recent developments at the school, including answers to questions relating to biblical theology's impact for good or ill upon systematics. One crucial point of clarification for those closely attuned to the Westminster dispute: Shepherd's renunciation of the active obedience of Christ in soteric justification in the pages of this book is not a late development. It was implicit in his teaching from the very outset. Shepherd's interpretation of biblical doctrine and his grasp of historical theology remain hopelessly garbled and distorted. Concerning Shepherd's abandonment of the Reformed doctrine of the active obedience of Christ, Frame demurs, adding this concession: "There is room for disagreement here." We need to understand that "these are technical matters of theological exegesis, and godly scholars have different views of them" (xi). Such reasoning we have come to expect from Frame.

To round out the argument of the book we note three other peculiar doctrines crucial to New Covenant Theology, all contrary to the teaching of Scripture: (1) the introduction of the concept of "covenantal election " (different from decretive election and national election, *i.e.,* the election of theocratic Israel in the covenant transacted at Sinai); (2) the two-sided feature of *every* covenant in the Bible, promissory and obligatory, the former best exemplified in the Abrahamic covenant (faith) and the latter in the Mosaic (the obedience of faith); and (3) an essentially theonomic (or Reconstructionist) reinterpretation of the law's abiding normativity, which includes the civil and ceremonial laws of Moses.

**Closing comments**. *Backbone of the Bible* is dedicated to the memory of Greg L. Bahnsen "who preached—and practiced—the covenant" (iii). To one degree or another the authors are all theonomists, though the alignment of Frame and Shepherd to theonomy remains somewhat awkward and tenuous. More appropriately, this volume might well be viewed as a kind of *festscrift* honoring Shepherd who lost out on the real thing. But like Shepherd's *The Call of Grace,* this collection of writings lacks *gravitas* and requisite scholarship. It is all the more surprising that publications like these should cause such widespread disruption in the churches and find so welcome a reception by many today. Clearly, Reformed churches and schools have failed somewhere along the line. In the final analysis, the explanation for the success of these promoters of New Covenant Theology is due to a conversion of several factors in contemporary theology, most notably, the rise of the New Perspective on Paul in biblical studies and recent evangelical reassessment and appropriation of the theology of Karl Barth, one now hailed by many as an evangelical rather than a modernist (contra the reading of earlier critics like Carl Henry and Cornelius Van Til).

The contributors are not in agreement on all details, but they are unified in their central convictions. Though Shepherd tries to adopt a more irenic approach in his two essays, that posture quickly dissipates. The issues are ones to which he and his critics are passionately drawn. Hence the heightened level of rhetoric, much as in the days of the Protestant Reformation when doctrine faithful to Scripture was being forged and defended against false teaching. Frame says he is awaiting a new consensus on the core doctrines of the Reformation: for him, the old consensus no longer bears weight (xi). Two opposite assessments are presented to students of the Bible: one for and one against the Shepherd theology. Within the Westminster community the reliability and trustworthiness of three theological interpreters—Norman Shepherd, John Frame and Richard Gaffin (who is not given his rightful due in this book)—remain in the balance. Frame need not state the obvious, namely, "how deep [Shepherd's] influence on [him] has been" (vii). Westminster Seminary, East and West, has progressed very little beyond the circumstance of the late 1960s and mid-70s when the Shepherd dispute first erupted on campus. The fans of fire have spread, in some cases consuming the uninformed.

[An abbreviated version of this review appears in *TrinJ* 26 NS (2005) 149–150.]

# Appendix B

## God of Promise: Introducing Covenant Theology

*Michael Horton*
**(Grand Rapids: Baker, 2006)**
[This book review is republished from *JETS* (forthcoming). The *Addendum* is new material.]

REPRESENTATIVE REFORMED spokespersons have described Michael Horton's book, *God of Promise: Introducing Covenant Theology*, as a "masterful survey of the covenantal frame of God's self-disclosure" (J. I. Packer), "a rigorous and articulate defense of a traditional view of covenant theology" (Bryan Chapell), "a clear guide to an essential topic" (Gerald Bray), and "the ideal introduction to covenant theology" (Philip Ryken). These endorsements have been provided by the Baker Publishing Group. After reading these words of high praise and commendation, one wonders if anything more can or should be said! Given the importance of the subject and the present-day controversy swirling around it, we are obliged to say more by way of assessment and critique.

As preface to my review of Horton's timely and attractive topic, I would emphasize for the sake of our readers that a great deal of diversity is to be found in the Reformed covenantal tradition: The theological streams include, principally, Continental Reformed theology, (pietistic-)Puritanism, and the Dutch-Reformed tradition. By reason of crossover and admixture, elements of these three, distinctive traditions can be found among many modern-day expositors of covenant theology (otherwise known as "federalism"). Despite differences in formulation and emphasis, an underlying agreement or consensus stands. When we speak of "the Reformed perspective" on the theology of the covenants within international Calvinism, we are distinguishing it from other, competing perspectives, e.g., that of neoothodoxy and nonfoundationalism. According to the school of neoorthodoxy, there is no contrast between law and gospel ("grace"). This crucial element in the teaching of historic Protestant-Reformed orthodoxy has been jettisoned to one degree or another in the thinking of T. F. Torrance, Sinclair Ferguson, and Carl Trueman, as well as in G. C. Berkouwer and Herman Ridderbos. Postmodernist assumptions have led John Franke and, to a lesser extent, Keven Vanhoozer to question the validity of the older Protestant dogmatics (i.e., scholastic orthodoxy), which has based the confessional teachings of the church on an authoritative reading/interpretation of the Bible. (Accordingly, the Protestant creeds are considered to be secondary norms for Christian life and faith.) The postmodern philosophy of language, or linguistic analysis, applied to biblical interpretation, insists that church doctrine can only be a *provisional and relative* approximation of the truth of God. The illuminating work of the Spirit is circumscribed by the finite, *fallible* capacity of the human interpreter. (Lost here is the doctrine of Scripture's perspicuity.)

Happily, Horton seeks to traverse a different path by following in the steps of classical Reformed theology. Aiming for a mature statement of covenant theology, the author introduces his readers to six major aspects of the subject: (1) a systematic overview of the Bible in terms of "the Big Idea," wherein covenant is seen as the architectonic principle of biblico-systematic theology (what involves the interpretive movement from "Scripture to system"); (2) a summary of the covenants in the Old and New Testaments, utilizing the traditional Protestant antithesis between the Law and the Gospel; (3) a discussion of the role and significance of common grace in the wider field of redemption in the postlapsum world (where the wheat and tares grow together until the final harvest); (4) an explanation of the relationship between (theocratic) Israel and the church; (5) a description of the covenantal signs and seals of the kingdom of God; and (6) the case for the necessity of good works in the Christian life, good works being the fruit and evidence of the believer's state of justification.

In the course of discussion some attention is paid to the history of doctrinal development (ancient to modern times). Above all else, however, this book addresses the topic of covenant theology from the vantage point of the Westminster tradition, as that has been borne by the Westminster Seminaries in Philadelphia and Escondido. In this regard, however, apologist Horton falls short in adequately introducing his readers to the *defense* of Reformed covenant theology. The author's mainly positive reading of covenant theology (one that is, for the most part, non-controversial) can readily be misread, given the fiercely-disputed nature of the subject within the Westminster community (and far beyond). Nothing is to be gained by shielding readers from the unpleasant, wearying side of this ongoing struggle for the propagation of the Gospel of grace in our day. With a view to this objective—clarification and resolution of disputed issues in contemporary Reformed covenant theology—we are hopeful that Horton's explication will make a contribution. Better yet, it is hoped that the collegial society of evangelical Bible interpreters (otherwise known as the Evangelical Theological Society) will continue to provide a forum to discuss and debate the critical issues raised in this dispute for the sake of authentic evangelicalism.

Though not a "central dogma," the biblical doctrine of the covenants (plural) is formative in the exposition of Scripture. Horton, like the present reviewer, is indebted to the work of Meredith G. Kline, who stands in the line of dogmatician and biblical theologian Geerhardus Vos and historic Reformed federalism. (I have elaborated on the relationship between Vos and Kline in my paper "New Vistas in OT Narrative: Geerhardus Vos and Meredith G. Kline as Exemplary Reformed Interpreters," read at the April 2005 Eastern regional meeting of the Evangelical Theological Society.) Horton instructs his readers concerning the origination of Scripture as a covenantal document within the context of the ancient Near Eastern world, specifically, in terms of the role and prominence of suzerainty treaties and grants. All this is familiar territory for OT interpreters. (The author refers also to the works of G. E. Mendenhall, W. Eichrodt, G. von Rad, and D. R. Hillers, among others.) Horton proceeds to distinguish between law covenants (like the one made with Israel at Mount Sinai) and promise covenants (like the ones made with Abraham and David).

With respect to interpretations emanating from the Westminster school(s) in recent decades, here is where matters become far more complicated and convoluted. For Horton, as a follower of Kline, it will not do to ignore the changes that have taken place in Kline's thinking over the course of five decades. The discussions of covenant theology that were provoked by the controversial teachings of Norman Shepherd in the 1970s (prior to his dismissal from Westminster Seminary in 1982 for doctrinal error), provided the context for vigorous, renewed study of covenant theology—both from the standpoint of the biblical text and the history of Reformed doctrine. Out of this came needed clarification and modification of traditional teaching. (I have labored to develop and articulate these changes in the work I first began at Westminster in 1973.) Horton is selective in his engagement with the seminary controversy. Foremost in this introduction to Reformed federalism is Horton's treatment of the differences in theological formulation between Kline and O. Palmer Robertson. What is notably missing, however, is any explicit mention of the views of Shepherd (although there are allusions to them). Nor does Horton interact adequately with the New Perspective (e.g., the views of E. P. Sanders, J. D. G. Dunn, and N. T. Wright) or with the Federal Visionists (e.g., the writings of A. Sandlin and S. Wilkins). These are matters too important to sidestep.

Given Horton's and Karlberg's attraction to the Vos-Kline tradition, one that is consistent with historic Reformed teaching, a few observations and clarifications are to be noted in this review. When Kline speaks of the necessity of an appropriate measure of national fidelity on the part of theocratic Israel under the old, Sinaitic covenant, what is a covenant of works (*of sorts*), it is a matter of the retention of the typological kingdom of God (life in the land of promise), not the reception or maintenance of spiritual salvation (what is grounded exclusively upon the obedience of the true Servant of the Lord, David's greater Son, the One greater than Moses). *This point must not be missed: The obedience required of the saints of God under the old covenant (which falls under the rubric of the "Covenant of Grace," extending from the Fall to the Consummation) is identical to that under the new (call it the "obedience of faith," as termed by the apostle Paul).* In terms of the Mosaic economy of redemption, obedience to the law of Moses (individually or corporately) may—for typological purposes—represent or typify the (future) meritorious work of Christ secured for the elect of God in atonement for sin, in the once-for-all accomplishment of redemption (i.e., spiritual salvation). Under the new covenant, the obedience or disobedience of sinners redeemed by grace is no longer judged according to the strictures of the old, Mosaic law. The people of God are now under grace, not law. This is one of the implications of the transition in covenantal history—from shadow to reality.

It is misleading to describe the Mosaic covenant as a "temporal covenant" (38). It is temporal in one regard, eternal in another (as part of the ongoing administration of the "Covenant of Grace"). Likewise, the contrast between the external and internal writing of the law requires careful explication. For the saints under the old covenant (the elect of God), there is the Spirit's writing of the law upon the tablets of flesh, upon the heart. (Reformed soteriology requires nothing less.) The contrast drawn in these terms by the OT prophet Jeremiah (and cited by NT writers) pertains to the peculiar, typological arrangement within the Mosaic economy, what is lacking altogether in the new. This explains the external/internal contrast. (Likewise, the outpouring of the Spirit on Pentecost does not imply that the

Spirit did not work efficaciously among the elect under the old covenant.) This teaching on the continuity/discontinuity between the old and new covenants continues to divide Reformed and dispensational interpreters. (It ought not divide Reformed interpreters, though such is regrettably the case in contemporary exposition. Many have succumbed to a dispensational understanding of the Spirit's work in the two economies.)

The Reformed theology of the covenants, true to Scripture, must come to grips with the distinction between the holy and the common. Both the ancient Israelite theocracy and the NT church are holy institutions, set apart from the world. Hence, for example, the sabbath ordinance (what is a sign of the covenant) belongs only to the people of God, not to unbelievers. It would be mockery for the ungodly to observe God's sabbath ordinance when they remain outside the covenant (as covenant-breakers in Adam). Included in this distinction between the holy and the common is the difference "between God's general care for the secular order and his special concern for the redemption of his people" (116). Horton explains: "What happens 'east of Eden' is this: culture is no longer sacred but secular, yet the secular is not literally "godless," a realm beyond God's concern and involvement" (118). Presumably, Horton means to say that God's common grace is manifested in the world of humankind generally. Good acts are performed by the ungodly, though of no benefit whatsoever for spiritual salvation (hence, Luther's distinction between civil and spiritual righteousness). Thinking through this doctrine consistently means (among other things) that the diaconal work of the church is restricted to the family of God, not to those outside the covenant community (the world-at-large). God's care for all peoples manifests itself in the institution of the state overseeing the welfare of its citizens. The fact that Christians have responsibilities in both kingdoms does not legitimate community programs conducted by the church to meet societal needs (including collaborative faith-based government initiatives). We must not confuse God's general providence of the affairs of the world with his special governance and superintendence of the church. There is a proper separation of church and state, each having its distinct function and purpose as ordained by God.

Lastly, by way of clarification (and correction), greater care must be given to the explication of the nature and significance of the sacraments. Recent Reformed expositions of the eucharist have labored hard to explain how Christ is *really* communicated in the sacrament (cf., especially, the teaching of the Federal Visionists). Horton tells us that the reality of grace (in the person and work of Christ) is "not only signified but is actually communicated and certified by the sacraments" (152). Horton takes up

Ridderbos' rebuke of those who "spiritualize" baptism, failing to realize that baptism "[actually] brings us to Christ's death" (155). The sacraments of the church do none of this. *Only sacramentally speaking are we united to Christ in baptism and renewed in the eucharist.* Christ is truly present in the sacrament (by the presence of faith exercised by the recipient); but he is not present *ex operato* (by the working of the sacrament). Christ is present in the bread and the wine sacramentally speaking, not "actually." There is a big difference here. Preferable is Horton's assertion: "The benefits offered by the sacraments are the same as those offered by the gospel itself: Christ and all his treasures. The sacraments signify and seal to the individual believer the promise that is heard in the preaching of the gospel" (167). It is the true, spiritual presence of Christ in Word and Spirit—in the gospel and in the sacrament. The sacraments are outward, visible signs and seals of God's saving grace to the elect (as Kline stresses, election is the "proper purpose" of redemptive covenant). We are not to conclude, however, that the sacraments are mere "outward" signs and seals. Grace is truly ("actually") communicated through union with Christ by the Spirit of God: Baptism sacramentally marks the beginning of spiritual union with Christ; the Supper reminds us of our continual need to feed upon Christ in the bonds of Christian love and fellowship.

The only question remaining is that addressed to contemporary readers and disputants: Does Reformed federalism continue to speak to the issues of the day, as raised most recently by advocates of the New Perspective and by the Federal Visionists? Bryan Chapell himself has offered a generous critique of the New Perspective. Since the time-tested results of that teaching are not yet in, it is too soon for him to offer a definitive judgment. And so, in the meantime, Chapell commends Horton's presentation as "a traditional view" of Reformed teaching on the covenants. What is urgently needed today is an informed response to the challenges facing the churches, Reformed and evangelical. Perhaps Horton can help others to provide just that.

## *Addendum*

The exchange between Dick Wynia ("The Definitive Introduction to Covenant?" *Christian Renewal* [March 8, 2008] 17–25) and Michael Horton ("Response to Dick Wynia's review of Michael Horton, *God of Promise: Introducing Covenant Theology*," *Christian Renewal* [May 10, 2006] 22–26) is very illuminating. What makes this exchange so illuminating is that Wynia's position is virtually identical to that of Richard Gaffin. Horton well understands this, hence his final acquiescence and accommodation of contrary views on covenant and justification. The effect of this posturing is that Horton's own position ends up garbled. His stance, like that of Westminster West, is one of compromise—compromise for the sake of unity and peace among the brotherhood. What we actually find here is another instance of covenant confusion. (The same compromise and accommodation are reflected in Horton's recent interview with Douglas Wilson on his radio program, *The White Horse Inn*.)

Now to the some of the highlights of the theological banter: Wynia depicts Horton's work as "somewhat idiosyncratic" (to use Horton's expression). *God of Promise* appears to Wynia to be "an apology for Meredith G. Kline's particular brand of covenant theology [rather] than an introduction of covenant theology as I have come to understand it" (17). In Wynia's opinion, Kline's view is "non-representative" of Reformed thinking. So much for Wynia's indoctrination in orthodox Reformed federalism, past and present! Wynia dismisses the classic Protestant-Reformed antithesis between law and grace as misleading and theologically inaccurate. He opines:

> In Horton's brand of covenant theology, it is not only the existence of the covenant of works, but the character and the features of this covenant that are critical. For Horton, one must not only recognize that there was such a covenant—as virtually all Reformed theologians do—but, that it was one that featured a strict principle of justice, and that it offered, during a time of probation, the opportunity for Adam to genuinely and justly merit eternal life by obedience (i.e., works). To call the existence, and the strict works character of this covenant into question, according to Horton, is to call the necessity of the imputation of Christ's active obedience (as the last Adam) to believers into question, too. The claim that the doctrine of the imputation of the active obedience of Christ "stands or falls" with this view of the covenant of works is repeated throughout the book. [page 19]

Later in the review Wynia asserts:

> Horton's view cannot stand up to the implications of all of the Biblical evidence. I am afraid that it does not fully recognize the unity of God's saving work in Jesus Christ, as presented by Scripture.
>
> One of the main reasons for that, it seems to me, has to do with the *a priori* commitment to the contradiction and incompatibility of law and promise. Another reason seems to be the imposition of the structure and characteristics of Ancient Near Eastern treaty forms on the Biblical covenants. [page 25]

# Appendix B

The heart of the matter is this (in Wynia's own words):

> Horton raises a serious concern when he addresses the issue of the imputation of Christ's active obedience. It seems to me that his (proper) desire to maintain the necessity of the imputation of Christ's active obedience drives his view of the covenant of creation, or the covenant of works, which God made with Adam in Genesis 2. But does the doctrine of the imputation of Christ's active obedience stand or fall with the strict works, or merit view of the covenant with Adam? Or do we simply need to maintain that there was a covenant between God and Adam; therefore, Christ's active obedience as the last Adam is necessary for our salvation? I do not believe that we need to say that Adam could genuinely earn or merit eternal life for himself and his descendants through his obedience. The 'work' is obviously disproportionate to the reward. It seems clear that the terms of the covenant of works are not defined by strict justice; Adam could not truly earn eternal life by his obedience. But, according to the terms of the covenant, he could receive eternal life by his obedience; therefore, his obedience was completely necessary. And, therefore, Christ's active obedience is also completely necessary. [page 25]

Is Christ's obedience meritorious, in the thinking of Wynia? Apparently not, and Horton shares my concern (to a different degree, however). Simply put, there is no genuine law/gospel antithesis in Wynia's formulation. Although he recognizes a covenant with Adam before the Fall, it is not a covenant of works founded on the principle of "strict justice." Accordingly, Wynia's reference to the active obedience of Christ is pointless—utterly pointless. He concedes that works are necessary for Adam in the covenant of creation (and so also for the Second Adam in the procurement of redemption). But they are not meritorious for the reason that the reward is disproportionate to the meager work required of Adam (focused as it was on the prohibition not to eat of the tree of the knowledge of good and evil). Wynia conjectures: "It seems clear that the terms of the covenant of works are not defined by strict justice; Adam could not truly earn eternal life by his obedience. But, according to the terms of the covenant, he could receive eternal life by his obedience; therefore, his obedience was completely necessary. And, therefore, Christ's active obedience is also completely necessary" (25).

Positively, Wynia very much likes what in reads in chapter 8 of *God of Promise*. "In general, this is a strong chapter, particularly in our North American theological climate" (22). At the same time, however, Wynia laments Horton's failure to cite others (like authors of the Liberated churches in the Netherlands) in support of the recent reassessment of the "Reformed" doctrine of the sacraments (one that differs from historic orthodoxy). In the end, Wynia concludes: "Our differences are 'intramural'—differences of brothers in the Reformed home" (22). And Horton can live quite comfortably with this assessment of the family debate.

In Horton's "Response" he is clearly on the defensive, ending up far too concessive, as already indicated. Horton refers to the contrary formulations of the "revisionists," but does not identify any of them by name (a safe measure, to be sure). The reader is left wondering whether Wynia might be one of these radical revisionists, only to learn later that he is not. Responding to the heart of the matter, Horton writes: "In my peculiar brand, the covenant of works is based upon 'a strict principle justice.' But is there anyone who believes in the covenant of works who thinks that it is a lax principle of justice" (24)? Is Horton's position really "peculiar"? I think not, and Horton certainly knows better, and has said so. (Just one more misstatement/contradiction/ambiguity in his thinking.)

And what about Horton's own covenant confusion? If law and gospel are antithetical, as Horton rightly contends, then greater care and precision in theological formulation must be exercised than is the case in *God of Promise*. Horton pleads misunderstanding: "First, I explicitly state (especially in chapter 9, but elsewhere as well) the ways in which law and gospel are not incompatible. Yet they certainly are incompatible when it comes to the way we inherit everlasting life. This sense of the law-gospel contrast was affirmed by every major Reformed theologian" (25). This reviewer is not at all satisfied that Horton grasps—with clarity and conviction—the work of Kline and Karlberg regarding the controverted points of doctrine addressed by today's disputants. Nor does Horton, as a historian of doctrine, sufficiently recognize the need to clarify (and reformulate, to some degree) traditional Reformed covenant theology. Surely the present-day controversy warrants closer attention be given to problems inherent in scholastic federalism.

Horton asks: "Pastor Wynia does not think that the imputation of Christ's active obedience requires a strict principle of works. Christ's obedience 'was necessary for our salvation'—that's all we need to say apparently. However, why was it necessary? How? With respect to Adam, 'the "work" is obviously disproportionate to the reward.' But why is this obvious? And if Christ is the Second Adam, how can his work be said to be disproportionate to the reward?" Again, he puts the question to Wynia: "Did he not fulfill all righteousness" (26)? Good questions, but I think that Horton can well anticipate Wynia's answer. Wynia has been clear; Horton has not. The intramural debate ends on good footing: "Despite these differences, I join with Pastor Wynia in encouraging healthy and godly discussion of these important issues. We do share a lot of common ground and we should build from there to reach a new consensus in our day" (26). Sounds like the latest effort at compromise and accommodation, "Presbyterians and Presbyterians Together: A Call to Charitable Theological Discourse," a movement spearheaded by Sam Logan, John Frame and others (see below). Westminster Theological Seminary, which views herself as the "doyen" of Reformed theological institutions, is plotting the strategy and crafting the urgent course of action deemed necessary to gain the upper hand in exercising leadership within the broader Reformed community.

Sadly, Westminster East has betrayed the Gospel of sovereign grace for wealth and connections in the politico-ecclesiastical world of our day. (Arminianism has become the surrogate for Calvinism; this blatant devolution of doctrine is part of a recurring pattern in the history of Reformed theology.) Equally sad is the fact that Westminster West leaves as its legacy a message of compromise. In the final analysis, the institution means more than the Gospel. James T. Dennison's new, brief biography of Geerhardus Vos (and his comments on Vos' regard for Westminster Seminary in its founding days) is informative and relevant—and searching with regard to the current theological dispute (see his "Introduction" to *The Letters of Geerhardus Vos* [ed. James T. Dennison; Phillipsburg: Presbyterian and Reformed, 2005]). Surprising is the conclusion—coming from the pen of Dennison—that the Gospel and the truth of God's Word cannot be institutionalized; they are the product of God's unfettered Spirit and grace. What Dennison's biography shows is that men of strong conviction, like Vos and Kline (I would hasten to add), make their appearance on the scene of church history, leave their indelible mark, and exist as mysteriously and inexplicably as they first appeared. They do not fit into with this world's system—including the institutional arm of the church mired in ecclesiastical intrigue and deceit. Their denominational ties are tenuous at best. Elusive and enigmatic figures they remain, earthen vessels whose singular desire is to explicate—with insight, passion and conviction—Scripture's teaching concerning the heavenly, eschatological treasure which is not of this world. If we have anything to learn from the history of the present-day controversy over justification and the covenants, it is that we must move beyond the ambiguities and misformulations of the past—deeply imbedded as they are in the Reformed tradition we cherish and respect. These misstatements do not create an obstacle, but a challenge for theologians in the ongoing work of the church as a distinctively confessional organism. Orthodox Presbyterian Church historians D. G. Hart and J. R. Muether conclude their 14-part series on "Turning Points in American Presbyterian History" (*New Horizons* 27/4 [April 2006] 11–12) without any mention of the Shepherd controversy and its divisiveness. This is not the first time that they have sidestepped this very grave dispute. Sad to say, more important to them is preservation of the Puritan doctrine of sabbath-day observance. We do well to heed the words and wisdom of Vos preached in one of his sermons:

> Now I do not mean to affirm that in all cases there need be the preaching of false doctrine which involves an open and direct denial of the evangelical truth. It is quite possible that both to the intention and the actual performance of the preacher any departure from the historical faith of the church may be entirely foreign. And yet there may be such a failure in the intelligent presentation of the gospel with the proper emphasis upon that which is primary and fundamental as to bring about a result almost equally deplorable as where the principles of the gospel are openly contradicted or denied. There can be a betrayal of the gospel of grace by silence. There can be disloyalty to Christ by omission as well as by positive offence against the message that he has entrusted to our keeping. [Quoted in *The Letters of Geerhardus Vos*, 82 n. 211].

TO BE sure, one of the most difficult challenges in Reformed theology is the interpretation of the Mosaic covenant, specifically, the proper understanding of the place of law—antithetical to (gospel-)grace— in the Mosaic administration of the Covenant of Grace. The following comments may offer some help to those wrestling with this issue (these comments were first drafted in correspondence with inquiring students):

(1) The Mosaic law does not call for works of self-righteousness. Nowhere in the divine order of things do such works find a home. As a *hypothetical* principle, it does surface explicitly on occasion (as in Jesus' discourse with the rich young ruler). More generally, it is implicit in the doctrine of law, as taught in Scripture. If one could keep the law perfectly, he/she would gain the right to life eternal. The fact is, after the Fall no one can keep God's law perfectly. Only Adam before the Fall was so able to do—not to earn salvation (which does not pertain in the original order of creation), but to receive/earn/merit confirmation in righteousness. By virtue of his creation in the image of God (as son of God), Adam already was righteous. Now it was a matter of being *confirmed* in righteousness. The doctrine of probation is a vital and essential ingredient. The (Pauline)

concept of "the obedience of faith" does not pertain here either. It is simply misleading—and erroneous—to employ that terminology with respect to the pre-Fall setting.

(2) The works-principle of inheritance operative in the Mosaic economy was not hypothetical, but actual. It pertained to temporal blessing in the land of promise. Of course, the design of the Sinaitic covenant was to frustrate Israel, and in so doing point her to Christ alone as the true Servant of the Lord, the faithful covenant-keeper. He alone delivers the elect from spiritual bondage to sin; he alone leads the exiled into true freedom, entrance into the eternal, heavenly kingdom.

(3) Salvation is always by grace through faith in Christ (even under the old, Mosaic economy), never by works. *Legalism* is works-salvation (and nowhere commended in Scripture); the *legal* demand of the covenant of creation and of the Mosaic covenant (regulating temporal life in Canaan) has nothing to do with the obtainment of salvation, which is by grace alone, apart from the works of the law.

(4) By virtue of the reintroduction of the works-inheritance principle (on the typological level only), the Mosaic covenant can be spoken of as a republication of the original covenant of works (*modified to accommodate the postlapsarian situation*).

(5) The moral law (so-called) reflects the holiness of God. But there is a specific context for the moral code—a *covenantal* context. For example, we are not to murder. Yet, God commands Abraham to offer up his own son, Isaac. Without getting into all the particulars (for here we have an example of what Professor Meredith Kline rightly discerns as "the intrusion ethic"—anticipating the final Day of the Lord, the day of judgment), had Abraham held to the revealed moral law as a standard independent of God, its author, Abraham would have had reason to disobey. This particular command is given to Abraham as a prophetic anticipation of the offering up of God's own Son for our salvation. (In the case of Jephthah, because of his vow to God, he *did* slay his only-begotten—an event that is part of the progressive unfolding of God's plan of redemption in the history of the Covenant of Grace.)

(6) The Fourth Commandment has generally not been understood to be part of the moral law, but rather part of the ceremonial law of Moses. The biblical doctrine of the sabbath is a rich and complex idea. (At the beginning of history—before the Fall—sabbath-observance was an eschatological sign of the end of the age.)

(7) Conforming to God's moral character takes on concrete, everyday significance in terms of the specific covenant he has made with us. The

sons and daughters of God are to obey the Word of God as revealed in the context of the covenant, old or new (whichever the case). The canon of Scripture—old or new—is the holy standard for believers. Presently, our standard is contained in the documents of the new covenant. (Of course, the Christian Scriptures comprise the Old and New Testaments.)

(8) Conformity to the law of God (naturally and supernaturally revealed, i.e., through general and special revelation) is our duty, not the (meritorious) means of finding acceptance with God, i.e. salvation. Before the Fall, Adam enjoyed communion and fellowship with God by virtue of the covenant relationship. But the covenant at creation *also* entailed the federal, representative principle of headship—and the terms of this covenant initially placed Adam on probation. It is the case that Adam would have earned (or merited) *confirmation in righteousness*. At the outset, Adam was just and righteous in God's sight, having been created in his own image as son of God.

(9) Under the new covenant, conformity to the law of God is requisite, not optional. But this "obedience of faith," as the apostle Paul calls it, is not the ground of justification. The ground of our justification is exclusively the vicarious obedience of Christ. (Such was true under the old covenant as well—in anticipation of the coming Servant of the Lord, Jesus the Christ, who would suffer for our sake in the procurement of our redemption. Atonement requires the active and passive obedience for the satisfaction of divine law—for the purpose of fulfilling all righteousness.)

(10) As to the operation of the works-inheritance principle under the Mosaic economy of redemption: Believers under the old covenant were required, like new covenant believers, to render conformity to the revealed law of God (i.e., "the obedience of faith"). According to God's own purpose and determination, the obedience of the Israelite (individually or corporately) could be and was judged in accordance with the antithetical works-inheritance principle, rather than faith-inheritance principle. Thus, for example, Moses was barred entrance into the land of promise because of his disobedience. But as numbered among the elect of God, Moses was heir of life eternal (a resident of true Canaan). With respect to the latter, the imputed righteousness of Christ was the legal basis for Moses' acceptance as a sinner redeemed by grace. The requirement of obedience to the law of God is not restricted to the typological sphere. The obedience/disobedience of the people of God is treated differently on the typical and the antitypical levels, and that according to God's design and purpose. The reason for the two levels within the Mosaic economy of redemption lies with the symbol-

ico-typological significance of life in the temporal land of Canaan, replica of the heavenly Kingdom of God.

Moisés Silva in "Faith Versus Works of Law in Galatians" (*Justification and Variegated Nomism: Volume II. The Paradoxes of Paul* [ed. D. A. Carson, P. T. O'Brien, and M. A. Seifrid; Grand Rapids: Baker, 2004] 217–48) wrestles once more with one of the critical texts in the current dispute, Leviticus 18:5—but to no avail. Contradiction in theological statement and manipulation of the biblical text continue to prevail in Silva's thinking and methodology. Among the better contributions in this important collection of writings is P. T. O'Brien's essay, "Was Paul a Covenantal Nomist?" Evangelicals are far from reaching a consensus on the controverted doctrines (here, it is to be noted, evangelicalism has moved far from its Reformation roots). Judaism (in all its variations) is not Christianity. It is not just a christological reading of the Old Testament, but a fundamental misinterpretation of the law of Moses, Israel's pedagogue, that lies at the root of the religious opposition. Judaism confounds grace and works in the procurement of salvation. Historically, Protestantism and Roman Catholicism differed sharply on role of faith and works in salvation. That is no longer the case today. Is the New Perspective a partial corrective to the teaching of the Protestant Reformation? Silva says *Yes*, I say *No*. The more important question is whether or not the covenant at creation brings into view the alleged harmony between law and grace (the doctrine of nonmeritorious reward as advocated in the Gaffin-Shepherd school).

At long last, Meredith G. Kline's masterpiece, *God, Heaven, and Har Magedon: A Covenantal Tale of Cosmos and Telos* (Eugene, Ore.: Wipf and Stock, 2006) has finally seen the light of day. In this book Professor Kline provides his readers a fresh presentation of Reformed covenant theology—more precisely, a restatement and rethinking (in places) of past formulations. It is the capstone of his biblical-theological reflections on the history of redemption laid out in the pages of Scripture, Old and New Testaments. Focal attention is given to the eschatological fulfillment of the original word of promise given to Adam, son of God redeemed by sovereign grace—earthling adopted, justified, sanctified, and (in principle) glorified for life in the heavenly kingdom yet to come. Most important in this study, as in several of his preceding works, is the reformulation of the operation of the dual principles of inheritance, law and gospel-grace, within the Mosaic administration of the Covenant of Grace. This reformulation comes as the culmination of years of discussion and debate among covenant theologians, especially those within the Westminster School.

My participation in these discussions began as early as my matriculation at Westminster Theological Seminary in 1973, beginning with the M.Div. program (1976), followed by the Th.M. program in New Testament (1977). My 1980 doctoral study, entitled "The 'Mosaic Covenant and the Concept of Works in Reformed Hermeneutics: A Historical-Critical Analysis with Special Attention to Early Covenant Eschatology," was written in the midst of the Shepherd controversy that had been raging on campus. The controversy had erupted in 1975. (The intensity of the dispute on campus slowly dissipated after 1982—when Shepherd was dismissed—with new appointments to the faculty and with changes in administrative leadership at the seminary. The climate now overwhelmingly favors the Gaffin-Shepherd interpretation.) Further study of the theology of the covenants—including engagement with later "refinements" in the Gaffin-Shepherd formulation, the New Perspective on Paul, and the Federal Vision—has led to numerous publications of mine. Many of these writings have been collected in *Covenant Theology in Reformed Perspective* (2000), its sequel, *Gospel Grace: The Modern-day Controversy* (2003), and in this present volume. Literature on this dispute from both sides of the divide continues to grow. (See, *for example,* Brian Schwertley, "The Crisis in the OPC and PCA," *The Westminster Guardian* [June 2006] 2–8.)

The most recent attempt to blunt criticism of the New Theology appears in the document "Presbyterians and Presbyterians Together" (May 2006). Among signers associated with Westminster Seminary are Sam Logan, Will Barker, John Frame, Tremper Longman, Doug Green, and Mike Kelly. Others who have signed include such names as John Armstrong, Andrew Sandlin, and Michael Williams. (The last named serves on the faculty of Covenant Seminary.) And the list of signers continues to grow (the document is posted on the world-wide web at www.presbyterianstogether.org). In a lecture delivered by Chancellor Sam Logan on the campus of Westminster Seminary on Commencement Day 2006 it was announced that the institution was charting a new direction: Machen's movement has been deemed too "intellectual," insufficiently "practical" for the necessary work and mission of the seminary (as now contemplated). Changes have been in the wind for a long time. Early on, the publication *The Presbyterian Guardian* was named as the denominational magazine of the Orthodox Presbyterian Church. The present outlook of the denomination—reflecting the thinking of New Westminster—has shifted to *New Horizons*. No longer the guardian of Presbyterianism (*i.e.,* Reformed orthodoxy), the church publication seeks to reach out to a more eclectic readership, emphasizing

# Appendix B

diversity in theological viewpoints. The OPC website contains this historical note (written by John Muether):

> On August 30, 1979, the Board of Trustees of the *Presbyterian Guardian* voted to merge the magazine with the *Presbyterian Journal*.
>
> Frustrated with a subscription base of about 3,500, the Trustees joined with the *Presbyterian Journal* in order to "reach a wider audience (well over 20,000) with the Reformed faith." In his article, "Toward the Future of the Presbyterian Church" in the *Guardian*'s final issue, Edmund Clowney wrote, "there is no good reason for [the two magazines] to remain separate, and every good reason why there should be one clear journalistic voice serving Machen's hope for American Presbyterianism." For many, the merger was a precursor of a denominational union that was perceived on the horizon. In Clowney's words, the merger "marks the growing unity of Bible-believing Presbyterians in the United States." The anticipated church union, however, would not take place. The *Presbyterian Journal*, even with a united voice and expanded subscription base, would cease publication in 1987, with its Board of Trustees transferring its assets to World magazine.
>
> The 1979 merger ended the remarkable 44-year life of a magazine founded by J. Gresham Machen in 1935, an independent monthly dedicated to a predominantly Orthodox Presbyterian readership. Numbered among its editors were Ned B. Stonehouse, Paul Woolley, Leslie Sloat, Robert Nicholas, and John Mitchell.

From the beginning, the seminary and denominational controversy (most immediately in the OPC, with direct ramifications in the PCA and the URC) has been a struggle for truth and moral integrity. Upon the dismissal of Shepherd from the faculty, several adjunct professors, notably Professors Meredith Kline and Stanford Reid, were barred from future teaching at the seminary on grounds of their ardent opposition to Shepherd's teaching. If Shepherd was dismissed unfairly in the eyes of Gaffin and his cohorts, then it was appropriate that others bear the wrath of those now in control of the seminary (President Clowney had just retired at this same time). Kline's letter to the members of the faculty (dated February 7, 1983) challenged their actions, decrying their deliberate deceit and prevarication. Likewise, Reid voiced protest and displeasure with the seminary's intrigue and ongoing spread of false teaching. Reid's biographer, A. Donald MacLeod, has carefully documented Reid's long relationship with the seminary and his involvement in the Shepherd dispute in *W. Stanford Reid: An Evangelical Calvinist in the Academy* (Montreal: McGill-Gween's University Press, 2004). Strikingly, Kline's portrayal of the "concocted" scheme worked out by the seminary faculty suggests a rehearsal of humankind's first encounter with sin and temptation in Genesis 3 (see Kline's description of the Garden episode in *Kingdom Prologue*): Here we encounter narrative theology carried out in slavish imitation by the faculty and administration of Westminster—mocking truth and relishing falsehood. Even more lamentable is that circumstance which now prevails: supporters of the seminary and the OPC have compromised on the Gospel of sovereign grace, and have condoned the manner in which Westminster has conducted herself all these years. God have mercy! Doubtless, it will require a future generation to untangle the web that has been made and to free church theologians and ministers of the Gospel to proclaim the Gospel in its purity and simplicity, a work of the Spirit of God in reforming the church of Christ.

# Appendix C

## The Kingdom of Christ:
## The New Evangelical Perspective

*Russell D. Moore*
(Wheaton: Crossway, 2004)
[This book review appears in *JETS* 48 (2005) 410–15.]

Russell Moore's study provides an invaluable gauge on contemporary evangelical theology. It is well written and comprehensive in range. Though selective with respect to bibliographical sources, the book nevertheless contains an outstanding compilation of material, weaving together many strands of evangelical theological discussion in illuminating fashion. As a "traditional covenant theologian" reviewing this book (so the author has identified me), it would come as no surprise that I have significant differences with Moore's case for evangelical theological consensus. Even Moore is quite unsure what to make of the mosaic of contemporary evangelical thought. The book closes by questioning his opening thesis. Perhaps greater attention to and comprehension of the writings of Reformed covenant theology—and hence less attention to progressive dispensationalism (if only to be more evenhanded!)—might have given the author himself more opportunity to rethink and refine his own position, commendable as it is in many places. Interesting is his system of labeling theological positions across a very wide spectrum of evangelical opinion. At times, Moore's assessment and categorization are too neatly drawn; in actuality, the issues are far more complex and far more convoluted than his analysis would lead his readers to think. Two examples: Moore's misreading of the Christian political theory of Edmund Clowney; and his misreading of the amillennial covenant theology of Vern Poythress. As a consequence, Moore's argument for evangelical "consensus" becomes flimsy and somewhat forced. Much more distinction and refinement in statement are needed.

The author is a devotee of Carl Henry, a giant in twentieth-century (neo-)evangelicalism, a staunch defender of biblical authority. (Moore rightly laments Henry's failure to carry through his conviction by retaining the doctrine of biblical inerrancy as a theological nonnegotiable within conservative Protestant theology.) The heartbeat of *The Kingdom of God* is concerned with the intersection between evangelical theology and political engagement. In my judgment, American evangelicalism has inherited a quasi-Constantinian, and therefore unbiblical, understanding of the relationship between Christian ethics and social politics, a subject of intense, growing conflict, especially in recent years—since the Jimmy Carter presidency. Agreeably, all Americans, whatever their religious conviction, strive—or should strive—for peace in the world. In addition, evangelical believers seek—or should seek—peace in the church. But Scripture clearly indicates that peace will not ultimately be obtained in this present (evil) age, not in the church and not in the world. Discord and disharmony are the fruits of sin; they will not be fully eradicated until the consummation of history. What concord and harmony are reached is often short-lived. Peace is elusive; to think otherwise is delusive. (Only the coming Prince of Peace will achieve this blessing for time eternal.) One final observation before moving on: Peace in society and peace in the church are two entirely different objectives. Peace in the church requires unity in the (essential) fundamentals of Christian doctrine. Whole-hearted obedience to the Word of God in faith and in practice is basic to the church's witness. Christian ethical behavior and church discipline are descriptive (and prescriptive) of life within the community of faith, not in society-at-large. But this takes us well ahead of our summary review of the argument in *The Kingdom of God*.

After introducing the reader to his topic of study, "evangelical theology and evangelical [political] engagement," we are treated to an analysis of the three defining doctrines informing this book: eschatology, soteriology, and ecclesiology. Simply put, in Moore's words, "the failure of evangelical politics points us to something far more important that underlies it—the failure of evangelical theology" (11). But things have changed dramatically, or so the reader is led to believe in the opening chapter. The emergent consensus among evangelicals that Moore thinks he has uncovered is an acknowledgment that the eschaton, or the consummation of earth's history, "is to be understood as part of the overall goal of the history of the cosmos—the universal acclaim of Jesus as sovereign over the created order

(Phil. 2:9-11) and the glorification of Jesus through the salvation of the cosmos (Rom. 8:29)" (56). On first appearance, this prospect looks scriptural enough. But the question is this: How is the consummate Kingdom of Christ—the eschaton—brought into being? Do the cultural endeavors of Christians as the corporate embodiment of the church, the Bride of Christ, prepare the way? Do they lay the foundation for the new earth? Although it is this earth and this cosmos that will be renewed, how is renewal effected? Bottom line: What presently is the business of the church in the world? This is the chief issue, with sundry other related ones.

To answer this question, argues Moore, we must deal substantively with basic Bible doctrine, specifically, the doctrine of things to come (grappling with the now burgeoning literature on "inaugurated eschatology"), the doctrine of salvation (considering the redemption of the fallen cosmos as well as humanity), and the doctrine of the church (understanding what it means to be God's prophetic voice in the secular world). Curiously, it is the alleged rapprochement—the "new evangelical perspective" (or "consensus")—among progressive dispensationalists and modified covenant theologians that has seemingly won the day. *Or has it?* Whatever convergence may be taking place, it is surely not all for the best. The battle among these two Protestant traditions has been around for a long time, and shows no signs of diminishing. What Henry saw as mere "skirmishes"—occasions for "navel-gazing"—are much more than that (21). Hermeneutical method, substantive doctrine, careful exegesis of crucial biblical texts are what is at stake. George Eldon Ladd shared some of the same socio-theological aspirations held by Henry, but these two pivotal thinkers had their sharp differences, as Moore very clearly indicates. What Moore likes about Ladd's analysis is the charge leveled against covenant theologians: "While dispensationalists severed the Kingdom from the present activity of the Messiah, Ladd argued, the amillennialists severed it form the goal of history by relegating the Kingdom to the arena of the human heart, the church, or the supra-temporal heavenly state" (32). Adopting a "restorational eschatology," Moore favorably cites Michael Williams' critique of the eschatological views of Geerhardos Vos, another pivotal thinker prominently featured in this book. Where Ladd fell short, however, was in his failure to grasp "the essentially spiritual nature of the Kingdom of God" (35).

This brings us to Chapter Two, which addresses the core doctrine in *The Kingdom of God*, namely, eschatology. Commendably, the impact of Vos' work in contemporary Reformed theology is given proper recognition in these pages. But what Moore does not grasp is the (radically) new direction taken by the Westminster school as represented by systematicians

Norman Shepherd and Richard Gaffin. (The former receives no treatment by the author, which may well explain why he misreads Gaffin's place in the stream of contemporary theological development. Compare my *Gospel Grace: The Modern-day Controversy* [Eugene: Wipf and Stock, 2003].) Moore's portrayal of the Westminster school—with comparison made to changes taking place at Dallas Theological Seminary—is simply inaccurate. Moore categorically states: "Richard Gaffin is correct to see that Kingdom eschatology reverses an older tradition within Western theology, at least as old as Anselm, which concentrates the work of Christ most heavily on the benefits of His death, rather than on *both* His sacrificial death and His resurrection from the dead" (61, *italics added*). Is it a matter of reversing or buttressing and enhancing the Western tradition? Where this debate becomes particularly contentious is with regard to the classic Protestant doctrine of justification by faith (alone). On the one hand, Moore commends "a reconsideration of a variety of problematic issues, ranging from the law/gospel relationship to the work of the Spirit in redemptive history, [where] nearly every eschatological question at issue is related to the 'already' and 'not yet' aspects of the reign of Christ" (60). On the other, Moore questions the direction of contemporary theology, demurring "the growing reluctance within evangelical theology to speak of the 'courtroom language' of forensic justification" (115). I wish more attention had been given to this wayward trend, including some analysis of the New Perspective on Paul and the Mosaic law and how that impacts the "new [eschatological] perspective" of evangelicals, what is, after all, the subject of this book. For Luther and Calvin, it is the *threefold use* of the law of God—the civil, normative, and pedagogical—that is the broad topic under discussion. Where does Moore stand on this issue—for or against the Protestant reformers? If the latter, then he stands with Gaffin and New Westminster. Clarification, please.

Turning to some of the specifics of Moore's eschatological panorama, he anticipates "a unique place for the fulfillment of geopolitical blessings to a reconstituted Israelite nation" (44). The new perspective, in Moore's estimation, "shields evangelical theology from perceiving the present nature of the Kingdom as merely spiritual or existential, or as languishing in suspended animation unto the eschaton. At the same time, these developments in evangelical eschatology remedy what theologian Adrio König has identified with precision as the 'eclipse of Christ' in contemporary eschatology" (57). With this conviction Moore is so bold as to say: "[Anthony] Hoekema and other modified covenantalists place the future consummation within a 'new creation' model of fulfillment in the new earth. In this, they are in agreement not only with progressive dispensationalists but also with classical dispensationalists in finding the older amillennial view of prophetic promises to be *biblically bankrupt*" (51, *emphasis mine*). I totally disagree. Another specific: the coming of the eschatological Spirit at Pentecost makes possible the *permanent* indwelling within new covenant believers. "Some Reformed theologians," observes Moore, "even do not hesitate to use the term 'dispensational' to describe the once-for-all character of the coming of the Spirit at Pentecost. This is a healthy development" (61). Conducive for consensus, maybe, but bad for the articulation of a Reformed soteriology. At this point I raise a fundamental question regarding Moore's soteriological estimate of human ability. I do so, when I read him denouncing the Reformed doctrine of supralapsarianism, which our author seemingly equates with double predestination (the decree of election *and* reprobation). Championing the new consensus, he reasons: "This Christologically focused Kingdom soteriology therefore protects evangelical theology from a resurgent supralapsarianism that defines this glory theocentrically in terms of the supra-temporal glorification and reprobation of individuals" (105). At the same time he castigates the open theists for their mitigation of God's sovereign control over all human affairs. Is God absolutely sovereign, or does the sinner have some limited, autonomous control over his future destiny? Divine reprobation, exercised in accordance with divine justice, includes God's act of passing by those who are not the objects of his discriminating love (preterition). How can it be? is the proper question to be asked by sinners—sinners saved on account of God's sovereign grace, chosen in Jesus Christ. As Moore himself rightly affirms, God "meticulously govern[s] the affairs of the cosmos" (230, n.57). So also the eternal destiny of every human being.

Then there is the question of the "millennium." According to the new perspective, "the Millennium is seen not as a separate dispensation from the eternal state, but as an initial phase of it" (63). Here Moore confuses time and eternity, undercutting the "cataclysmic" nature of the end of the age, the radical in-breaking of the new heavens and new earth. This all-to-common misconception is repeated throughout the book. Moore takes exception to the "Augustinian 'spiritual vision' eschatology, with which it is impossible to reconcile the 'earthy' feel of the prophetic promises, not only of the Old Testament but of the New as well" (62). All along the way Moore gives expression to a particular reading of the Old Testament prophetic idiom; consistent with premillennial dispensationalism, Moore follows a literalistic approach to future, apocalyptic portrayals in the Bible. This school of interpretation is still very far apart from amillennial covenant theology. And Moore is well aware of that fact.

Given his eschatological reading of the Bible, Moore proceeds in the third and fourth chapters to reformulate the doctrines of salvation and the church in accordance with this newly-formulated evangelical perspective. Salvation is christological—and it is *holistic*. Although Moore commends Henry for recognizing that humanity's problem is fundamentally spiritual, not political or economic, he nevertheless seeks to make a stronger case for evangelical political engagement than his protégé did. Following the argument of Robert Saucy, Moore faults covenant theologians for failing to grasp the national and political character of the new covenant church "as a multi-national Spirit body," a feature that is "impossible to relegate to the eternal state" (96). This brings into play, again, important and complex issues in biblical hermeneutics, issues that sharply distinguish dispensational and covenantal systems of interpretation. While Moore rejects the position of Louis Berkhof, "arguably the most influential American Reformed theologian of the twentieth century" (97), I contend that amillennial covenant theologians have for the most part correctly understood the vital and essential distinction between cult (worship and ministry as practiced by the community of believers) and culture (what is, broadly speaking, the carrying out of the creational mandate to exercise dominion over the earth, an enterprise shared by believers and unbelievers). Related to this is the important distinction in Reformed theology between the "common" and the "holy," a distinction largely missed by premillennialists and, more broadly, neo-evangelicals. What Moore identifies as "new earth" amillennialism (100) is a repudiation—or, at the very least—a reformulation of covenant theology that is inherently inconsistent with its own principles of interpretation, i.e., with Reformed theology's distinctive hermeneutical/typological methodology.

"The cosmic extent of salvation," writes Moore, "is seen as the Second Adam offers up to the Father a created order in which He has subdued every enemy (1 Cor. 15:24-26), and there is nothing unclean in the garden over which He rules (Rev. 21:1-8)" (106). Viewing the arrival of the eschaton as beginning in the millennium, what Moore sees as the initial stage of the (final) kingdom of Christ, how does this interpretation really differ from postmillennialism? He posits: "If redemption is the restoration of the creation order, not its repudiation, then evangelical theology must take seriously a creation mandate that values human culture as an aspect of human vicegerency over the earth" (122). He further clarifies: "In the emerging 'new earth' understanding of the salvific transformation of the cosmos, human cultural endeavors are not simple temporal concerns, which will be consumed and forgotten in the static, timeless salvation enjoyed at the eschaton. Instead, creation is to be redeemed, albeit not by human effort, but by the cataclysmic coming of Christ, the Messiah, for whose inheritance the universe was created in the first place.... Furthermore, the New Testament seems to imply that some cultural human endeavors from within the stream of human history will be sanctified and will continue in the new order of the everlasting Kingdom of God" (Rev. 21:26) (122). Among Reformed interpreters this point of view is more reflective of the tradition of Amsterdam than that of Princeton. No consensus here.

What is the practical import of the new evangelical perspective on social engagement? Moore explains: "Political solutions are first implemented within the community of the local church. When political solutions are offered to the outside world, they must always be couched in language that recognizes the futility of cultural reform without personal regeneration and baptism into the Body of Christ" (172). This nicely sums up the principal argument in *The Kingdom of Christ*. Only the church—as the redeemed people of God, the new humanity—can make a lasting impact in society as God's instrument working to establish the eternal kingdom in this present order of things. The church's sanctified political theory and practice serve to usher in the eschaton. In this increasingly pluralistic world (post September 11) this is not what needs to be said. And more importantly, Moore's viewpoint, in my estimate, does not have the support of Scripture. Even so, Moore's book should provoke thoughtful, ongoing dialogue and debate. Whereas the book opens with the prospect of genuine evangelical consensus, it closes by seeing the real threat of evangelicals "splintering apart" (175). Moore warns: "the long-term ramifications of this debate cast uncertainly on the prospects of ever developing an evangelical theological consensus" (182). Quite a reversal on the part of our author—and without a doubt, a cause for rethinking the issues. I submit that what we find in amillennial covenant theology is realism, not pessimism. The dawning of the kingdom of Christ comes with the present reign of God in the hearts of the redeemed, as Berkhof correctly understood. The business of the church is the proclamation and defense of the Gospel, not the drafting of a political agenda or the implementation of a social program (not even the establishment of medical clinics at home or abroad). It is the role of the common grace institution of the state to maintain the well-being of her citizens and to exercise justice and equity in all human affairs. This Reformed conviction *in no way* absolves Christians of their duties and responsibilities in the political and social arenas. No grounds for abdication or nonengagement—except in the case of those called to preach the Word!

# Appendix D

## The Pattern of Sound Doctrine: Systematic Theology at the Westminster Seminaries.

*Edited by David VanDrunen*
**(Phillipsburg: Presbyterian and Reformed, 2004)**
[This book review appears in *SBJT* (forthcoming).]

THIS COLLECTION of thirteen essays—what is a *festschrift* in honor of Robert Strimple—attempts to present both a rationale for and an explanation/critique of the Westminster school, theological successor to Old Princeton. (Other seminaries have also appeared within American Reformed presbyterianism to carry on the work and witness of Old Princeton.) In this account by faculty members one bitter dispute in the history of Westminster, in Philadelphia and in Escondido, California, receiving special mention is the controversy that continues to swirl around the teachings of Norman Shepherd, former professor of systematics. This dispute has altered the course of Westminster for the worse, and to the detriment of international Calvinism.

Part One ("Historical Studies") opens with Darryl Hart's comparison of Old Princeton's "unoriginal Calvinism" with Westminster's creative urge not only to say something new in theological exposition, but also to reshape the method and discipline of Reformed systematics for the twentieth/twenty-first century. Westminster's first president, Edmund Clowney, offers personal reflections on John Murray, the school's highly-esteemed professor of theology, ignoring the divisive issues he faced as chief executive of the institution. (I had hoped for more, much more from his pen.) The relationship of systematic theology to other disciplines within the theological curriculum is the subject of Part Two. While Michael Horton tackles the "uneasy union" between biblical theology and systematics, John Frame

# Appendix D

stakes out his peculiar niche at Westminster, specifically, his role in reshaping Van Tillian apologetics—what amounts to Frame's own personal apology. (Frame now teaches at Reformed Seminary in Orlando.) This section closes with Dennis Johnson's understanding of practical theology as an expression of systematic theology. Part Three is given to four specific issues of theological import at Westminster: the doctrine of justification by faith alone (Robert Godfrey); the free offer of the gospel (Scott Clark); human language as theological medium (Richard Gaffin); and the doctrine of the covenants (David VanDrunen). To one degree or another, each of these four have been controversial within modern-day Reformed orthodoxy. Hence, they serve as a barometer of Westminster's own fidelity to Scripture and historic Calvinism. (Westminster still regards herself as the bastion of Protestant-Reformed orthodoxy, the "doyen" of Calvinistic schools.) The final part sets Westminster theology in the wider context of church life and ministry. John Muether reflects on Westminster's devotion to the "whole counsel of God," Reformed theology in its breadth and depth. The tie between seminary and constituency is the topic of Dirk Bergsma's essay. Jay Adams addresses the contentious debate relating to the place of biblical-theological exposition in preaching. Concluding the *festschrift* are Clair Davis' thoughts on the implications and ramifications of Westminster theology for the cultivation of genuine Christian piety and spirituality, a subject with which he has wrestled throughout his career.

Given the history of Westminster, the most important entry in this collection, in my judgment, is that by VanDrunen. It is his contention—well justified—that the different conceptions of theology as a *system* of doctrine held by Westminster's systematicians have undermined or brought into serious question her Reformed witness. In writing this lament VanDrunen notes that there is "much at stake" (196). Before summarizing his diagnosis of the health of systematics (and his remedy), we assess the leading indicators of theological activity at Westminster as judged by the other contributors to this volume. Hart observes the shift from the solid posturing of theological stalwarts like Charles Hodge and B. B. Warfield to the ambiguous, uncertain meandering of the more recent systematico-biblical theologians. Here Hart faults Murray, Van Til, Gaffin, Frame, and Tim Trumper for abandoning the old line. As a consequence, "systematics lost its regal standing and has vied especially with biblical theology for supremacy. The methods of systematics no longer provide the coherence they once did at Old Princeton. Hence, creativity and constructive Calvinism have become virtues in the Westminster tradition in the way that unorginality was the hallmark of the Princeton theology" (24-25). Horton pleads for the reintegration of systematic and biblical theology without providing clear direction. Elsewhere I have questioned Horton's own forage into foreign territory (see my *Gospel Grace: The Modern-day Controversy* [Eugene, OR: Wipf and Stock, 2003] 287-294). Here, once again, Horton accents the dramatic, existential element of biblical narrative in terms of the covenant relationship between the Creator and the creature. He sees covenant as the "integrative structure rather than a central dogma" of Reformed theology, and calls for "a reinvigorated and revised covenant theology [*á la* Gaffin]" (66-67). Horton's work sounds a very different note to that of VanDrunen. I take strong exception to suggestion made by several in this work that the problem at Westminster lies with the inherent rivalry between biblical and systematic theology (something I do not see among these disciplines); rather, the problem arises with the introduction of dogmatic presuppositions alien to Scripture. The new breed of systematicians has not liberated itself from dogma, as many have been led to believe. There is dogma faithful to Scripture, and dogma that is not. (Westminster West does evince some careful rethinking of the issues. Light appears on the horizon.)

As Frame himself admits, the reference he makes to the Shepherd controversy is not relevant to the development of his essay, but he feels compelled to justify himself, Shepherd and his theological entourage. Along the way he points out that it was Shepherd who invited him to join the Westminster faculty in 1967. Frame also misleadingly invokes the past endorsement of Shepherd by Van Til, Westminster's revered, but aged apologist and theologian. Godfrey attempts to set the record straight on this dispute, adding that the deeper problem, in his opinion, is the matter of creedal subscription. In the case of Gaffin, Frame, and Trumper, argues Godfrey, fidelity to the Reformed standards is undermined by their call for a "sympathetic-critical" regard for the confessions. Along similar lines, Muether denounces Frame's biblicism and misrepresentation/caricature of Machen's followers, portraying them as head-hunters and obstructionists in the cause of (New) Westminster. Davis seeks a more irenic tact, one which regards Shepherd's misfortune as mere theological confusion and miscommunication on his part, not theological error. But that assessment is *false*. All told, this *festschrift* indicates that these are not pleasant, congenial days for Westminster—not on any account.

Recurring in these pages is the charge that Murray himself minimized the importance of systematic theology, and in so doing invited ambiguity and uncertainty into the theological programme and polemic of Westminster. VanDrunen bemoans the faculty's meager output in the field of systematics. None of the theology professors have engaged in systematics to any significant degree. Rather, their penchant for systematic coherence and consistency must be gleaned from isolated, exegetico-theological expositions. VanDrunen contends: "Though the existence of a system of theology has been affirmed at Westminster in the past only with some ambiguity, I argue that its defense must be taken up with renewed vigor in the next generation. In response to doubts that the development of a system of theology is even possible, I point to the Reformed doctrine of the covenants as the place where a system of theology can be centered and from which it can emerge in orderly coherence and biblical fidelity" (196). Here lies the heartbeat of Reformed theology, the "center" and "architectonic structure" of the entire theological enterprise (209). (Nothing new here for those who are students of traditional covenant theology, but refreshing to read nevertheless.)

Others issues addressed in these essays include the following: the role of natural theology in Van Tillian apologetics (Frame); the Van Til/Gordon Clark dispute regarding the doctrine of divine incomprehensibility (Scott Clark and Frame); Reformed theology of worship (Johnson); the central place of exegesis in the theological enterprise (several authors); and the principle of *sola scriptura* in confessional orthodoxy (Muether). According to Frame, natural theology (what he defines as cogent, rational ideas produced in the human mind, derivative of divine image-bearing) is merely "one step removed" from God's intrinsic knowledge, truth that is divinely revealed in Scripture and in nature (85). Frame's novel approach, called perspectivalism, attempts to resolve disputes among Christians who in diverse ways give expression to their faith and comprehension of divine truth. (In my reading of Frame, he has thoroughly distorted the work and argument of Van Til and Murray.) An important theological component in all these discussions is the matter of the relationship between divine archetype and human ectype, which includes the inscripturated Word. Johnson contends that practical theology is systematic theology in application (echoing the programme of his former colleague, Frame). Practical theology—or better, *pastoral* theology—is, in my view, derivative of systematics, a distinct department within the theological curriculum having its own specific task. Johnson rightly points out that this discipline in the seminary and in the church presently suffers "an identity crisis" (102). The solution to this crisis demands renewed appreciation for and allegiance to confessional Protestant-Reformed systematics (church dogmatics), still the queen of the theological sciences. In closing, Davis muses on the significance of "Sonship theology" (crafted by colleague and practitioner Jack Miller), raising doubts about its introspective, "mystical tendencies" (287). Readers of this book are left with much to ponder.

The bibliography of Strimple's writings leads one to question just how adept Strimple was in the field of Reformed systematics. What have Strimple's writings to contribute to the discussions taken up in this volume? The answer is little, if anything. Strimple's theological output has been exceedingly meager. So why the *festschrift* in his honor? It would appear that the poor health of systematic theology at Westminster (and the sister disciplines) cries out for help. Whether this book review is construed as an obituary for Westminster or an occasion calling for her resuscitation will depend upon the final outcome, consolidation within the institution. From the standpoint of the yet, unresolved Shepherd controversy, one thing is absolutely certain: Only radical surgery will cure her. Is there a skilled physician in the House of Westminster?

[Additional note: Compare the review of this book by William Dennison, *CTJ* 40 (2005) 380–383. The Dennison brothers (Jim, Charles, and Bill) have long been ardent promoters of the Ridderbos-Gaffin approach to biblical theology. The fledgling Northwest Theological Seminary, founded by Jim, has as its distinctive purpose the promotion of this theology and methodology (one that differs from the biblical-theological and dogmatic approach of Geerhardus Vos and Meredith Kline). The critical issue here is the proper relationship between biblical theology and systematics. In his closing remarks, Bill has this to say: "We cannot help but notice that such divisions [including that between Westminster East and West] have found their way into Christ's church. Indeed, healthy differences and debate will always exist in the church, but one wonders if the volume has crossed the line of intramural and brotherly debate" (383). Obviously, a great deal of thinking and talking is going on these days. One of the outcomes of all of this is the document "Presbyterians and Presbyterians Together: A Call to Charitable Theological Discourse" (www.presbyterianstogether.org ), urging "healthy differences and debate." It was Will Barker, dean of the faculty at Westminster East, who informed me that I had "crossed the line" in my criticisms of Professor Richard B. Gaffin, Jr. The hope of reconciling two contrary theologies will not be met. The call for charity is a foil for doctrinal accommodation and compromise.]

# Appendix E

## Given For You: Reclaiming Calvin's Doctrine of the Lord's Supper

*Keith A. Mathison*
**(Phillipsburg: Presbyterian and Reformed, 2002)**
[This book review appears in *JETS* 48 (2005) 174–78.]

THIS BOOK takes up the subject of the Lord's Supper, one of the (two) sacraments of the church. There are many mysteries to the Christian faith, this surely being one of them. Unfortunately, many readers of Keith Mathison's study will be left shaking their heads, mystified or confused on issues historical and theological. What did John Calvin and the Calvinist tradition actually teach? Was there uniformity? More importantly, what does Scripture teach concerning the mysterious operation of the Holy Spirit in and with the Word and sacrament?

Particularly alarming in contemporary Reformed theology is the rapid and widespread advance of a reinvigorated sacramentalism, in slightly different cloak. (One example of this trend is found among the Auburn Federalists, a little known group but highly influential and representative of recent "Calvinistic" thinking.) Part One of *Given for You* lays out the author's grasp of the historical context of Reformed teaching pertaining to the eucharist, covering the span of time from Calvin all the way up to the present. The biblical material is the subject of Part Two, highlighting the shadowy nature of OT revelation and its fulfillment in the new covenant reality of Christ's body and blood shed for the remission of sins. The third Part addresses other various issues of a theological and practical nature, including comparison of Calvinist doctrine on the Lord's Supper with that of other Christian traditions, the matter of frequency of observance, the use of wine (not grape juice), and paedocommunion. The closing appendix,

"The Lord's Supper before the Reformation," provides a brief overview of Christian interpretation prior to the Protestant Reformation.

The hero in Mathison's account is the nineteenth-century German-American theologian John Nevin, with whom the great Princeton systematician Charles Hodge had sparred. What we have in this book, then, is a reassessment of the controversy that ensued between Nevin and Hodge. How important is this particular doctrine, one of many mysteries of the Christian faith? In Nevin's estimate, it is of paramount importance. It involves "more than a change in a peripheral doctrine" (140); rather, it is "a central element of the Christian faith" (141).

The testimony of history suggests that there was not unanimity within the Reformed tradition on the nature and significance of the sacraments, whether we consider the Lord's Supper or baptism. Reformed thinking has never fully jelled on this subject. What we do find, however, are a variety of formulations and explanations of the "working" of the sacraments, some views standing in tension with others. It is essential that great care and distinction be given to the diversity of expression. There is need to sort through differences, some more subtle than others. Before critiquing Mathison's historical and theological assessment, we note several formative aspects of the discussion and debate among Reformed theologians by way of a summary of the author's treatment of the subject.

The chief reason for the diminution of Calvin's doctrine among the Reformed churches, Mathison contends, is the impact that Ulrich Zwingli's teaching has had, teaching that Mathison regards to be nonReformed. To Zwingli is attributed the view that the Lord's Supper is but a "bare memorial," not a real means of grace (i.e., a spiritual feeding upon the body and blood of Christ). And Calvin's view, Mathison tells his readers, is the *authentic* Reformed view. (Some historians of doctrine refute the common reading of Zwingli's sacramental theology. More study of Zwingli's thought is certainly demanded here.) In the judgment of Hodge, Calvin had it wrong (in part). Research in the history of doctrine also indicates that later Reformed theologians had objected to views attributed to Calvin. It may fairly be asked: What precisely were the views of Calvin? Was Hodge himself guilty of misreading Calvin, as Mathison claims?

Our author points out in the opening section of his book that one of the critical facets of Calvin's doctrine relates to "the heavenly location of Christ's natural body" (6). How, then, does Mathison understand this datum of special revelation? The answer to this question is crucial for our evaluation of Mathison's theology of the Lord's Supper. Is Christ's presence at the Supper physical, spiritual, or both (as Mathison later argues). The author's opening affirmation, following the clear, unambiguous statement of Calvin, instructs his readers that the physical body of Christ is now in heaven, not on earth, not on the Table—not even "suprasubstantially" speaking, what suggests a change in the substance of the Supper (see below). Is Mathison consistent in his own affirmation of faith? What we can say is that Christ is present at the Table in the same manner that he is present with believers indwelt by the Spirit and united to Christ by faith.

Turning to attempts to reconcile differences between Martin Luther and Calvin on the physical presence of Christ in the sacrament, Mathison suggests that the failure to reach agreement at the Marburg conference did serve as an incentive to Calvin. Calvin "wanted to achieve what Luther and Zwingli had not been able to achieve—common ground among the different branches of the Reformation. Calvin seems to have deliberately sought to find a biblical middle ground between the Lutheran and Zwinglian positions. It would be a mistake, however, to say that Calvin's mediating position was as close to Zwingli's view as it was to Luther's view. Calvin sympathized with Luther's position. He did not have the same enthusiasm for Zwingli's position" (5).

Mathison wants to see a physical, not merely spiritual, presence of Christ in the Supper. Quoting Calvin on the doctrine of mystical union: "I do not restrict this union to the divine essence, but affirm that it belongs to the flesh and blood, inasmuch as it was not simply said, My Spirit, but, My flesh is meat indeed; nor was it simply said, My Divinity, but, My blood is drink indeed" (18). This leads Mathison to reason: "We see that for Calvin, the Incarnation was crucial because Christ had to take upon himself human flesh in order to mediate divine life to us. According to Calvin, the flesh of Christ functions as something of a 'channel' or 'conduit' through which the divine life is poured into those who are in union with him. He is the true Vine, and we are the branches" (21). And as further clarification of his understanding, Mathison explains: "The difference here is subtle, but important. Some were arguing that when Christ commanded his followers to eat his flesh and drink his blood, he was merely urging them to believe in him. According to this position, believing in Christ is all that is meant by 'eating his flesh and blood.' Calvin rejected this view, saying that eating is a result of faith, not faith itself. In other words, faith is the instrument by which we truly eat and partake of the body and blood of Christ" (30–31).

This brings us to the crux of the dispute, as Mathison sees it: Do we commend Nevin's doctrine or Hodge's. Nevin argues for an "objective" signification to sacramental feeding upon Christ in the bread and wine. The meal is "not simply suggestive, commemorative, or representational. . . .

The invisible grace of the sacrament, according to the doctrine, is the substantial life of the Savior himself, particularly in his human nature" (142-43). *Here is the essence of the matter:* According to Nevin, "The modern view [represented by Hodge] rejects the older idea that unique grace is offered in the Supper that is not offered elsewhere. . . . The modern view rejects the older idea that there is an objective force in the sacrament of the Supper. In the new view, everything is subjective" (143-44). Conversely, in explaining Puritan theology, as illustrative of Reformed teaching, J. I. Packer (rightly) indicates that "The typical Puritan view of the Lord's Supper was not a bare memorialism, as if eucharistic worship was a matter merely of recalling Christ's death without fellowshipping with him in the process. It was, to be sure, no part of the Puritan belief that the communicant receives in the Supper a unique grace which he could not otherwise have; the Puritans would all agree with the Scot, Robert Bruce, that 'we get no other thing in the Sacrament, than we get in the Word'. But there is a special exercise of faith proper to the Lord's Table, where Christ's supreme act of love is set before us with unique vividness in the sacramental sign; and from this should spring a specially close communion with the Father and the Son" (*A Quest for Godliness: The Puritan Vision of the Christian Life* [Wheaton: Crossway Books, 1990] 213). Clearly, we have an unreconcilable difference of opinion. Nevin's view, in my reading, is sacramentalist. Parenthetically, saving grace is not bestowed incrementally, which is to say that we do not receive Christ or his benefits in bits and pieces. We are united to Christ in his person and work as the incarnate Son of God; we are the beneficiaries of his complete saving work by means of the efficacious application of redemption by the Spirit of Christ.

"As far as Nevin is concerned," writes Mathison, "the modern Reformed view of the Eucharist is a complete abandonment of the substance of the sixteenth-century doctrine in favor of a rationalistic conception" (146). The appropriate word here is subjectivistic, not "rationalistic" (whether or not we agree with Nevin's assessment of the church's diverse understanding of this doctrine in its historical development). More to the point, however, it is Nevin's view that is rationalistic (i.e., speculative and unbiblical). After affirming Calvin's doctrine, Nevin eventually comes around in his book to offer an improvement upon Calvin's otherwise ambiguous teaching.

In my judgment, it is Hodge who upholds a position more in conformity to biblical and confessional teaching. Mathison notes the following salient points, by way of summation: "Hodge's review [of Nevin's book] is roughly divided into four main sections. In the first section, he explains that there are several reasons why determining the true Reformed doctrine of the Lord's Supper in the sixteenth century is difficult. The first problem is the mysteriousness of the subject itself. The second problem has to do with 'the fact, that almost all the Reformed confessions were framed for the express purpose of compromise.' The third problem is the ambiguity of the terminology involved, and the fourth problem is the difficulty of knowing where to look for the authoritative exhibition of the Reformed doctrine" (149).

There are many other features and ramifications of this debate that merit our close attention. These include the doctrine of the imputation of Adam's sin to the entire human race, the imputation of Christ's righteousness (the meritorious ground of the sinner's justification) to those chosen in Christ (namely, the elect), the nature and necessity of the incarnation and atonement of Christ, decretive election, the dual sanctions of redemptive covenant (blessing and curse), and the sacraments as a sealing ordinance. On these issues Nevin and Hodge were at odds.

Where does Mathison leave his readers? The thesis he would have us consider is this: "Because Calvin taught that Christ's body is made present in the sacrament by the working of the Holy Spirit, his view of Christ's sacramental presence has sometimes been referred to as a doctrine of 'spiritual presence.' Unfortunately, this term is often misunderstood to mean that only Christ's Spirit or divine nature is present in the sacrament. Calvin explicitly denied any such idea. The term *suprasubstantial* might avoid some of these misunderstandings because it communicates the idea that there is a real participation in the substance of Christ's body and blood, as Calvin taught, but that this participation occurs on a plane that transcends and parallels the plane in which the physical signs exist. It communicates Calvin's focus on the presence of Christ in the sacrament, not the presence of Christ in the substance of the elements" (279-280).

Despite terminological and conceptual differences, how does Mathison's doctrine of *suprasubstantiation,* in the final analysis, differ from Rome's doctrine of *transubstantiation*? I see little, if any, substantive difference between the two views. (It should be said, however, that Mathison forthrightly rejects Rome's doctrine of the mass as an ongoing re-sacrifice of Christ.)

The question I pose to Mathison and his readers is this: What does it mean to distinguish—but not separate—the sign from that which is signified in the sacrament (the latter being the spiritual reality of feeding upon Christ by means of the sovereign, gracious operation of the Holy Spirit)? If one insists on a literal, one-for-one union between sign and reality, then one inevitably ends up with sacramentalism. For Calvin, it was the sovereign Holy Spirit who made effectual our spiritual feeding upon Christ in the Supper. It is the Spirit, not the sacrament, that unites us to Christ by grace through faith.

Before concluding this review, I want to return to the idea that there is "nothing new" in the Supper that is not already available to the believer in union with Christ. What more could we possibly receive that we have not already received in regeneration and union with Christ (a union which brings to us *all* the benefits of Christ's atoning death)? But rather than stating it in the negative, I want to insist that our participation in the Lord's Supper is a genuine means of grace for those united to Christ and, ultimately, a means of destruction for those who partake in unbelief. Participation in the Supper has individual and corporate, i.e., ecclesial, blessing and benefit. The symbolism of the Supper, what is both a memorial and an eschatological meal, is exceedingly rich in Scripture. To be sure, our understanding of the doctrine of the Lord's Supper (and our understanding of divine truth in its totality and particularity as revealed by God to finite creatures) is fraught with mystery; our spiritual participation in and enjoyment of this sacramental token—received by faith—is itself a sublime, mysterious experience. Doubtless, some Reformed interpreters need to say more than they have in their formulation of the doctrine of the sacraments; others have said too much, going beyond the explicit teaching of Scripture. I believe that Mathison has transgressed this sacred boundary.

# Appendix F

## The Covenant of God and the Children of Believers: Sovereign Grace in the Covenant

*David J. Engelsma*
**(Grandville, Mich.: Reformed Free Publishing Association, 2005)**
[This book review appears in *JETS* (forthcoming).]

"THE PLACE of children in the covenant is still controversial in Reformed churches. There is sharp disagreement over the meaning of infant baptism and the proper rearing of the baptized children of believing parents. This is shameful" (ix). So begins David Engelsma in *The Covenant of God and the Children of Believers,* much of which was previously published in the *Standard Bearer,* the magazine of the Protestant Reformed Church. Controversy continues to loom large among all branches of Christianity, not only within the Reformed camp. Although Engelsma primarily engages the Dutch Reformed tradition (Continental European and North American), his analysis is of wide-ranging interest across the evangelical Protestant theological spectrum. And although the author is quite dismissive of Baptist thinking on the subject, perhaps we might give him reason to reconsider—for the sake of unity in truth, and truth in unity (as witness to genuine Reformed catholicity). Indeed, the Reformed Baptist tradition has something substantive to contribute in the ongoing debate.

Publication of this book is part of the resurgence of interest in the theology of the sacraments (including, more broadly, the theology of the covenants). Engelma's discussion offers a valuable contribution, even though his own view is contradictory in places and also speculative, e.g., with regard to knowledge of those numbered among the elect of God. Regrettably, Engelsma's critique of other positions at times lacks balance and sobriety. This does not help foster constructive dialogue. More importantly, Engelma's denunciation of teaching that is truly heretical is apt to lose its sting for most readers.

The study is divided into six parts. Part One lays out Engelma's formulation of what he understands to be "the Reformed doctrine" of children in the covenant. This is followed by analysis of objections to this view (represented as the teaching of the Protestant Reformed Church, of which Engelsma is a member). Parts Two through Four contain Engelsma's response to the Baptist, the Netherlands Reformed, and the Canadian Reformed ("Liberated") objections. Parts Five and Six engage the contemporary scene, addressing the controversy now raging in evangelical Reformed Protestantism. Here the author delves insightfully, though briefly, into the teaching of the New Perspective on Paul, the Federal Visionists, and, most notably, the teaching of Norman Shepherd. The roots of the modern-day heresy (the focus of Parts Five and Six) are located in previous Reformed thinking (the focus of Parts Two through Four). With regard to teaching critiqued in the opening section, Engelsma dismisses most of it as not in any legitimate sense "Reformed." Here we will have to part company with the author. Much of the thinking laid out in this portion of the book falls within the parameters of Reformed teaching, however inconsistent and incoherent that teaching may be at times. Four appendices, containing book reviews, reinforce the argument of the book and provide the reader additional resource material.

We begin our review/evaluation by considering Engelma's conceptualization of the covenant of God. Our author states: "The covenant is the relationship of friendship between the triune God and his chosen people in Jesus Christ" (4). This will not do, if we take seriously the doctrines of Creation, Fall, and Redemption. Better to define covenant "as a relationship, as a bond of communion" (5). And better yet, covenant is a relationship *under sanctions* (something that mostly eludes Engelsma's thinking). Our author locates the essence of the covenant in the creature's (or the believer's) enjoyment of God—as recipient of his love, communion and fellowship. More supremely, we are told, covenant life is participation in the trinitarian life of God, who is himself life-in-community (by way of the interpenetration of the three persons of the Godhead in eternal self-subsistence). Covenant "is the revelation to us and the sharing with us of God's own inner, trinitarian life. God's own life is friendship. The life of God is family friendship" (8). This formulation of covenant Engelsma developed in his 1994 Th.M. thesis written at Calvin Theological Seminary. (For the record, Engelsma differs sharply with the theology of the Christian

Reformed Church.) But to the contrary, covenant pertains to God in relation to his creation—a relationship first established under dual sanctions, the blessing and the curse. Relationship in covenant is not applicable to the trinitarian life of God as Family—Father, Son, and Holy Spirit. (Actually, the theological term is "Trinity," not "Family," though the latter is the popular one today. Perhaps it sounds more inviting for those eagerly seeking to be adopted into the family of God!)

The central focus of Engelsma's treatise is the question regarding the place of children in the covenant (more precisely, in the "Covenant of Grace"). "The children of believers are included in the covenant as children, that is, already at conception and birth. They receive forgiveness of sins through the blood of Jesus, the Holy Spirit of sanctification, and church membership—as children" (10). This surely sounds like the doctrines of presumptive regeneration, eternal justification, and sacramentalism—at least with respect to the *children of godly parents*, as Engelsma continually qualifies. Yet, these are teachings that Engelsma (rightly) renounces. Clearly, there are a number of very important issues that must be untangled and clarified.

According to Engelsma, there is no promise that all baptized children are saved: the promise of God is extended only to the elect children of godly parents. But how do we know if the parents who bring their children for baptism are godly or not? Presumably, Engelsma would answer: God alone. That answer would be correct. What *is required* is a credible profession of faith on the part of the parent(s). Contrary to the explicit teaching of scriptural texts cited by Engelsma himself on many occasions, the election of God is according to his own sovereign good will and determination (see, e.g., Rom 9). There simply is no guarantee that the children of godly parents are saved (i.e., numbered among the elect). The household principle that informs the administration of redemptive covenant in its historical outworking is not identical with the principle of sovereign, electing grace. *All this to say, redemptive covenant is broader than election.* Denial of this fundamental truth lies at the root of Engelsma's covenant confusion. (Here is where the Baptist tradition is rightly critical of Reformed teaching—more precisely, one stand of Reformed thinking.)

Just a word about the Reformed confessions: Invariably these contain—here and there—theological inconsistencies and contradictions requiring correction and reformulation. This is not the place to address shortcomings, as I see them. The problem in Engelma's argument is that he has been selective in his own reading of confessional Reformed theology. The issues are far more complex and ambiguous than Engelsma would have his readers believe. The reality of this circumstance in history of Reformed doctrine gives license to Norman Shepherd and others to assert what they understand to be the "true intent" of the framers of the confessions—a highly speculative enterprise, to be sure. Better that we content ourselves with what actually lies before us on the written page. And, as Engelma would fully agree, in the final place it is the teaching of Scripture, not the secondary standards of the church, that is decisive.

Engelsma explains: "It is the *covenantal election of God* that determines the viewpoint that believing parents and churches take toward the children and that governs the approach in rearing them" (21, emphasis mine). What in the thinking of Engelsma is "covenantal election," and how does it differ from the view of Shepherd? How does sovereign, decretive election relate to redemptive covenant in its historical outworking? One of the favorite texts among disputants is Ephesians 1. The question is this: Is Paul's address to the elect saints at Ephesus from the standpoint of decretive election, or is it in terms of "covenantal election," i.e., (external) membership in the covenant community? The latter view maintains that one can be numbered among the elect today, but may fall from grace tomorrow (by defection from the covenant). As I read Scripture, the church of Christ is composed of both elect and nonelect (both the wheat and the tares). The tendency among many theologians is either to equate membership in God's covenant with decretive election or to distinguish two kinds of election, decretive and covenantal, the latter being losable, as in the case of ancient, theocratic Israel. (On this latter view, "covenantal election" is equated with Israel's national election under the old economy). Neither view will do: The covenant of God in the history of redemption is *broader than election.* Yet it must be said, the *proper purpose* of redemptive covenant is election unto salvation. (Baptism, like the preaching of the Word, is a genuine *means of grace.*)

In my estimate, it is primarily with the theological position of the Canadian Reformed Church that *substantive differences* come into sharp focus. The issue, once again, is the doctrine of election and the covenants. The "liberated" theologians will have no part of that teaching which defines the blessing of redemptive covenant in terms of sovereign, decretive election (wherein salvation is fixed and unlosable). This "election theology of the covenant" is forthrightly repudiated. Since God alone knows who the elect actually are, we are told that we must refrain from viewing individuals in the covenant community as truly elect or reprobate. Taking our cue from the apostle Paul (as read by the "liberated" theologians), we are to regard church members as elect *from the standpoint of the historical covenant.* We are not to contemplate individual election *from the standpoint of God's*

# Appendix F

*eternal foreordination* (which is unavailable to us). Doubtless, one of the sources for Shepherd's radical reformulation of covenant theology is this contention of the "liberated" Reformed churches favoring the doctrine of "universal, resistible, losable grace in the covenants" (99). Engelsma adds: "Imbedded deeply in the very heart of 'liberated' covenant doctrine is a fatal weakness regarding, if not antipathy to, God's eternal election. This comes out in 'liberated' theologian and founding father Benne Holwerda's astounding teaching that virtually every New Testament mention of election, including Ephesians 1:4 and Romans 9:11, refers, not to God's eternal decree, but to an act of God in time" (128).

Well into the book Engelsma asserts: "An 'election theology' of covenant demands a distinction between being in living covenant fellowship with God by covenant grace and merely being in the sphere of the covenant by natural birth" (125). This assertion conflicts with Engelsma's earlier insistence that redemptive covenant be defined in terms of sovereign election and with his rejection of the distinction between external and internal membership in the covenant. Our author cannot have it both ways. Having boxed himself into a corner, Engelsma finds no other recourse than the standard distinction between the external/internal spheres of the covenant. "However one may choose to name it, the distinction between being in the covenant and being in the sphere of the covenant is biblical" (126).

The remaining hundred pages of the book expose heretical teachings taking residence in Reformed churches and educational institutions to a very alarming degree. Not only advocates of the New Perspective on Paul, the Federal Vision, or the Shepherd-Gaffin formulation (*i.e.,* the New Westminster school), but advocates of the "Openness of God" are charting a radically different course for present-day "Reformed evangelical" theology. "Central in the contemporary debate is biblical justification" (148). My book, *Gospel Grace: The Modern-day Controversy* (Eugene, OR: Wipf and Stock, 2003), tackles this issue, with special attention to the teaching of New Westminster. (The publication date of my prior writing, *The Changing of the Guard: Westminster Theological Seminary in Philadelphia* [Unicoi, TN: The Trinity Foundation, 2001] is misprinted in *The Children of God.*) Though not of substantive weight, I strongly differ with Engelsma's attempt at harmonizing Paul and James (by speaking of two kinds of justification, rather than two *aspects,* the constitutive and the demonstrative) and with his exegesis of Romans 2:13 (which I understand to teach two actual classes of individuals, the godly and the ungodly). These differences aside, I concur fully with Engelsma when he writes, "There is no excuse for Reformed people to be deceived by Shepherd and his allies" (151). The effect of all this false teaching is an accelerating rapprochement between Rome and Protestants (or those who once expounded and defended the Protestant faith). "The clear and necessary implication of Shepherd's rejection of Luther's 'alone,' of course, is that one is not justified by faith alone. Rather, as Rome has always taught, one is justified by faith *and by works of some sort,* though not 'works of the law'" (165).

Engelsma laments the fact that many who repudiate these heretical teachings are unable to offer a thorough critique because they do not define the covenant as he and the Protestant Reformed Churches do. "They do not get to the root of the evil. They cannot. With the rare exception, they are themselves committed to a conditional covenant" (181). As a leading critic of the New Theology, I am dismayed in reading Engelsma's final assessment of the current dispute and deeply lament the fact that exegetes and theologians—those standing in the tradition of historic Protestant-Reformed Orthodoxy—cannot rise above partisan differences to denounce *with one clear voice* what is clearly heretical in our theological circles. The reason for this inability to come together is quite simple: We cannot agree on the biblical concept of (redemptive) covenant. In my judgment, it is necessary that faithful interpreters of Scripture come to recognize that redemptive covenant is broader than sovereign, decretive election. Only then can we legitimately and consistently oppose the view positing a faulty distinction between external and internal membership in the covenant community. And only then can we understand aright the "household principle" in the administration of the Covenant of Grace in redemptive history—in its progressive unfolding (including the process of differentiation between the elect and nonelect).

Engelsma concludes: "There is one, and only one, doctrine of the covenant that magnifies and safeguards the sovereign grace of God in his work of salvation in the sphere of the covenant. This is the teaching that the grace of God *in the sphere of the covenant,* as everywhere else, is particular. God's gracious covenant and covenant grace are for the elect alone" (202). Previously we were told to distinguish between (true) membership—*in the covenant*—and what, ultimately, is hypocritical membership—*in the sphere the covenant.* Part of the blame for this confusion in formulation rests with the statement made in the *Westminster Larger Catechism*: "The covenant of grace was made with Christ as the second Adam, and in him with all the elect as he seed" (quoted on p. 205). Better is the Reformed doctrine of the "Covenant of Redemption," which recognizes the vital distinction between the eternal covenant between the Father and the Son (in the Spirit) on behalf of the elect and the historical administration of redemptive covenant (the "Covenant of Grace") made with elect and nonelect. The operation of the "household principle" in the administration of God's covenant is conclusive. All this to say, even the theology of the Westminster divines can be improved upon in terms of clarity and consistency!

I do have to wonder when Engelsma writes, "As a Reformed minister and parent, I have no interest whatever in conversion as the basis for viewing baptized children as God's dear children, loved of him from eternity, redeemed by Jesus, and promised the Holy Spirit, the author of faith" (86). Is conversion not necessary for baptized children? Earlier in the treatise, Engelsma answered in the affirmative. Because we do not know if a baptized child is saved, we are to commend to him/her the life of faith and repentance (conversion may be sudden or imperceptible). We cannot presume the regeneration of the baptized infants of godly parents, anymore than we can presume the regeneration of adults who are baptized on the basis of a good confession. Engelsma is wrong to say that his view regarding the infant baptism of the elect children of godly parents *is* "traditional, confessional Presbyterian (Reformed) doctrine (222). It ain't so! And if it were, it ain't biblical! (Like Engelsma, I am not commending revivalism as advocated by pietistic Puritans and Dutch precisionists—Jonathan Edwards' ministry as illustrative. We are to nurture our children—and adults—in the faith of our fathers, knowing that the regenerating and renewing work of the Spirit is requisite for true growth in grace.)

Then too, I have to wonder when Engelsma writes, "If the Reformed churches face these questions [raised in the book], they will also be led to consider whether the covenant is a warm, living relation of love, rather than a cold contract; whether the covenant in Scripture is itself the highest good—the very blessedness of salvation—rather than a mere means to some other end; and whether Christ is the head of the covenant of grace" (181-182). The implied caricature of alternative views will not do, neither in terms of the teaching of Scripture, nor in terms of the history of Reformed doctrine.

Lastly, by way of critique: Engelsma's rhetoric is, in places, comparable to that frequently used by Shepherd. There is need to move beyond this polemical style to forthright, theological statement that is exegetically faithful to Scripture in its totality and comprehensiveness (i.e., exegesis that combines the fruits of biblical and systematic theology). Proof-texting merely points readers to a particular exegetico-theological tradition, however consistent or eclectic that tradition might be. Commendably, Engelsma does not mince any words when it comes to heretical teaching. One can only hope and pray that discerning readers will weigh carefully the criticisms offered in this book, sweeping as they are, and properly identify the true miscreants in this present-day battle for the Gospel of particular, sovereign grace—the Gospel of justification by faith alone.

Additional space here would permit comment on other related issues, such as the role and importance of Christian nurture (including the place of evangelism in Christian schools), the necessity of church discipline (including excommunication when requisite), the question whether the covenant is conditional or unconditional (including the matter of the warnings against covenant unfaithfulness, specially as addressed in the Letter to the Hebrews), the extent and efficacy of the atonement, federal headship, the sole instrumentality of faith in soteric justification, the assurance of believers, and the perseverance of the saints. Much is at stake in our systematic formulation of the theology of the covenants. The subject of infant baptism simply opens up an array of crucial issues, as it has always done.

# Supplemental Bibliography

[To my two previous studies, *Covenant Theology in Reformed Perspective* and *Gospel Grace*].

Beale, Gregory K. *The Temple and the Church's Mission: A Biblical Theology of the Dwelling Place of God.* New Studies in Biblical Theology. Downers Grove: InterVarsity, 2004.
Carson, D. A., P. T. O'Brien, and M. A. Seifrid, eds. *Justification and Variegated Nomism: Volume II. The Paradoxes of Paul.* Grand Rapids: Baker, 2004.
Clark, R. Scott, ed., *Covenant and Justification: A Westminster Seminary California Faculty Symposium (*Phillipsburg: Presbyterian and Reformed forthcoming).
De Jong, Brian L. "What Machen Meant." *New Horizons* 27 (June 2006) 23–24.
Dennison, Charles G., *History for a Pilgrim People* (Willow Grove, Pa.: The Committee for the Historian of the Orthodox Presbyterian Church, 2002).
Edgar, William. *Truth in All its Glory: Commending the Reformed Faith* (Phillipsburg: Presbyterian and Reformed, 2004).
Elliott, Paul M., *Christianity and Neo-Liberalism: The Spiritual Crisis in the Orthodox Presbyterian Church and Beyond* (Unico: Trinity Foundation, 2005).
Engelsma, David J., *The Covenant of God and the Children of Believers: Sovereign Grace in the Covenant* (Grandville, Mich.: Reformed Free, 2005).
Evans, William Borden. "Imputation and Impartation: The Problem of Union with Christ in Nineteenth-Century America Reformed Theology" (Ph.D. dissertation, Vanderbilt University, 1996).
———. "Union with the Second Adam" (Th.M. thesis, Westminster Theological Seminary, 1986).
Ferry, Brenton C., "Cross-Examining Moses' Defense: An Answer to Ramsey's Critique of Kline and Karlberg." *Westminster Theological Journal* 67 (2005) 163–68.
Frame, John M., "Machen's Warrior Children." In *Alister E. McGrath and Evangelical Theology: A Dynamic Engagement,* ed. S. W. Chung (Grand Rapids: Baker, 2003).
Franke, John R., *The Character of Theology: A Postconservative Evangelical Approach* (Grand Rapids: Baker, 2005).
Golding, Peter. *Covenant Theology: The Key of Theology in Reformed Thought and Tradition* (Ross-shire: Focus, 2004).
Greidanus, Sidney. *Preaching Christ from the Old Testament: A Contemporary Hermeneutical Method* (Grand Rapids: Eerdmans, 1999).
Griffith, Howard. "High Priest in Heaven: The Intercession of the Exalted Christ in Reformed Theology, Analysis and Critique." Ph.D. dissertation, Westminster Seminary, 2004.

## Supplemental Bibliography

Hart. D. G., *John Williamson Nevin: High-Church Calvinist*. America Reformed Biographies, D. G. Hart and S. M. Lucas, series editors (Phillipsburg: Presbyterian and Reformed, 2005).

Hill, C. E. and F. A. James III, eds., *The Glory of the Atonement: Biblical, Historical and Practical Perspectives—Essays in Honor of Roger Nicole* (Downers Grove: InterVarsity, 2004).

Holifield, E. Brooks. *Theology in America: Christian Thought from the Age of the Puritans to the Civil War* (New Haven: Yale University, 2003).

Horton, Michael. *God of Promise: Introducing Covenant Theology* (Grand Rapids: Baker, 2006).

Husbands, M. and D. J. Treier. *Justification: What's at Stake in the Current* (Downers Grove: InterVarsity, 2004).

Inman, Benjamin T., "God Covenanted in Christ: The unifying role of theology proper in the systematic theology of Francis Turretin." Ph.D. dissertation, Westminster Theological Seminary, 2004.

Kang, Kevin Woongsan. "Justified by Faith in Christ: Jonathan Edwards' Doctrine of Justification in Light of Union with Christ." Ph.D. dissertation, Westminster Theological Seminary, 2003.

Karlberg, Mark W., "Today's Church: Standing or Falling?" [Part 1]. *The Outlook* 54.4 (April 2004) 5–8.

———. "Judgment According to Works: The Crux of Today's Dispute" [Part 2]. *The Outlook* 54.5 (May 2004) 6–8.

Kline, Meredith G. *God, Heaven and Har Magedon: A Covenantal Tale of Cosmos and Telos* (Eugene, Ore.: Wipf and Stock, 2006).

Mathison, Keith A. *Given For You: Reclaiming Calvin's Doctrine of the Lord's Supper* (Phillipsburg: Presbyterian and Reformed, 2002).

MacLeod, A. Donald. *W. Stanford Reid: An Evangelical Calvinist in the Academy*. Montreal: McGill-Gween, 2004.

McGowan, A. T. B., "Justification and the *Ordo Salutis*." *Foundations* (Spring 2004) 6–18.

Moore, Russell D., *The Kingdom of Christ: The New Evangelical Perspective* (Wheaton: Crossway, 2004).

———. "What Hath Dallas to Do With Westminster? The Kingdom Concept in Contemporary Evangelical Theology." *Criswell Theological Review* NS 2 (2004).

Muether, John R., "Machen Memoir: Fifty Years Later." *New Horizons* 25.5 (May 2004) 11–12.

Murray, Iain H., *Evangelicalism Divided: A Record of Crucial Change in the Years 1950–2000* (Carlisle: Banner of Truth Trust, 2000).

Noll, Mark A., *America's God: From Jonathan Edwards to Abraham Lincoln* (New York: Oxford, 2002).

——— and Carolyn Nystrom. *Is the Reformation Over? An Evangelical Assessment of Contemporary Roman Catholicism* (Grand Rapids: Baker, 2005).

Noll, M. A., N. O. Hatch, and G. M. Marsden. *The Search for Christian America* (Westchester, Ill.: Crossway, 1983).

Rainbow, Paul A., *The Way of Salvation: The Role of Christian Obedience in Justification* (Carlisle: Paternoster, 2005).

Ramsey, Patrick. "In Defense of Moses: A Confessional Critique of Kline and Karlberg." *Westminster Theological Journal* 66 (Fall 2004) 373–400.

Sandlin, P. Andrew, ed. *Backbone of the Bible: Covenant in Contemporary Perspective* (Nacogdoches, Tx.: Covenant, 2004).

Schwertley, Brian. "The Crisis in the OPC and PCA." *Westminster Guardian* (June 2006) 2–8.

Smith, Ralph. *The Eternal Covenant: How the Trinity Reshapes Covenant Theology* (Moscow, Id.: Canon, 2003).

———. *Paradox and Truth: Rethinking Van Til on the Trinity* (Moscow, Id.: Canon, 2002).

Trumper, Tim J. R., "A Fresh Exposition of Adoption: II. Some Implications." *Scottish Bulletin of Evangelical Theology* 23 (2005) 194–215.

VanDrunen, David, ed., *The Pattern of Sound Doctrine: Systematic Theology at the Westminster Seminaries* (Phillipsburg: Presbyterian and Reformed, 2004).

Vanhoozer, Kevin J., *The Drama of Doctrine: A Canonical-Linguistic Approach to Christian Theology* (Louisville: Westminster John Knox, 2005).

Waddington, Jeffrey C., "Jonathan Edwards's 'Ambiguous and Somewhat Precarious' Doctrine of Justification." *Westminster Theological Journal* 66 (2004) 357–72.

Waldron, Samuel E., "John Calvin versus Norman Shepherd on *Sola Fide*." *Reformed Baptist Theological Review* 2 (2005) 87–106.

Ward, Roland S., "Why works works: Biblical revelation unfolds from the covenant of works." *Australian Presbyterian* 579 (March 2006) 11–12..

Wells, David F., *Above All Earthly Pow'rs: Christ in a Postmodern World* (Grand Rapids: Eerdmans, 2005).

# Name Index

## A
Adams, Jay, 44, 132
Armstrong, John H., 121
Augustine, 1

## B
Bahnsen, Greg L., 50, 105
Barker, William, 121, 135
Barth, Karl, 23, 30, 52, 62, 71, 105
Bavinck, Herman, 30, 76, 80
Beale, Gregory K., 19, 23, 95
Beisner, E. Calvin, 20
Belz, Nat, 46
Bergsma, Dirk, 132
Berkhof, Louis, 91, 129–30
Berkouwer, G. C., 30, 38, 45, 108
Bird, Michael F., 24
Bohlmann, Ralph A., 56
Booth, Randy, 101
Bray, Gerald, 107
Bruce, Robert, 139
Brueggemann, Walter, 26, 33
Buber, Martin, 33
Buddha, 85
Bullinger, Heinrich, 1, 25
Bultmann, Rudolf, 62
Bush, George H. W., 84
Bush, George W., 84

## C
Calvin, John, 1, 21, 25, 46, 53, 86, 136–41
Carnes, Tony, 52
Carson, Donald A., 24
Carter, Jimmy, 84, 125
Chapell, Bryan, 45, 57, 107, 112
Childs, Brevard, 26, 33
Clark, Gordon, 76, 80, 134
Clark, R. Scott, 39, 132, 134
Clowney, Edmund P., 36–37, 40, 43–44, 56, 68, 122, 124, 131
Cocceius, Johannus, 44
Confucius, 85
Conn, Harvie, 51, 70
Cullmann, Oscar, 97

## D
Davis, D. Clair, 44, 132–34
De Jong, Brian L., 97
Dennison, Charles G., 80, 135
Dennison, Jr., James T., 116, 135
Dennison, William D., 135
Dick, John, 103
Dillard, Raymond, 51
Dooyeweerd, Herman, 45
Duncan, J. Ligon, 97
Dunn, James D. G., 71, 110

# Name Index

## E
Edgar, William, 97
Edwards, Jonathan, 148
Eichrodt, Walter, 109
Elliott, Paul M., 61–81
Engelsma, David J., 20, 54, 142–49
Enns, Peter, 21, 51, 58, 74, 78
Estelle, Brian, 97
Evans, William B., 54

## F
Facke, Gabriel, 26, 33
Ferguson, Sinclair, 38, 51–52, 60, 108
Ferry, Brent C., 22, 51–52
Fesko, John V., 78
Fisher, Allan, 54
Franke, John R., 50, 56, 58–59, 78, 108
Frei, Hans, 26, 33
Frame, John M., 23, 38, 42–44, 47, 51, 65, 68, 74, 77, 80–81, 101–6, 116, 121, 131–34
Fuller, George, 69

## G
Gaffin, Jr., Richard B., 14, 16–18, 21–24, 30, 34, 38–40, 42–50, 52–56, 60, 65, 69–75, 77–81, 97, 102, 106, 112, 121–22, 127, 132–33, 135, 146
Gallant, Timothy, 21
Garlington, Donald B., 22, 77
Gidley, James S., 77
Godfrey, W. Robert, 39, 44, 51, 57, 65, 104, 132
Golding, Peter, 50
Goppelt, Leonhard, 19
Green, Douglas J., 21, 51, 74, 121

Greidanus, Sidney, 19
Grenz, Stanley, 26, 34, 58
Griffith, Howard, 53

## H
Hart, Darryl G., 41–42, 54, 80, 96, 116, 131
Hauerwas, Stanley, 26, 34, 58
Henry, Carl F. H., 89, 96, 105, 125
Hesselink, I. John, 52
Hillers, Delbert R., 109
Hodge, Charles, 43, 56, 96, 103, 132, 137–40
Hoekema, Anthony, 97, 127
Holifield, E. Brooks, 24, 127
Holwerda, Benne, 146
Horton, Michael S., 39, 41–43, 55–56, 73, 79, 107–23, 131–33
Hutchison, William R., 96

## I
Inman, Benjamin T., 53

## J
Johnson, Dennis, 132, 134
Johnson, Gary, 79
Jordan, James B., 21

## K
Kang, Kevin W., 53
Kelly, Michael, 121
Kennedy, D. James, 79, 85–88
Kinnaird, John, 70, 74
Kline, Meredith G., x, 19–20, 23, 25–35, 48–49, 52, 68–69, 74, 78–79, 89, 98, 103, 109–10, 113, 115–16, 118, 120, 122–23, 135
König, Adrio, 127
Knudsen, Robert, 70

# Name Index

## L
Ladd, George E., 90, 96–97, 126
Letham, Robert, 39, 79
Lillback, Peter A., 20, 39, 51, 59, 74–75, 79, 85–88, 94
Lincoln, Abraham, 85
Lindbeck, George A., 26, 34
Logan, Jr., Samuel T., 38, 51, 59, 69, 116, 121
Longman III, Tremper, 78, 121
Lusk, Rich, 50
Luther, Martin, 21, 28, 36, 46, 53, 86, 138, 147

## M
MacIntyre, Alastair, 26
MacLeod, A. Donald, 21, 34, 51, 53, 122
McElwain, Martha, 75
McGowen, A. T. B., 52
McLaren, Bruce, 58
McWilliams, David, 38
Machen, J. Gresham, 36, 38, 62–63, 73, 121–22
Mangum, R. Todd, 78
Marcion, 1
Mathison, Keith A., 19, 54, 136–41
Meacham, Jon, 96
Mendenhall, George E., 109
Millbank, John, 85
Miller, C. John, 134
Mitchell, John, 122
Moo, Douglas, 24
Moore, Russell A., 55, 88–99, 124–30
Muether, John R., 51, 80, 116, 122, 132, 134
Muhammad, 85
Muller, Richard A., 54

Murray, Iain H., 51
Murray, John, 16–17, 23–24, 29–31, 38–39, 43, 52, 56, 63–65, 74, 131–32, 134

## N
Nevin, John, 137–40
Nicholas, Robert, 122
Niebuhr, Reinhold, 62
Niell, Jeffrey D., 102
Nixon, Richard, 84
Noll, Mark, 21, 46, 94
Nystrom, Carolyn, 21, 46

## O
O'Brien, Peter T., 120
Olson, Roger, 58

## P
Packer, James I., 107, 139
Perrin, Nicholas, 79
Piper, John, 22
Poythress, Vern S., 68, 74, 77, 124

## R
Rainbow, Paul A., 80
Ramsey, Patrick, 22, 34, 52, 78
Reagan, Ronald, 84
Reid, W. Stanford, 21, 34, 122
Ridderbos, Herman, 38, 45, 75, 97, 108, 135
Robbins, John W., 57, 65–68, 73, 76, 80
Robertson, O. Palmer, 21, 34, 51, 56, 78, 97, 110
Ryken, Philip, 107

## S
Sanders, Edmund P., 71, 110
Sandlin, P. Andrew, 101–3, 110, 121

Saucy, Robert, 98, 129
Schwertley, Brian, 121
Scott, James W., 78
Seifrid, Mark A., 24
Shepherd, Norman, 14, 16–18, 20–24, 30, 34, 36, 38–40, 42, 44–48, 50–54, 56–57, 65, 68–81, 97, 102–6, 109–10, 117, 121–22, 123, 127, 131, 133, 135, 143, 145–48
Silva, Moisés, 21, 51, 120
Sloat, Leslie, 122
Smith, James, 58
Smith, Jay E., 60
Smith, Ralph, 20
Sproul, Sr., R. C., 103
Spykman, Gordon, 45
Stonehouse, Ned B., 122
Streett, R. Alan, 60
Stendahl, Krister, 28
Strimple, Robert B., 31, 39–41, 65, 74, 104, 135

## T

Templeton, Jr., John M., 51–52
Thielman, Frank, 23
Thielmann, Ronald, 26, 34
Tipton, Lane, 52, 53, 58
Torrance, Thomas F., 52, 108
Trueman, Carl, 51–52, 56, 108
Trumper, Timothy J. R., 38, 42, 44, 77–78, 132–33
Turretin, Francis, 30

## V

Van Til, Cornelius, 20, 29–30, 38, 63–65, 68, 74, 76, 80, 105, 132–34
VanDrunen, David, 39, 41, 43, 56, 57, 96, 132–34

Vanhoozer, Kevin J., 73, 108
Venema, Cornelis, 20
Ventrella, Jeffery, 101
Vlachos, Chris Alex, 19
Voetius, Gisbert, 44
Von Rad, Gerhard, 109
Vos, Geerhardus, x, 25–35, 38, 42, 55, 68, 75, 80, 89, 97, 110, 116–17, 126, 135

## W

Waddington, Jeffrey C., 53
Wagner, Roger, 101
Waldron, Samuel E., 54
Ward, Roland S., 97
Warfield, Benjamin B., 55, 132
Washington, George, 85
Waters, Guy P., 21, 54, 79
Webber, Robert, 58
Wells, David F., 51, 60
White, Fowler, 20
White, John, 51
Wilkins, Steve, 110
Williams, Michael, 97, 121, 126
Wilson, Douglas, 113
Winthrop, John, 79, 84
Woolley, Paul, 122
Wright, George E., 42
Wright, N. T., 23, 42–43, 71, 110
Wynia, Dick, 112–23

## Y

Young, Edward J., 31

## Z

Zwingli, Ulrich, 137–38

www.ingramcontent.com/pod-product-compliance
Lightning Source LLC
Chambersburg PA
CBHW051746230426
43670CB00012B/2187